THE COVENANT
WITH
BLACK
AMERICA

TEN YEARS LATER

THE COVENANT

WITH

BLACK

AMERICA

TEN YEARS LATER

COMPILED AND EDITED BY

TAVIS SMILEY

SMILEYBOOKS

Distributed by Hay House, Inc.
Carlsbad, California • New York City
London • Sydney • Johannesburg
Vancouver • Hong Kong • New Delhi

Distributed in the United States by: Hay House, Inc.: www.hayhouse.com® • *Published and distributed in Australia by:* Hay House Australia Pty. Ltd.: www.hayhouse.com .au • *Published and distributed in the United Kingdom by:* Hay House UK, Ltd.: www .hayhouse.co.uk • *Published and distributed in the Republic of South Africa by:* Hay House SA (Pty), Ltd.: www.hayhouse.co.za • *Distributed in Canada by:* Raincoast Books: www.raincoast.com • *Published in India by:* Hay House Publishers India: www .hayhouse.co.in

Cover design: Amy Grigoriou • *Interior design:* Tricia Breidenthal

Interior graphs and illustrations used with permission.

Library of Congress Cataloging-in-Publication Data

Names: Smiley, Tavis, date. editor.
Title: The Covenant with Black America - ten years later / compiled and
    edited by Tavis Smiley.
Description: Carlsbad, California : Hay House, Inc., [2016]
Identifiers: LCCN 2015042597 | ISBN 9781401951498 (tradepaper : alk. paper)
Subjects: LCSH: African Americans--Social conditions--1975- | African
    Americans--Politics and government. | United States--Race relations. |
    African American leadership.
Classification: LCC E185.86 .C58883 2016 | DDC 305.896/073--dc23 LC record avail-
able at http://lccn.loc.gov/2015042597

Tradepaper ISBN: 978-1-4019-5149-8

10 9 8 7 6 5 4 3 2 1
1st edition, January 2016

Printed in the United States of America

The eyes of the future are looking

back at us and they are praying

for us to see beyond our own time.

—Terry Tempest Williams

TABLE OF CONTENTS

INTRODUCTION

What a difference a decade makes.

At least that was my hope.

Ten years ago when I had the honor of compiling and editing the historic text *The Covenant with Black America,* I had no idea that a decade later, life for Black fellow citizens would be even more challenged—politically, economically, socially.

To be clear, a decade after this groundbreaking #1 *New York Times* best-selling text, Black America has lost ground in every leading economic category.

Additionally, all across America, the vicious assault on the civil and human rights of Black people has outraged citizens of conscience, and led to a renewed sense of social protest and political activism. Led primarily by a younger generation that has, ironically, been let down by our failure to respect their dignity and humanity. It's not that difficult to understand why a generation that's been politically marginalized, economically exploited, and culturally manipulated would feel so angry and aggrieved.

I could spend these almost 300 pages assessing and assigning blame for how this happened. Responsibility and accountability matter.

And yet, at this critical juncture, with so little time to waste in order to save the soul of Black America, I'm more compelled in this book to first remind us of the plan laid out ten years ago—well in advance of the 2008 presidential election cycle—by presenting the ten covenants as they appeared in the original edition, with minor cosmetic edits. And, second, to share fresh data, courtesy of the

Indiana University School of Public & Environmental Affairs (SPEA) that might help us to redeem the time that's been lost.

As we head into yet another important presidential election cycle, you will learn on the pages that follow that Black health disparities still exist. Black children are still failing in our nation's classrooms. Our system of jurisprudence is still unequal. The digital divide is still firmly in place. We still lack environmental justice for all in America. And 150 years after the Civil War, Black folk still wonder whether their lives truly matter.

It's time to claim our democracy. Which starts by reclaiming the hopes, dreams, and aspirations of Black America from the lost and found.

We have to be intentional.

We have to have a plan.

Ten years later, time is not on our side.

—Tavis Smiley
Los Angeles, California
November 2015

✛ ✛

STATEMENT OF PURPOSE

MARIAN WRIGHT EDELMAN

> *If there is no struggle, there is no progress. Those who profess to favor freedom and yet deprecate agitation, are men who want crops without plowing up the ground, they want rain without thunder and lightning. They want the ocean without the awful roar of its many waters. This struggle may be a moral one, or it may be a physical one, and it may be both moral and physical, but it must be a struggle. Power concedes nothing without a demand. It never did and it never will.*
>
> —FREDERICK DOUGLASS,
> "WEST INDIA EMANCIPATION" SPEECH, AUGUST 4, 1857

I am so tired of feeling afraid for my children's and grandchildren's futures and waking up at night wondering whether human life will end on America's and our watch for children everywhere in our violence-saturated world. So I hope you will stand with me and others to stop those who prey on children, pick on children, and put children in harm's way.

Black children are disproportionately denied a fair chance and are disproportionately poor. An unlevel playing field from birth contributes to many poor Black children getting pulled in to a cradle-to-prison-to-death pipeline that we must dismantle if the clock of racial and social progress is to not turn backward.

Imprisonment is the new slavery for the Black community. On average, states spend over three times as much per prisoner as per public school pupil. What does that say about what we value?

The United States—the most militarily powerful and materially rich nation in the world—is so spiritually poor it chooses to let children be the poorest age group and to suffer multiple preventable deprivations. Millions of children lack health care when they are sick, lack enough food to stave off hunger, are homeless when their parents cannot find or afford housing, and lack safe and quality childcare and after-school programs when parents have to work. Millions of poor children are denied an early Head Start and quality preschool experience to help them get ready for school. Millions more children in our schools cannot read or write and are dropping out or being pushed out of school, en route to juvenile detention and adult jail rather than to jobs or college. And millions of children are struggling to grow up in working poor families who are playing by America's rules, but still cannot earn fair wages from their employers or get enough support from their government to escape poverty or better themselves.

We can and must do better.

This *Covenant with Black America* calls upon all parents, educators, preachers, social service providers, community leaders, and policymakers to act now and create a brighter future for our children. The words of writer and environmental activist Terry Tempest Williams make clearer the urgency of this book's message: "The eyes of the future are looking back at us and they are praying for us to see beyond our own time."

✢ ✢

I.

SECURING
THE RIGHT TO
HEALTH CARE
AND WELL-BEING

INTRODUCTORY ESSAY
BY DAVID M. SATCHER, M.D.

The health of African Americans has suffered greatly because of social disparities that rendered us, and therefore our treatment, less than equal in quality and access. There are major disparities in health care and health outcomes. For example, if we had eliminated disparities in health in the last century, there would have been 85,000 fewer Black deaths overall in 2000. Among others, these include: 24,000 fewer Black deaths from cardiovascular disease; 4,700 fewer Black infant deaths in the first year of life; 22,000 fewer deaths from diabetes; and almost 2,000 fewer Black women would have died from breast cancer.

In addition to health outcomes, disparities in health also relate to access to care. Access to health care is determined by many factors—insurance status, living in underserved communities, being underrepresented in the health-care professions, being uninformed about health-care services and need, and feeling insecure about or untrusting of the health-care system. These are major barriers to access.

To eliminate disparities in access, we must deal with all of these barriers. For example, there are almost 44 million Americans who are uninsured.[1] African Americans and Hispanics are most likely to be uninsured as are American Indians, about whom we have less specific data at present. Thus, we must be committed to effecting changes in policies such that universal access is a reality in this country.

Since African American health professionals are five times more likely to serve African American patients and Hispanic health professionals are five times more likely than majority professionals to serve Hispanic patients, we must work to elevate the representation of minorities in the health professions.[2] Today, whereas underrepresented minorities make up almost 30 percent of the population, they make up only 10 percent of the physicians in America.[3]

Any discussion of access must also include a discussion of quality of care received. Well-demonstrated studies reveal that the health professions, while clearly part of the solution to disparities, are also clearly a part of the problem of health disparities. Consider that African Americans receive a lower quality of care in many areas in cardiovascular care, diabetes, surgery care, and the early diagnosis of cancer, to mention a few. Studies of other populations are not as well developed, but there are clear indications that similar trends exist.

Culture plays a major role in the provision of quality health care, and the culture of medicine is predominantly white European. The provider must have the ability to identify with, relate to, and accommodate the culture of the patient. In many cases, the culture of patients influences how, when, and where they present with illness and how they express it. Likewise, the culture of health-care providers influences how they interact with patients, how they diagnose problems, and how they treat those problems. All of these are serious factors that contribute to people being uninformed, feeling insecure or untrusting, and being uninspired to seek medical care.

While access to and quality of health care are paramount to eliminating health disparities, their roles are not as significant as environment and lifestyle. According to a major study, the environment accounts for 20–30 percent of morbidity and mortality; genetics for 15–20 percent, and lifestyle for 40–50 percent. Lifestyle is a major consideration in the elimination of disparities in health.

According to the Leading Health Indicators of Healthy People 2010 and the Surgeon General's Prescription developed in 1999, the most important lifestyle indicators are physical activity; good nutrition, especially consumption of fruits and vegetables; overweight and obesity; the avoidance of toxins, especially tobacco; responsible sexual behavior, including emphasizing abstinence where appropriate; and minimizing unplanned pregnancy and STDs if sexually active.[4]

While all of these are important and even critical to eliminating disparities in health, the epidemic of overweight and obesity—and its disproportionate impact on African Americans and other minorities—is a clear point of attack. Obesity is a major risk factor for cardiovascular disease, including hypertension and strokes; diabetes; and cancer of the breast, colon, and prostate. We must also address policies at all levels of government to ensure support for education and good nutrition.

Environment makes a major contribution to disparities. For example, we know that Black and Hispanic children are more likely to be exposed to toxic substances or lead-based paint than their white counterparts.[5] Other toxins relate to the fact that Black and Hispanic children are most likely to grow up close to hazardous waste sites where the toxins are not as well-defined.

There are also gender differences among African Americans that relate to income gains experienced by African American women and the provision of Medicaid, which is more amenable to Black women than to Black men. Violence and gun-related deaths have taken a toll on African American men. Disproportionate numbers of Black men are incarcerated as a result of policies that mandate imprisonment as opposed to treatment for substance abuse.

Finally, we cannot overlook mental health. Mental health is fundamental to overall health and well-being. Mental disorders are real and indeed they, too, are physical disorders. Mental disorders are so common in the United States that one in five Americans has a diagnosable mental disorder each year. This includes 44 million adults and 13.7 million children.[6] Mental disorders are as disabling as cancer or heart disease in terms of premature death and lost productivity. They interfere with quality of life/productivity and cause unnecessary pain and suffering. They also interfere with the development of positive and fulfilling relationships.

African Americans are not exempt from mental illness and mental disorders. Indeed, African Americans have a greater burden of mental illness because of difficulty in accessing treatment. Since 1980, suicide has doubled among young Black males. Eighty to 90 percent of people who die by suicide are suffering from a diagnosable mental illness or substance abuse or both. In 2000, suicide was the 11th leading cause of death. Suicide deaths outnumber homicide deaths by five to three.[7] None of us can take our mental health for granted; there is a continuum between mental health and mental illness.

Many things must change to secure the right health care, healthy living, and well-being in America. The solution to this pervasive problem of health disparities is that we must advocate for system changes that include universal health insurance, guaranteed primary medical care, proportionate representation in health professions, bias-free interventions, nonviolent and exercise-friendly neighborhoods, nutritious food outlets, educational equality, career opportunities, parity in income and wealth, homeownership, and hope. There are individual, community, and governmental responsibilities for achieving these goals. Somehow we must bring these different levels of responsibility together in a concerted effort to eliminate disparities in health care and health outcomes.

I believe that there are reasons to be hopeful that with concerted efforts from the Black community and other leaders, we will successfully reverse the current trends. Today, there are national goals to eliminate racial and ethnic health disparities. I am encouraged by several new government programs created to address health disparities; an example is the National Center on Minority Health and Health Disparities of the National Institutes of Health.[8] Some health plans are now monitoring the quality of care provided to African Americans and other ethnic minorities compared to the majority population. Now more than ever, people are engaged with this issue. So I feel that we can all be hopeful, even though there is still a lot of work to be done.

Some time ago, I completed Stephen Ambrose's book *Undaunted Courage*. In it, he depicts the bravery, commitment, unusual insight, and fortitude possessed by those who led the expedition that expanded our borders from sea to shining sea. I also read Tom Brokaw's book *The Greatest Generation,* which salutes men and women of all races and ethnic groups who, through courage and commitment, gave their best efforts to protect freedom in the world and help position America for such a great second half of the 20th century. In both cases, what is noteworthy is the willingness of individuals to conquer territory that heretofore has been left unchallenged. That is what we are called on to do today. America's new frontier is not the wilderness, or the air, or the sea; it is the inner cities, the barrios, and the reservations, where disparities persist and where dreams are dim.

✤

DAVID M. SATCHER, M.D., Ph.D. is the Interim President of the Morehouse School of Medicine; before his December 2004 appointment, he served as the Director of the School's National Center for Primary Care. In February 2002, he completed his four-year term as the 16th Surgeon General of the United States; during that tenure, he simultaneously served as Assistant Secretary for Health. In both capacities, he led the federal government's effort to eliminate racial and ethnic disparities in health care. This initiative was incorporated into one of two major goals of Healthy People 2010, the nation's public health agenda for the next several years. For more information: http://www.msm.edu.

THE FACTS ON HEALTH CARE

INFANT MORTALITY

- Black infants are nearly two-and-one-half times more likely than white infants to die before their first birthday.[9]

DISEASE-RELATED RISK FACTORS

- More than one out of every three Black people are plagued by hypertension; this is the highest rate in the world. Hypertension can damage kidneys and lead to stroke, heart failure, and heart attack when it is not treated.[10]

- White adults are more likely to receive treatment than African Americans for hypertension complications, even though African Americans are affected at higher rates.[11]

- Of all men ages 20 and older, 36.4 percent of African Americans have high blood pressure, compared to 25.6 percent of white men.[12]

- Nearly 70 percent of Black adults between the ages of 20 and 74 are overweight; more than half of ALL Black women are overweight.[13]

PREVALENCE OF DISEASE

- Black women are close to 80 percent more likely to die of a stroke than white women, and 30 percent more likely to die of a heart attack.[14]

- More than 2.2 million African Americans have diabetes.[15]

- African Americans with diabetes have a 27 percent higher death rate than whites with the disease.[16]

- African Americans are 13 percent of the nation's population and account for 56 percent annually of new HIV infections. A quarter of these new infections are among people under 25 years of age.[17]

- Two-thirds of new AIDS cases among teens are Black, yet they are only 15 percent of the national teen population.[18]

- African American and Latino children make up more than 80 percent of pediatric AIDS cases.[19]

- Black women are diagnosed with AIDS at a rate 25 times that of white women. [20]

- HIV-positive African Americans are seven times more likely than whites infected with the virus to die from HIV-related illness.[21]

- African Americans are three times more likely to be hospitalized and also three times more likely to die from asthma.[22]

- More African American women die from asthma than those of any other ethnic group; the mortality rate is more than 2.5 times higher than that of white women.[23]

- Black people are 10 percent more likely to suffer from cancer and 30 percent more likely to die from cancer than whites.[24]

HEALTH CARE

- Nearly one-third—32 percent—of African Americans do not have a regular doctor. By contrast, only 20 percent of white Americans do not have a regular doctor.[25]

- Close to 1.8 million African American children in the United States do not have health insurance.[26]

- Fourteen percent of African Americans receiving HIV treatment have private insurance.[27]

- In a study of Black inner-city children with asthma, doctors prescribed long-term control asthma medications for only 42 percent of those who needed them.[28]

HEALTHY LIVING

- Nationally, half of all Black neighborhoods lack access to a full-service grocery store or supermarket.[29]

- Nationwide, predominantly white neighborhoods have four times more supermarkets than predominantly Black neighborhoods.[30]

- When there is a supermarket in a community, studies show that there is a 32 percent increase in fresh fruit and vegetable consumption.[31]

- Fifty percent of Black adults do not participate in light, moderate, or vigorous physical activity regularly as opposed to 35 percent of white adults.[32]

- White youths are 14 percent more likely to engage in regular exercise than African American youths.[33]

- Seventy-one percent of African Americans across the United States live in counties that violate federal air pollution standards, compared with 58 percent of white Americans.[34]

- There are 1.7 acres of park space for every 1,000 people in African American neighborhoods in Los Angeles, compared with 31.8 acres in white neighborhoods.[35]

What the Community Can Do

According to the World Health Organization, health is defined as "a state of complete physical, mental, and social well-being and not merely the absence of disease or infirmity."[36] The *Webster II New College Dictionary* defines health as "a condition of optimal well-being." In other words, health is more than not being sick; health is a state where individuals are performing at their best in both mind and body.

A common approach to health emphasizes the individual's role in her/his own health status: people get sick because they are not taking care of themselves. This perspective puts the responsibility of health entirely on the individual and fails to consider how the community in which people live has an impact—positive or negative—on health.

Overall, ethnic and racial minorities, and specifically African Americans in the United States, face a social and an economic environment of inequality that includes greater exposure to racism, discrimination, violence, and poverty[37]—all of which result in lower health status. Addressing health disparities means understanding how socioeconomic status and racism result in social and economic inequities that determine where we live, what we eat, where we work, how we exercise, what we breathe, what we drink, what we perceive as our life options, and how well informed we are about our health.

By working together, we are capable of bringing about positive change and building healthy, strong, vibrant, and inclusive communities. To strengthen the ability of community members to have input on healthy living decisions affecting them, to increase advocacy skill building, and to actively engage the African American community in its well-being, we must strengthen existing community coalitions, develop strategic collaborations, and demand the integration of community concerns and input into policy decision-making processes.

What Every Individual Can Do Now:

- Take responsibility to improve your diet; eat at least one additional fruit or vegetable daily.

- Walk one mile every day. Take the stairs instead of the elevator at work or in your apartment building.

- Make sure your children have healthy diets, get their daily exercise, and are fully immunized.

- Gather information about disease and health risks. Schedule regular exams with your health-care professional.

- Talk to your neighbors and organize a healthy living committee; create awareness of the situation in your

community, coordinate outdoor activities, start a
walking group, and demand that the local storeowners
stock fresh produce.

MOST OF ALL:

- Hold all leaders and elected officials responsible and
demand that they change current policy.

What Works Now:

These action statements are not submitted in isolation. The principles contained in them have been actualized in various communities across America wherein residents decided to "take matters in their own hands." Following are representative examples of these real-life activists.

Myser Keels: West Fresno Food Maxx Supermarket

In 1995, little new development was occurring in West Fresno, California, a once thriving community composed of mostly African American and some Latino residents. For many years, residents had hoped that the Fresno City Council would allocate funds to improve neighborhood conditions. Concerned residents gathered to prioritize what they most wanted from the city to spur development and decided construction of a supermarket was at the top of their list. The small food stores in the area charged high prices for little selection, and many residents had to depend on the bus to access the selection, quality, and prices available at supermarkets in other parts of the city.[38]

Residents began advocating for a supermarket in their community. Myser Keels, a leader of and spokesperson for The Affordable Housing Coalition, which included churches and community groups, said, "We want choices. We've been waiting too long to get the city to bring in a big store. The few stores in our area only have limited supplies of what we need. It's just a tragedy that we don't have a decent shopping center in our area."[39] The coalition held a news conference in front of a supermarket in another part of the city, where members carried empty grocery bags and demanded that the Fresno City Council set aside money from its $11 million Community Development Block Grant to build a shopping center in their community. Over several years, these concerned residents continued to strategize and advocate in a variety of settings. They attended public hearings conducted by the city on Community Development Block Grant funds and met with city council members, the director of the city's redevelopment agency, and other public officials. Coalition members got residents to sign petitions and turned out hundreds of residents at city council meetings. They also worked with the media, held news conferences, wrote editorials, built relationships with local reporters, and received ongoing coverage of their struggle in the *Fresno Bee.*

Once their supermarket campaign gained political support, the coalition continued to move the project forward. They ensured that the city allocated redevelopment funds to help build the supermarket; helped local government officials negotiate with local property owners to secure the land for the site; worked to ensure that jobs went to local residents; urged the city to make an agreement with a developer; got a police station built to ensure security at the shopping center; and urged the city to approve final zoning for the market.

The supermarket is now open, serving the largely African American community successfully for more than five years.

Fayette County Public School District and PTA

Over the past 20 years, access to healthy food has improved, resulting from concerted grassroots organizing and strategic advocacy for policy reforms.[40] Elected officials agree that grassroots efforts are necessary to pass reform legislation, and PTA organizations nationwide are effective in changing children's nutrition policy in schools.[41] The Fayette County (Kentucky) Public School District negotiated a healthier vending contract to ensure the nutritional well-being of its students.

There are 51 elementary, middle, and high schools in Fayette County's Public School District. Of these 51, African American students are the majority at 11 schools, they make up between 20 percent and 72 percent at 27 of the schools, and over 50 percent of the students are on free or reduced lunch meal plans at 21 of the district's schools.[42]

The PTA worked with the school district to set nutritional standards for snacks and renegotiated its vending contracts to shift the proportion of healthy options from 1 percent to 40 percent in the snack selections, and 21 percent to 72 percent of the beverage selections. In addition, the prices for healthier options were lowered, and the machines now feature pictures of young people being physically active. These changes were the result of two years' worth of advocacy in support of healthier school vending. Elementary schools in the district have been and will continue to be free of vending machines.[43]

Louisiana Bucket Brigade

The Bucket Brigade was started in California, but it was in Mossville, Louisiana, that the program achieved its most provocative and successful results.[44] Founded by African Americans in 1812, the community of Mossville has 17 industrial facilities within half a mile of the city's boundary, including the largest concentration of vinyl plastic manufacturers in the United States, oil refineries, a coal-fired power plant, and chemical production facilities.[45]

The people of Mossville grew very ill with numerous diseases and ailments—cancer, heart problems, and respiratory disorders.[46] Many suspected that their exposure to the toxic contaminants from the heavily polluting facilities in the community was the cause of these adverse health effects.[47] They were fed up with the lack of concern for their health and decided to form a "bucket brigade" to begin taking samples of the contaminated air. The bucket, a low-cost device that communities can use to monitor their exposure to toxic pollutants for themselves, is sent to a lab for analysis after individuals complete the simple collection process.[48] The samples of different chemicals found violations of Louisiana standards of as much as 220 times the state's standards.[49]

Within a year, the bucket brigades had spread throughout the cancer alley of Louisiana with much media attention, leading to the formation of a new nonprofit, the Louisiana Bucket Brigade. The Environmental Protection Agency (EPA) brought in high-priced monitoring devices that confirmed the astronomical levels of pollution, and the enforcement authorities meted out the consequences accordingly.[50] Offending companies were forced to pay fines and use high-tech monitoring devices. The EPA's regional office next funded community groups' bucket monitoring and through their efforts, there is much less pollution. This "stemmed from a few citizen activists with their buckets."[51] There are now bucket brigades in California, Louisiana, Pennsylvania, Ohio, and Texas, and they have even reached as far as Durban, South Africa.

What Every Leader and Elected Official Can Do

- Improve data collection and analysis at local, regional, state, and national levels.

- Create universal access to quality health care and treatment.

- Ensure residents in low-income neighborhoods have decent places to engage in physical activity and purchase healthy food.

- Strengthen regulations on hazardous toxic substances that have negative impacts on health and the environment.

- Develop and implement trainings for health-care professionals to meet the needs of diverse patient populations.

Improve Data Collection and Research

Data collection and research are crucial to understanding the health status of our nation: indicating who is doing well, who is not, and analyzing factors that promote or hinder health. According to the National Center for Health Statistics at CDC, policy-makers, planners, researchers, and others use these data in the health community to monitor changes in the use of health-care resources, to monitor specific diseases, to examine the impact of new medical technologies, and to discover root causes of disease and illness. Since the analysis can only be as good as the data gathered, it is essential to improve data collection and analysis on local, regional, state, and national levels to ensure that all populations are represented in a comprehensive and thorough manner.

Officials at all levels of government must identify and create funding sources and mechanisms for collecting and analyzing prevalence, health outcome, and risk factor data at the regional and community levels. In addition, health advocates need to promote collaboration between government agencies to collect standardized prevalence data that allow comparison among states, regions, counties, and other localities.

Create Universal Access to Quality Health Care and Treatment

People of color and residents of low-income communities have less access and face more barriers to quality health care and treatment than do their better-off and nonminority counterparts. Barriers include a lack of health facilities nearby, the cost of care and prescriptions, or the lack of neighborhood-based resources and social support to engage in healthy behaviors.

To increase access to quality health care and treatment, three crucial factors must change: (1) Health coverage must be expanded to reduce disparities in access to current, innovative treatment modalities and quality medications. (2) Elected officials need to mandate that health plans provide broader coverage for medication and equipment prescribed by physicians that could promote increased home management. (3) It is necessary to advocate for health plans to expand coverage to pay for home assessments, for remediation efforts, and for equipment intended to address environmental toxins.

Increase Levels of Physical Activity and Access to Healthy Foods

People who live in low-income neighborhoods face many barriers to health, including lack of access to safe parks or green space, where they can engage in physical activity, and lack of access to grocery stores that offer affordable and nutritious food. Low levels of physical activity and poor diet are linked to obesity, which can result in high blood pressure, cardiovascular disease, diabetes, and other negative health outcomes.

To ensure residents in low-income neighborhoods have decent places to engage in physical activity and purchase healthy food, policy-makers need to implement public policies that mandate safe, attractive local parks and encourage local involvement by churches, parks and recreation departments, and others to maintain facilities. It is equally important that they reform the way schools are designed and built in order to open indoor and outdoor recreational sites on school grounds for community use after school hours.

Healthy living advocates have to urge local and state government officials to provide low-cost financing for grocery stores in underserved neighborhoods through tax breaks, low-interest loans, and other incentives. In striving to achieve healthy-living alternatives for all, policy-makers must also build partnerships among local government, Farmer's Market Associations, hospitals, health maintenance organizations (HMOs), and other local institutions and businesses to implement creative programs to provide healthy food to residents in low-income communities.

Promote Environmental Justice

In the United States, a disproportionate number of toxic-waste sites are located in or near low-income communities and communities of color. This is the result of environmental racism: discrimination in environmental lawmaking and law enforcement, and targeting communities of color as sites for toxic-waste disposal and polluting industries.

To protect community members and the environment from hazardous toxic substances that affect health both directly and indirectly, government officials need to strengthen regulations on hazardous substances that have negative impacts on health and the environment. Health advocates must also encourage the use of Medicaid funds for environmental assessment and needed physical remediation. It is imperative that local and state officials support and promote public education campaigns targeting the general public, as well as specific neighborhoods, with demonstrated high levels of environmental hazards that contribute to illnesses and diseases such as lead poisoning, asthma, birth defects, and cancers. To aid in preventing these diseases, city planners must improve the design and construction standards in new public and state-assisted housing to improve ventilation and reduce the likelihood of mold problems. Finally, to continue to include health professionals in the fight for universal healthy living, state education boards should integrate training in environmental health effects into medical school curricula and post-graduate training. (Note: Environmental justice is discussed more fully in Covenant IX.)

Broadly Train Health-Care Professionals

To provide the best treatment for all people who live in the United States, health-care professionals need to feel comfortable and skilled working with patients from different backgrounds. This includes not only race, ethnic, and cultural backgrounds, but also how to have successful doctor/patient relationships regardless of physical ability/disability, age, sexual orientation, gender, size, education, economic background, English language ability, or preferences in Eastern or Western approaches to health.

By developing and implementing training for health-care professionals, they will be able to meet the needs of diverse patient populations and identify additional resources required to provide adequate care. To do this, policy-makers need to require culturally competent training for health-care professionals and other service providers, including school and childcare personnel and athletic coaches; and to provide additional resources, such as translators and medical information in multiple languages, including Braille and sign language. Further, access to training that improves understanding of the valuable role of nontraditional, alternative healing practices must be increased.

A Final Word

If we take responsibility for our own diets and make sure we provide nutritious food and physical activity for our children and our families, and if we hold our elected officials to ensuring access to adequate treatment and healthy living options for all, then we can secure the right to health care and well-being.

CWBA

TEN YEARS LATER

SECURING
THE RIGHT TO
HEALTH CARE
AND WELL-BEING

Since 2006, we have seen many changes to the political land-scape of health policy in the United States—changes that suggest improvement to racial gaps in the right to health care and well-be-ing. Although the U.S. suffered a massive economic recession with larger losses in employment for Black fellow citizens than for whites,[1] 2010's Affordable Care Act (ACA) expanded access to health care for low-income Americans and already appears to have markedly improved racial gaps in insurance status. However, the implemen-tation of ACA's reforms began only recently, and on the whole the period since 2006 has seen the continuation of large gaps in most of the areas surveyed a decade ago. The sections below survey changes over the time since the publication of this book's original edition in the areas of mortality and chronic conditions, HIV infection rates, health insurance and health-care access, and healthy living.

Mortality and Disease-Related Risk Factors

Disparities in health by race are notable from birth itself, although there are some narrowing of gaps in recent times. Life expectancy at birth for whites in the U.S. was 78.94 years in 2010, while for Black Americans it was almost 4 years less, at 75.08. In 1999–2001, the gap was closer to 6 years, at 77.43 and 71.81 years respectively.[2] Black infant mortality has declined from a rate of 13.8 deaths per 1,000 live births in 2004 to 11.3 deaths per 1,000 in 2013, which represents a narrowing of the gap as well but continues to be over two times as high as white infant mortality (Fig. 1).[3]

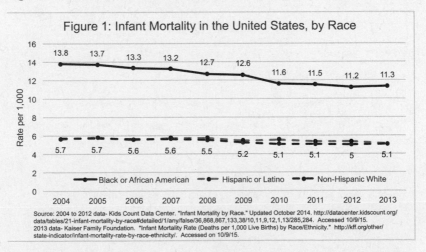

Figure 1: Infant Mortality in the United States, by Race

Source: 2004 to 2012 data- Kids Count Data Center. "Infant Mortality by Race." Updated October 2014. http://datacenter.kidscount.org/data/tables/21-infant-mortality-by-race#detailed/1/any/false/36,868,867,133,38/10,11,9,12,1,13/285,284. Accessed 10/9/15. 2013 data- Kaiser Family Foundation. "Infant Mortality Rate (Deaths per 1,000 Live Births) by Race/Ethnicity." http://kff.org/other/state-indicator/infant-mortality-rate-by-race-ethnicity/. Accessed on 10/9/15.

The teen birth rate, a related risk factor for infant mortality, has improved for all racial groups, with a narrowing of disparities. The rate of births for Black teens age 15–17 has reduced 51 percent between 2003 and 2013.[4] Thus, since the original publication of this book in 2006, Black America has experienced improvements in several dimensions of mortality and related factors.

In contrast to mortality, the prevalence of disease-related risk factors appears fairly stable or (in the case of female obesity) worsening over the recent past. The rate of hypertension for Black men was 42.5 percent in 2010–2012, compared to 29.6 percent among white men; the gap in rates for women was also similar, with Black women being more than 1.5 times as likely as white women to suffer from hypertension (Figs. 2 and 3). A study of women in Connecticut highlights the widening racial gaps in hypertension rates. According to Olivero, "In fact, nearly one out of every two African American women living in Connecticut suffers from hypertension, a life-threatening condition that can lead to heart attack, stroke, and kidney disease, research shows"[5]

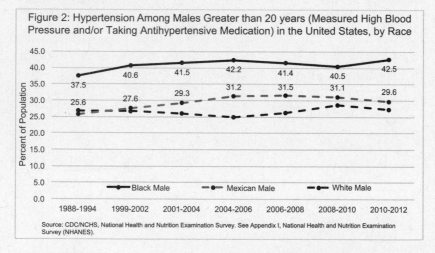

Figure 2: Hypertension Among Males Greater than 20 years (Measured High Blood Pressure and/or Taking Antihypertensive Medication) in the United States, by Race

Source: CDC/NCHS, National Health and Nutrition Examination Survey. See Appendix I, National Health and Nutrition Examination Survey (NHANES).

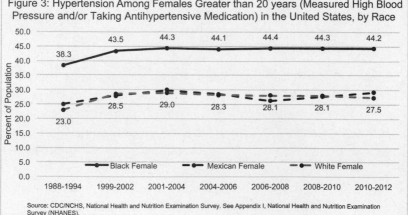

Figure 3: Hypertension Among Females Greater than 20 years (Measured High Blood Pressure and/or Taking Antihypertensive Medication) in the United States, by Race

Source: CDC/NCHS, National Health and Nutrition Examination Survey. See Appendix I, National Health and Nutrition Examination Survey (NHANES).

Although recently rates of obesity have been leveling off for some populations, the Black-white gap in obesity has been rising for females (Figs. 4 and 5). In 2010–2012, 57.5 percent of Black females over the age of 20 were obese, while for whites this was 32.3 percent. For men, the rate was about the same for whites as for Black Americans. In all, 82 percent of Black women are now overweight or obese, compared to 63.2 percent for white women.[6]

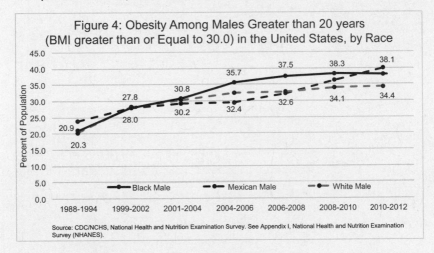

Figure 4: Obesity Among Males Greater than 20 years (BMI greater than or Equal to 30.0) in the United States, by Race

Source: CDC/NCHS, National Health and Nutrition Examination Survey. See Appendix I, National Health and Nutrition Examination Survey (NHANES).

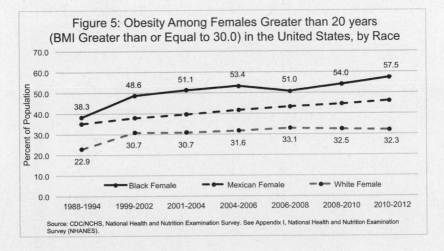

Figure 5: Obesity Among Females Greater than 20 years (BMI Greater than or Equal to 30.0) in the United States, by Race

Source: CDC/NCHS, National Health and Nutrition Examination Survey. See Appendix I, National Health and Nutrition Examination Survey (NHANES).

Rates of stroke also remain an area for concern, with the prevalence rate for Black citizens being about 1.5 times that for whites in 2006 and in 2010 (Fig. 6).

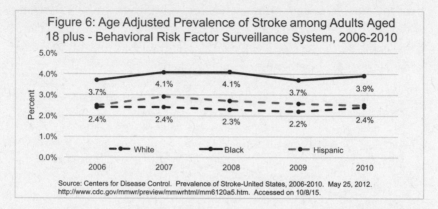

Figure 6: Age Adjusted Prevalence of Stroke among Adults Aged 18 plus - Behavioral Risk Factor Surveillance System, 2006-2010

Source: Centers for Disease Control. Prevalence of Stroke-United States, 2006-2010. May 25, 2012. http://www.cdc.gov/mmwr/preview/mmwrhtml/mm6120a5.htm. Accessed on 10/8/15.

Diabetes prevalence for Black Americans is 20.6 percent, about double that for whites; the gap has remained stable since the late 1980s (Fig. 7).

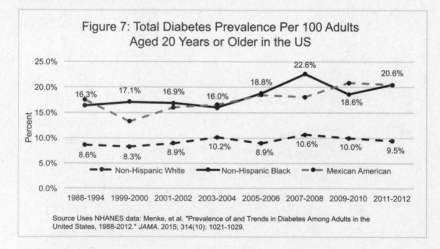

Figure 7: Total Diabetes Prevalence Per 100 Adults Aged 20 Years or Older in the US

Source Uses NHANES data: Menke, et al. "Prevalence of and Trends in Diabetes Among Adults in the United States, 1988-2012." JAMA. 2015; 314(10): 1021-1029.

HIV

In addition to chronic diseases, rates of infectious diseases also showed large disparities a decade ago. The HIV rate is of particular concern; diagnosis rates per 100,000 are currently at 70 for African Americans and 11 for whites (Fig. 8). A report from the CDC shows that in 2010, Black males accounted for 5,600 new HIV infections in the U.S., compared to 2,100 for white males. Black females accounted for 1,400 new infections while white females accounted for 280.[7]

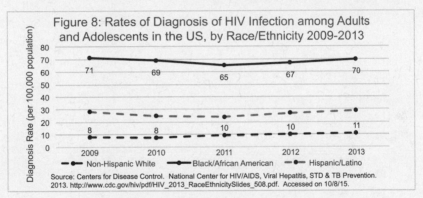

Figure 8: Rates of Diagnosis of HIV Infection among Adults and Adolescents in the US, by Race/Ethnicity 2009-2013

Source: Centers for Disease Control. National Center for HIV/AIDS, Viral Hepatitis, STD & TB Prevention. 2013. http://www.cdc.gov/hiv/pdf/HIV_2013_RaceEthnicitySlides_508.pdf. Accessed on 10/8/15.

Health Insurance and Health Care

Rates of uninsurance were around 9.4 percent for whites and 20 percent for African Americans in 2002. During the past two years, the racial gaps in health insurance have narrowed dramatically, as can be seen in Figure 9. While part of this may be due to economic recovery, the update to Covenant VIII demonstrates that the recovery has been less beneficial for racial minorities, thus it is more likely that these improvements in health insurance are early effects of the ACA. From 2012 to 2014, the rate of uninsurance among whites fell from 11.1 percent to 7.6 percent; for Black Americans this rate improved from 18.5 percent to 11.8 percent. Most noticeable in Fig. 9 is the change for Hispanic Americans, from 30.1 percent to 19.9 percent. There are corresponding improvements visible in access to care. Over the past two years, the percentage who reported being unable to see a doctor because of cost decreased from 16 percent to 14 percent for whites, and from 24 percent to 21 percent for Black Americans; for Hispanics the improvement was from 29 percent to 25 percent. In addition to reducing the extent of uninsurance, the ACA improves the quality of care (for example, by preventing exclusion of services for pre-existing conditions), and future work should monitor the extent to which these improvements in access to care reduce the persistent gaps in chronic disease prevalence.

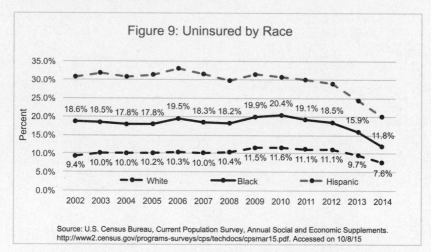

Figure 9: Uninsured by Race

Source: U.S. Census Bureau, Current Population Survey, Annual Social and Economic Supplements. http://www2.census.gov/programs-surveys/cps/techdocs/cpsmar15.pdf. Accessed on 10/8/15

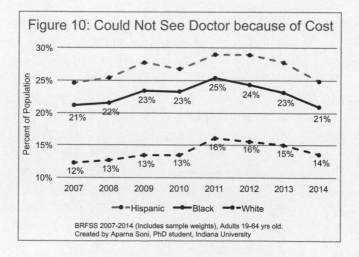

Figure 10: Could Not See Doctor because of Cost

BRFSS 2007-2014 (Includes sample weights), Adults 19-64 yrs old.
Created by Aparna Soni, PhD student, Indiana University

Healthy Living

In searching for potential ways to improve health outcomes, policy makers and researchers increasingly turn toward improvements in healthy-living measures, in addition to improved access to health care. Healthy living encompasses traditional public health risk factors, such as smoking, as well as external conditions, including exposure to environmental toxins. Recent research finds that up to one third of the difference in life expectancy among demographic groups can be explained by characteristics of workplaces related to health.[8]

Although rates of smoking initiation have reduced in recent years, the percent of 12th graders who smoke shows growing disparities between Black and white citizens in recent years.[9]

The original *Covenant* text reported that 50 percent of Black adults do not regularly participate in physical activity, compared to 35 percent for white adults. Since that edition's 2006 publication, a study in the *Journal of Public Health Policy* has found there may be reductions in the racial gaps identified earlier, perhaps due to public attention focused on disparities that existed, and that higher rates of poor outcomes among Black Americans are now unlikely caused by lower rates of physical activity.[10]

Also since the original publication of *The Covenant with Black America*, the Obama administration and the First Lady in particular have raised national awareness of inequities in neighborhood access to healthy foods and have advanced various policy initiatives. For example, in December 2009, 39 members of Congress from both the Republican and Democratic parties issued a resolution in the House of Representatives recognizing the need for national policy to address limited access to healthy food in underserved communities. However, progress has stalled on specific measures; policies included in the President's budget proposal, such as the Healthy Food Financing Initiative—which was to incentivize healthy food retail outlets to locate in underserved neighborhoods—have not received funding in Congress.[11]

Conclusion

In 2006, *The Covenant with Black America* brought unprecedented awareness of the disparities in health and related outcomes between whites and Black fellow citizens. While improvements are visible in some areas including mortality and physical activity, the racial gap in prevalence of chronic conditions and mortality risk factors has not narrowed. This update serves to direct the attention garnered by the original edition of the book toward persistent and troubling disparities; evidence from other spheres of life, including racial discrimination in sports refereeing, shows that increasing national awareness can play an important role in instigating meaningful change in racial disparities.[12]

The work of various social justice organizations dedicated to reversing disparities in criminal justice systems has increased media attention on the differences in well-being outcomes between Black and white Americans. But, gaps in health outcomes such as chronic conditions and access to care must also be monitored, especially as there is promising potential in the ACA to reduce these gaps.

—Prepared by Kosali Simon, Ph.D., School of Public and Environmental Affairs, Indiana University; Angshuman Gooptu, Doctoral Candidate in Public Affairs, School of Public and Environmental Affairs, Indiana University; Seth Freedman, Ph.D., Assistant Professor, School of Public and Environmental Affairs, Indiana University; Victoria Perez, Ph.D., Assistant Professor, School of Public and Environmental Affairs, Indiana University, Bloomington, Indiana

✦ ✦

II.

ESTABLISHING A SYSTEM OF PUBLIC EDUCATION IN WHICH ALL CHILDREN ACHIEVE AT HIGH LEVELS AND REACH THEIR FULL POTENTIAL

INTRODUCTORY ESSAY BY EDMUND W. GORDON

Without question, education is the key to progress and prosperity in the United States today. Whether fair or not, educational opportunity and academic achievement are directly tied to the social divisions associated with race, ethnicity, gender, first language, and social class.

The level and quality of educational attainment either open the doors to opportunity or close them.

Education starts at home, in neighborhoods, and in communities. Reading to children, creating time and space for homework, and demonstrating—through words and deeds—that education is important are the key first building blocks for high educational achievement. While schools are responsible for what children are taught, reinforcement at home is essential. As members of the Black community, we must take responsibility for educating all our children—whether ours by birth or otherwise—to uplift our people as a whole.

Gains made in the 1960s, 1970s, and 1980s have slowed. We have not been able to eliminate or significantly reduce the academic achievement gap between African American, Latina/o, and Native American students and their counterparts who identify themselves as Asian American or European American. Not only has the gap not disappeared, rather it appears to have also increased as academic achievement and/or social-economic status (SES) rise. That is, the gap is smaller between low-achieving and low-SES Blacks and whites than it is between high-achieving or high-SES Blacks and whites. In other words, higher academic achievement and higher social class status are not associated with smaller but rather greater differences in academic achievement.[1] African American males lag behind African American females in academic achievement. Schools that serve predominantly Black student populations are more likely to be underresourced than are schools serving predominantly white student populations.

Fifty years after the U.S. Supreme Court's decision declaring school segregation unconstitutional, most Black children attend public schools where minorities represent the majority of the student body. Students attending schools in predominantly white neighborhoods are less likely to experience teachers of poor quality than are students attending schools in predominantly Black communities. By almost all the common indicators of academic achievement and school quality, students who identify themselves as Black suffer in the comparisons with students who identify themselves as white.

The continuing shortage of African American, Latino/a, and Native American students who achieve at very high levels academically is the issue that guided the work of the National Task Force on Minority High Achievement, a group organized by the College Board in 1997. The report of the Task Force, *Reaching the Top*, concluded that it would be: "virtually impossible to integrate the professional and leadership ranks of our society . . . until many more students from these underrepresented groups become high achievers."[2]

As our nation and schools become increasingly diverse, the issue of closing the achievement gap becomes more urgent. Between 1972 and 1998, the proportion of students of color in public schools increased from 22 percent to 38 percent. The enrollment rates for students of color in the West and South already constitute 47 percent and 45 percent, respectively, of the student population. And what some of us do not realize, or may not even accept, is that these proportional increases suggest that the prosperity of our nation will be increasingly dependent on the knowledge and contributions of students of color. Thus, in our multifaceted roles as educators, policy-makers, parents, and community members, it is important that we stimulate high levels of academic achievement for all students, particularly those who have been least well-served by our schools.

Clearly the state of education in Black America is multidimensional and complex. Arguably, the most critical problem in education that faces Black America is the problem of the gap in academic achievement known to exist between Blacks and whites. Further, as we have indicated, not only is this problem manifested at all achievement and SES levels, but as we go up the ladder with respect to each, the achievement disparity also increases. Obviously, this society has not been able to make education function to optimize and equalize academic development among Blacks.

This failure is not unique to the United States. In other industrialized societies in which caste-like systems are in place, we see comparable differentials in the academic achievement of high-status and lower-status children.[3] There certainly appears to be a ubiquitous association between one's status in the social order and one's level of academic achievement that favors high status and privilege.

There are several possible explanations for these widely observed phenomena that are reflected in the academic achievement gap.

Persistent explanations place varying degrees of emphasis on assumed cultural and/or genetic differences between Blacks and whites. In this line of argument, assumed inferiority is the underlying premise, whether it be genetically or culturally determined.[4]

Some liberal scholars argue for cultural and behavioral differences that are not necessarily inferior but are, nonetheless, inappropriate to the demands of high levels of academic achievement, and these differences tend not to be addressed by typical approaches to schooling.[5] Other explanations have focused on the attitudes and behaviors of the students themselves. Here we have the Fordham and Ogbu finding of "fear of acting white" as a factor that directs the attention and behavior of Black students away from serious academic pursuit.[6] More recently, Steele has advanced the notion concerning "fear of stereotype confirmation" in which Black students' performance is assumed to be impaired by their anxiety concerning the possibility that if they try and do not do well, they will confirm the negative stereotype that others hold concerning them.[7]

From the Black community and other reasonably well-informed sources, we hear the argument that the achievement gap is a reflection of inadequate opportunities to learn. This argument rests on the historic finding of inequality in the educational opportunities available to children in America.[8] It is the inequality in educational opportunity that has been the driving force behind the school desegregation movement and behind much of the continuing effort at school reform. If that inequality in opportunity to learn and the inequality in achievement are ultimately to be eliminated, we think that the nation must undertake a multifaceted initiative to improve the state of education in Black America. Such an initiative would include interventions directed at:

- Reducing the relatively high levels of academic underproductivity observed in so many of our children and the schools that serve them;

- Stabilizing the social fabric of our families and communities to better protect and support the academic and personal development of our children;

- Reducing inefficiencies in and the underutilization of the power of schooling and supplemental education in the development of the sizeable group of children of color who now achieve at modest levels or barely survive with minimum performance in many of our schools; and

- Increasing the nurturance and celebration of developed ability in the group that Du Bois called "the talented tenth" of our people upon whom the Black community and the nation must depend for leadership.[9]

The National Urban League, through its former President/CEO Hugh Price, and the College Board have recently advocated that greater attention be given to high academic achievement of students of color.[10] We too have continuously promoted the idea of a national effort at the "Affirmative Development of Academic Ability."[11] This notion was first advanced at a conference sponsored by the National Action Committee on Minorities in Engineering some 20 years ago. In an exchange with Scott Miller, we proposed that for affirmative action to work in a society where opportunities to learn are unequally distributed, a parallel program directed at the affirmative development of academic ability might be needed.[12] The notion was picked up a decade later in the recommendations of the College Board's National Task Force on Minority High Achievement.

Thus, the Task Force recommends that an extensive array of public and private policies, actions, and investments be pursued, which would collectively provide many more opportunities for academic development for underrepresented minority students through the schools, colleges, and universities that they attend, through their homes, and through their communities. We summarize this as a commitment to affirmative development.[13]

In this line of argument, we have borrowed from Bourdieu to emphasize the variety of forms of capital upon which effective education rests.[14] (See Table 2:1.)

Table 2:1 Forms of Capital For Effective Education

KINDS OF CAPITAL	DEFINITION
HEALTH	Physical developmental integrity, health, nutritional condition
FINANCIAL	Income, wealth, family, community, and societal economic resources available for education
HUMAN	Social competence, tacit knowledge, and other education-derived abilities as personal or family assets
SOCIAL	Social network relationships, social norms, cultural styles and values
POLITY	Societal membership, social concern, public commitment, political economy
PERSONAL	Disposition, attitudes, aspirations, efficacy, sense of power
INSTITUTIONAL	Quality of and access to educational and socializing institutions
PEDAGOGICAL	Supports for appropriate educational treatment in family, school, and community

Access to these forms of capital is grossly unequally distributed. Schools and other social institutions seem to work when the persons served bring to them the varieties of capital that enable and support human development. If we are correct in assuming that the effectiveness of schools and other human resource development institutions is in part a function of the availability of such wealth-derived capital for investment in human development, we may have in this relationship a catalyst for pedagogical, political, and social intervention.

If the effectiveness of education rests on such resources and they are unequally distributed, it is reasonable to anticipate that the effects of education will be unequal. The achievement distribution data correlate highly with the data on access to these forms of capital. Our notion of affirmative development is conceptually grounded in possible approaches to offsetting the negative effects of the maldistribution of access to these forms of education-related capital. While the most direct approach to the solution of the problem of maldistribution would involve the redistribution of income, wealth, and related resources, it is not reasonable to expect that such a radical solution will resonate with 21st century America. It is possible, however, that even a compassionate conservative society will see it to be in the best interest of the nation to organize its social institutions and its services so as to remove the negative effects of such maldistribution on the academic and personal development of its people.

A national effort at affirmative development to complement continuing efforts at affirmative action should be much broader than the initiatives directed at improving the effectiveness of education. Within the education establishment, however, we know a great deal about the deliberate development of academic ability. We propose that the education community embark upon a deliberate effort to develop academic abilities in a broad range of students who have a history of being resource deprived and who as a consequence are underrepresented in the pool of academically high-achieving students.

The deliberate or affirmative development of academic ability should include more equitable access to the variety of assets and strengths referred to in the chart above as capitals and to such educational interventions that provide early and continuous high-quality learning opportunities, high-quality teaching and school facilities, and rich community supports that are stimulating, encouraging, and supportive of educational excellence. Broad political will, and courageous leadership from the Black community and beyond, must also present a strong and consistent demand for adequate investments to achieve the high-quality education of *all* children.

The state of education in Black America is considerably better than it was 100 years ago—better than even 50 years ago. Some evidence suggests that our progress has been uneven during the past half-century. There is no question, nonetheless, that there remain complex and serious problems. These problems are related to the significant gap between the academic achievement levels of peoples of color and the achievement levels of Asian American and European American peoples.

But even more problematic may be the changing and rising demands for intellective competence that are associated with urbanicity and postmodernity, at the same time that Blacks are trying to close the academic achievement gap. With such a moving target, the challenge may be exacerbated. What we need is a national commitment to the affirmative development of academic ability in Black and other populations that are underrepresented among the high achievers in our society. A cross section of what is being done in pockets all across America is highlighted in the balance of this chapter.

✢

EDMUND W. GORDON, Ed.D., is the Richard March Hoe Professor of Psychology and Education, Emeritus, Teachers College, Columbia University; John M. Musser Professor of Psychology, Emeritus, Yale University; and Senior Scholar in Residence, The College Board. He is the founder and director of the Institute for Urban and Minority Education at Teachers College. The noted developmental and educational psychologist has held appointments at several of the nation's leading universities—Howard, Yeshiva, Harvard, Columbia, City College of New York, and Yale. His scholarship is documented in his authoring more than 175 articles in scholarly journals and book chapters and authoring or editing more than 15 books and monographs. His special interests relate to educating low-status populations and the intersect of cultures and human behavioral development. For more information: http://iume.tc.columbia.edu/default.asp.

THE FACTS ON PUBLIC EDUCATION

EARLY CHILDHOOD EDUCATION

- Early childhood education is key to school readiness and sustained academic achievement, yet at age three, only 45 percent of African American children are enrolled, and at age four just 73 percent are registered.[15]

READING COMPREHENSION

- Just 12 percent of African-American fourth graders have reached proficient or advanced reading levels, while 61 percent have yet to reach the basic level.[16]

- In a national assessment of student reading ability, Black children scored 16 percent below white children.[17]

- Forty-six percent of Black adults, compared with 14 percent of white adults, scored in the lowest category of the National Adult Literacy survey. The results indicate that Blacks have more limited skills in processing information from articles, books, tables, charts, and graphs compared with their white counterparts.[18]

MATHEMATICAL PROFICIENCY

- Many Black 17-year-old students graduating high school have the math skills of white eighth graders.[19]

PROMOTIONS/RETENTIONS, SUSPENSIONS/ EXPULSIONS

- While 9 percent of white students have repeated a grade, twice as many, or 18 percent, of Black students have been held back at least once.[20]

- One out of three African American students in seventh through 12th grades has been suspended or expelled at some point, as opposed to 15 percent of white children.[21]

HIGHER EDUCATION

- Of Black 16- to 24-year-olds, 13 percent have not earned a high school diploma or GED; 7 percent of white young people are without a high school credential.[22]

- In 2000, 31 percent of African Americans ages 18 to 24 were enrolled in colleges and universities; nearly two-thirds of these students were female.[23]

- According to the most recent statistics, the nationwide college graduation rate for enrolled Black students is only 40 percent, compared to 61 percent of enrolled white students.[24]

What the Community Can Do

From the time of slavery to today, Black Americans have struggled to attain high-quality education. During slavery, educating Blacks was forbidden. Today there is a legal right to attend schools, but for many Blacks, a quality education is almost as difficult to obtain as it was more than a century ago. Schools are more segregated than they were 20 years ago, too many of which are predominantly Black and of low quality. We must demand that local communities provide the resources to educate *all* children, that the state and federal governments provide sufficient resources. The mandate of educating all of America's children rests on all of us.

What Every Individual Can Do Now:

- Read to your children or grandchildren every day.
- Create clean, quiet spaces for your children to do homework; check to make sure that assignments are completed.
- Get a library card for each member of your family.
- Arrange enriching family and neighborhood activities for children of all ages: museums, educational games, spelling bees, and science fairs.

- Become involved in your children's school—PTA, school committees; attend back-to-school events; if you do not have children in the school, consider becoming a volunteer.

MOST OF ALL:

- Hold all leaders and elected officials responsible and demand that they change current policy.

What Works Now:

Following are some strategies that you may want to consider emulating.

Thelma Harrison's "Mama, I Want to Read"

Thelma Harrison is the founder and director of "Mama, I Want to Read," a program that teaches reading skills to preschoolers and helps them prepare for kindergarten. The 87-year-old veteran of the civil rights movement started the organization in an inner-city neighborhood of Norfolk, Virginia.

With the skills these young children acquire under Harrison's tutelage, they are prepared to succeed in their early years of elementary school. She has developed relationships with parents, grandparents, teachers, and administrators. From offering teaching advice and curriculum suggestions directly to schools, to offering great wisdom, compassion, and love to families, Harrison has created lifelong bonds. She believes that "it does take a village" for children to succeed and spends each day ensuring that she does her part, as do the people she rallies to the cause, continuing tirelessly to build a strong foundation for our future.

Harlem Children's Zone

The Harlem Children's Zone (HCZ)[25] is one of the largest community-based programs devoted to combining learning in and out of school in the United States. Its mission: to change the odds for children and parents in a 60-block zone in central Harlem, an area with nearly 7,000 children, more than 60 percent of whom live below the poverty line and three-quarters of whom score below grade level on statewide reading and math assessments. President and CEO Geoffrey Canada's strategy focuses on more than academic achievement, however. He has developed a system in which academic excellence is one of the outcomes, achieved in a number of ways, but it also includes nurturing family stability, opportunities for employment, decent and affordable housing, youth development activities for adolescents, and a quality education for children and parents in the zone.

Over the past 15 years, Canada has increased the Harlem Children's Zone annual budget by $34 million by creating a national buzz and an interest for investors everywhere, making the HCZ a model for other growing community organizations across America. If the country is talking about Canada, just imagine the energy on Harlem's streets. Most if not all of the families in Harlem have either a child, a niece, a nephew, or know a young person in one of HCZ's programs.

The Harlem Children's Zone houses Promise Academy Charter School, an institution that strives to provide the highest quality education for up to 700 middle and high school children. Students are fortunate enough to have access to a modern library with research facilities, a state-of-the-art computer lab, a science laboratory, and a gymnasium.[26]

Other HCZ initiatives include: Baby College, a nine-week series of workshops offered to parents of children ages 0 to 3; Harlem Gems, a pre-K program; Peacemakers, which trains young people ages 18 to 24 to work with teachers in elementary school classrooms and operate after-school and summer programs; The Family Empowerment Program, which provides home-based supportive counseling as well as individual and family therapy, a parenting group, and an anger management group; and Summer Freedom Schools, described in detail below.[27] Canada and his dedicated staff are determined to touch every single child in Harlem, especially those who would otherwise slip through the cracks.

Children's Defense Fund Freedom Schools®

Each Children's Defense Fund (CDF) Freedom School[28] is a product of the relationships between the CDF and community organizations, churches, universities, and schools. There are at least 70 schools in more than 20 states and 40 cities that "create supportive, nurturing, literature-rich environments that set high expectations for all children through a focus on literacy, cultural heritage, parental involvement, Servant-Leadership, and social action."[29]

The Freedom Schools program was organized during the civil rights movement by the Student Nonvlolent Coordinating Committee and the Council of Federated Organizations. The Mississippi Freedom Summer Project of 1964 strived to "motivate young people to become critically engaged in their communities and to help them identify and design authentic solutions to local programs."[30] Proudly rooted in the American Civil Rights Movement, the Children's Defense Fund Freedom Schools program was reborn in 1993 by Marian Wright Edelman and the Children's Defense Fund Black Community Crusade for Children (BCCC); it draws on the vision, philosophy, and experience of those who conducted Freedom Schools as part of the Mississippi Freedom Summer Project of 1964.[31]

The program's key elements are educational enrichment and cultural awareness, parental involvement, intergenerational leadership, community involvement, and social action. These schools are unique because young African American children who would otherwise spend long summer days home alone or out on the streets have the opportunity to connect with other youth, form lasting relationships, sharpen their academic skills, and empower themselves as they learn about their rich heritage. Close to 5,500 children attended a CDF Freedom School in the summer of 2005.

What Every Leader and Elected Official Can Do

- Invest in child and parental development.

- Implement federal support at all levels of education.

- Ensure an education in which students truly amass knowledge and preparedness for the next level of schooling and life.

- Develop a universal, well-rounded, and comprehensive curriculum.

- Adequately train and compensate professional staff who teach in responsible ratios of adults to children and are trustworthy and culturally sensitive.

- Guarantee that all children have access to appropriate and sufficient facilities, curriculum resources, and materials.

Invest in Child and Parental Development

Government resources should be better invested to support the academic and personal maturity of children. Local officials should readily help to develop and fund after-school, mentoring, college preparatory, and collegiate scholars programs and leadership opportunities. School administrators should also identify supplemental enrichment programs for students. Children's learning processes are enhanced only when they have forums to exercise other parts of their ongoing development.

Continuing development of parents to ensure that they are capable of advocating for and orchestrating the supplementary support necessary for the holistic development of their children is also key to a complete, quality education. In large part, many parents are part of a working population that cannot advocate at their leisure because of work or other commitments. In being sensitive to those issues, schools must provide parents with ways to be active without taking time off work, phone conferences, making special arrangements with teachers on how to monitor a child's progress, and creating opportunities for parents to be involved before and/or after work. If schools make it possible and beneficial for parents to participate, every child will benefit.

Implement Federal Support at All Levels of Education

The United States government should provide public early childhood education, just as it does elementary and secondary education. It is proven that attending preschool and pre-kindergarten better prepares children to succeed at all levels of schooling. Because many preschools, or other types of early childhood learning programs, are not free, parents who cannot afford them simply do not send their children. They enter into kindergarten already at a disadvantage to their peers who have just completed preschool. In order to level the playing field from day one, early childhood education must be a basic right of all children, just as elementary, junior, and high schools are.

We must also demand access for all to higher education. Federal and state level officials have to work to greatly extend programs that provide scholarships and support to those who do not have the resources to afford college. Quality community colleges need to be more broadly available, and they should be required to have in-house programs to encourage students to transfer to four-year institutions. No student should ever be denied federal aid when applying to the higher education institution of his or her choice. In addition, this money should be in the form of grants, as opposed to loans. The fear alone of having to pay back a substantial loan with high interest rates turns many young people away. There must be nothing daunting about pursuing a higher education.

Ensure an Education in Which
Students Can Learn and Grow

Too often teachers and administrators are concerned with national school rank or are simply careless and promote children to the next grade before the students are ready. Every child in America, regardless of school reputation, must be duly educated so that he or she may have a fair and an equal chance of being a productive and successful member of society. We must not allow children to be promoted until they are prepared to move forward; at the same time, we must demand that educators take the time to keep our children learning at least at grade level. It is unacceptable for children to be left behind academically; we must find and offer whatever special resources are needed to help them learn and progress on par with others their age.

The objective of all educational institutions has to be just that, to educate. It is crucial that local officials enforce teaching so that children actually learn, as opposed to memorizing answers for government-issued standardized tests. As national requirements for elementary and secondary schools change, official tests are administered to all students and schools are categorized according to overall scores. This practice encourages teachers to teach the exams, rather than covering a wide range of grade-level appropriate topics. Knowledge must be the end result, not test scores.

Develop a Universal, Well-Rounded,
and Comprehensive Curriculum

Schools must provide for the early and continuous exposure of all children to rigorous, varied, and joyful learning experiences where personal effort is encouraged and rewarded. This includes educating them in the arts, foreign languages, and physical education as well as in all other required academic subjects. Those courses that are now considered to extend beyond basic education should be a part of every child's curriculum. Areas of study that stimulate other parts of a child's brain must not be reserved as a privilege of children who attend private schools or public schools in wealthy districts.

All schools that have been forced to cut music, visual arts, performing arts, and sports must have them restored. If government officials allocate substantive educational funding to all schools equally, then every child will have the opportunity to explore both creative and academic areas of interest. A truly educated child is not only proficient in math, science, history, and English, but also in painting, piano, and a foreign language.

Guarantee Adequately Compensated and Prepared Professional Staff in Responsible Ratios of Adults to Children

Educating our children is critical to cultivating and sustaining our society. Without education, crime rates would skyrocket; health breakthroughs would be limited, if they existed at all, with no doctors or nurses to cure or care for the sick, and so on. That scenario notwithstanding, teachers are inadequately compensated for their efforts and contributions to the well-being of this country. Logically, a contented teacher makes for a better teacher. While we must acknowledge and be grateful for the educators who are in the profession out of love for youth, many can barely survive on their salaries. Elected officials must raise the starting salary for educators nationwide.

Teachers have a responsibility as well: They should be required to go through yearly training to share and learn new teaching techniques, raise their awareness of cultural current events, and brush up on educative methods. School staff must be responsible for creating and maintaining trust and a safe space between staff members, between staff and students, between staff and parents, and between students and students such that prejudice real or perceived is avoided. In enforcing this policy, school officials must nurture relationships, especially with those parents and students who seem hard to reach.

Many of the nation's classrooms are extremely overcrowded, the worst instances with 40 students to one teacher. Schools must divide such classes in half and increase their staff. Focused, individual attention is necessary for students to progress, mature, learn at a healthy pace, and succeed.

Make the Necessary Tools Available

Every child has the right to his or her own desk, textbooks in good condition, new pencils, and other necessary supplies. Local officials must never accept the fact that students are forced to share curriculum resources and learning materials. Administrators have to be responsible for ensuring that they provide teachers with grade-appropriate and up-to-date texts and interactive learning materials that are relevant to today's society. Furthermore, all schools must maintain safe and clean playgrounds, classrooms, hallways, and bathrooms. We cannot allow our schools to house our children in makeshift classrooms or auditoriums. All of these factors contribute to a positive school experience.

A Final Word

If we are actively engaged in our children's learning and development from an early age, and if we hold our elected officials responsible for providing well-resourced educational facilities, programs, and staff, then we can establish a system of public education in which all children participate, achieve at high levels, and reach their full potential. Education must be guaranteed as a civil right and a civil liberty for every child in America.

ESTABLISHING A SYSTEM OF PUBLIC EDUCATION IN WHICH ALL CHILDREN ACHIEVE AT HIGH LEVELS AND REACH THEIR FULL POTENTIAL

Since the original 2006 publication of *The Covenant with Black America*, the goal of providing an equal, high-quality education to all of America's students has yet to be realized. Indeed, ten years later, students who identify themselves as Black still suffer in comparison with students who identify themselves as white. And Black males still lag far behind Black females in educational achievement. However, major education policy reform initiatives—some bipartisan in nature—have aimed at increasing access to educational opportunity and improve student outcomes via a few notable mechanisms: (1) school choice, (2) high-stakes accountability for schools and teachers, (3) intensive investments in early childhood education and comprehensive "wrap-around" services that complement traditional K–12 classroom instruction, and (4) curricular reforms. Some of these policy reforms have been enacted or encouraged at all levels of government—federal, state, and local (including school districts and schools)—and have resulted in notable changes in the delivery of public education. Further, many of these reforms focus particularly on improving access to education and outcomes among underserved children, including low-income students and students of color. A growing body of research now examines the effects of these reforms on student outcomes and should be used to inform how families, communities, and policy makers advocate for an improved system of public education for Black Americans.

The Status of Black American Education

As discussed in the original chapter, persistent reductions in the Black-white achievement gap occurred in the 1960s, 1970s, and 1980s. Since the 1980s, however, this gap has not narrowed further. For example, the Black-white math test score gap among nine-year-old students who completed the National Assessment of Educational Progress (NAEP) was 25 points in both 1986 and in 2012. According to NAEP data, only 18 percent of Black fourth graders currently achieve a rating of proficient or above in mathematics, and 33 percent have not reached a basic level of proficiency.[1] On average, Black students in 12th grade score about 20 percent lower on math assessments than their white peers.[2] The Black-white reading test score gap among 13-year-old students ranged from 18 to 32 points in the 1980s and was 23 points in 2012.[3] According to NAEP data, only 18 percent of Black fourth graders currently achieve a rating in reading of proficient or above, and 50 percent have not reached a basic level of reading proficiency.[4] On average, Black students in 12th grade score about 10 percent lower than their white peers on reading assessments.[5] The rate of in-grade retention is about 4.8 percent among Black students, as compared to just 1.5 percent among white students.[6] And, as of 2013, 19 percent of Black youth ages 18–25 did not have a high school diploma.[7]

Despite this stagnation in relative gains, however, the level of achievement among Black students has increased since the 1980s. In 1986, nine-year-old Black students scored an average of 202 points on the NAEP exam in mathematics (as compared to 227 points for white students), but scored an average of 226 points in 2012 (as compared to 252 points for white students). From 1984 through 2012, average NAEP reading scores among 13-year-old Black students grew from 236 to 247 points, while average reading scores grew from 263 to 270 points among 13-year-old white students. Further, the share of Black youth between the ages of 18 and 24 who are enrolled in college increased from 30 percent in 2000 to 36 percent in 2012.[8] Nearly two-thirds of these students were female.[9]

The past decade also produced several high-quality research studies that not only examined the Black-white achievement gap, but also explored the intersectionality of race with other attributes, including socioeconomic status. Though the Black-white achievement gap did not narrow substantially in the past 30 years, the achievement gap between low-income and higher-income children increased substantially. U.S. Gross Domestic Product (GDP) roughly doubled over the past thirty years, but that economic growth concentrated disproportionately among families above the 80th percentile of income distribution. Those families experienced average income growth of 34 percent, as compared to just 7 percent among families in the 20th percentile of the income distribution. Since the 1950s, the test-score gap between low-income and higher-income children increased by about 60 points on the Scholastic Aptitude Test (SAT), and the gap in years of school completed between students in the 20th percentile and the 80th percentile of income distribution increased by about one year.[10] The widening income-based achievement gap disproportionately impacts minority children due to their over-representation in low-income families. As of 2013, 27 percent of Black families earned incomes that fell below the federal poverty level—$18,751 for a family with two adults and one child—as compared to just 10 percent of white families.[11]

The past decade also brought increased attention to a prominent civil rights issue in education: the disproportionate exposure of students of color—and Black students in particular—to exclusionary disciplinary actions such as suspensions and expulsions. In 2014, only 5 percent of white K–12 students received an out-of-school suspension, as compared to 16 percent of Black students overall and 20 percent of male Black students.[12] Recently, the federal Departments of Education and Justice renewed their commitment to investigating civil rights violations related to the disproportionate suspensions and expulsions faced by students of color. The so-called discipline gap is likely to exacerbate race-based achievement gaps because students who receive a suspension or expulsion exhibit lower academic achievement outcomes[13] and are more likely to drop out of high school.[14] Further, the discipline gap also plays a role in the school-to-prison pipeline: students who experience a suspension or expulsion are substantially more likely to become involved in the juvenile justice system.[15] Since the 1970s, suspension and expulsion rates have more than doubled, due in part to the widespread adoption of "zero-tolerance" school discipline policies. In addition, the growing prevalence of "no excuses" charter schools—which disproportionately serve low-income and minority students—also contributes to the discipline gap because students attending those schools are more likely to experience a suspension or expulsion than students attending traditional K–12 schools.[16]

Reforms Aimed at Improving the Status of Black American Education

The first paragraph in this *Covenant* update identifies four areas of policy reform that characterize the past decade of education policy and aim to improve educational opportunity, equity, and outcomes among Black Americans. These policy reform areas are (1) school choice, (2) high-stakes accountability for schools and teachers, (3) intensive investments in early childhood education and comprehensive "wraparound" services that complement traditional K–12 classroom instruction, and (4) curricular reforms. After more than a decade of experimentation with various reforms in these areas, one thing is clear: no single education policy reform is a panacea. Fortunately, the last decade also accompanied a major expansion in the collection and dissemination of detailed student-level data that enabled several high-quality evaluations of these reform initiatives. These evaluations provide a solid evidentiary base for understanding the circumstances under which these reforms do work, for whom they work, and at what cost. Many of these high-quality education reform evaluations are published in highly ranked journals in the fields of education policy, public policy, and economics, and also may be located by searching the What Works Clearinghouse—an initiative of the Obama administration administered by the federal Institute of Education Sciences, and accessible via http://ies.ed.gov/ncee/wwc/. This clearinghouse is an online repository of education research studies on programs, products, practices, and policies that meet high standards for establishing credible evidence.

Families, communities, leaders, elected officials, government agencies, nonprofit organizations, and other policy makers should use this growing evidentiary base to inform advocacy efforts and policy reforms aimed at improving educational access and outcomes among Black Americans. Education advocacy efforts should not focus on a single, ideological approach to "solving" educational inequality, but rather should support evidence-based policies and practices that produce the best outcomes for Black Americans. For example, the stance that "school choice will improve outcomes for Black Americans" is overly simplistic, ideological, and inaccurate in many contexts. Rather, advocacy stances should reflect the evidence—for example, "research demonstrates that students benefit most from school choice in states with strict standards for authorizing charter schools."[17] Similarly, pro forma calls for greater school and teacher accountability are vague and likely less effective than advocacy efforts aimed specifically at making strategic, evidence-based investments in the professional development of teachers and administrators. A growing body of research also indicates that simply enabling greater access to early childhood education and other educational services does not level the playing field. Educational programs and services must be of sufficiently high quality to produce gains in student outcomes.[18] Finally, many recent curricular reforms reflect political preferences rather than evidence regarding what works best for enabling students to acquire knowledge. Puzzlingly, the Boston Public School pre-K program is one of the only early childhood programs in the nation to implement a standardized curriculum with a proven track record of improving children's learning outcomes and narrowing the Black-white achievement gap.[19]

The next decade of education advocacy should highlight further the Black-white discipline gap and identify evidence-based solutions for reducing the disproportionate exposure of students of color to suspensions and expulsions. More broadly, in the next decade of education policy, the challenges faced by Black Americans—and particularly low-income Black Americans—will become only more nuanced. Therefore, so too must the policy solutions.

—Prepared by Ashlyn Aiko Nelson, Ph.D., Associate Professor, School of Public and Environmental Affairs, Indiana University; Bee Smale, Research Assistant, School of Public and Environmental Affairs, Indiana University; Bloomington, Indiana

✢ ✢

III.

CORRECTING THE SYSTEM OF UNEQUAL JUSTICE

Introductory Essay by James Bell

> *Often the voice of conscience whispers*
> *Often we silence it*
> *Always we will have to pay*
>
> —Anonymous

Since before this country's inception, Black people have struggled against deeply ingrained race-based expressions of power, privilege, and exclusion. After post–Civil War Reconstruction was defeated in 1877 and the era of Jim Crow was ushered in during the mid-20th century, America's elite universities and well-respected "scientists" advanced claims of biological evidence connecting Black physical features to inferior intelligence and predisposition to criminal behavior. This "evidence" further fueled the national hysteria about a growing Black population and offered justification for criminalizing Black men.

Today, there is a more nuanced but equally damaging perception of poor Black people that has resulted in a cradle-to-prison super-highway (CPS). The CPS is a network of legislation, policy, practice, and structural racism that has fostered Blacks being incarcerated at unconscionable levels at increasingly younger ages for increasingly minor acts. It is no wonder then that many Blacks believe the term "racial justice" is an oxymoron.

After decades of prison construction and record incarceration rates, proponents of punishment continue to argue that serving time is an effective tool to combat crime. The incarceration epidemic has been buttressed by misinformation and exaggeration from high-profile politicians, psychologists, and criminologists. It has been rein-forced by sensational news accounts that daily parade Black men—young and not-so-young—in handcuffs and orange prison uniforms in front of the public. Conservative writer John Dilulio, a former Bush aide who worked in the White House for the first 180 days, greatly contributed to the incarceration frenzy by introducing the pejorative political catchphrase "super-predator" to describe these Black males.[1] To incite fear, those who advocate for harsher penalties for law vio-lators have used the term relentlessly, which in turn provides public support for a flawed justice system.

An examination of the data from the federal justice system reveals that warehousing these Blacks is extremely expensive, is nonrehabili-tative, and lacks evidence that it reduces crime. Notwithstanding this abysmal track record, incarceration continues to be a growth indus-try. Given the current system's unfair, disproportionate, and negative impact on the Black community, Blacks should be leading the effort to demand that resources be diverted from prisons to the interven-tions and treatments highlighted in this chapter that can make a real difference in the lives of our people.

The implications of the CPS for our children, families, and com-munities are far reaching and deserving of attention. For example, while the majority of Blacks incarcerated are men, Black women have also felt the brunt of these practices. Black women are eight times more likely to be incarcerated for similar offenses than are their white counterparts.[2] Indeed, women are the fastest-growing population in the penal system. Their primary offenses: a preponderance of drug and property crimes, along with other nonviolent and economically motivated crimes.[3]

The compelling stories of Dorothy Gaines, a nurse technician and mother of three, and Kemba Smith, a sheltered, only child of professional parents, illustrate how poor choices in mates and associates can come crashing down on contributing members of their communities. A few years after entering into a relationship with a relapsed crack addict, Gaines's home was raided. The state police found nothing at all there, yet she and her boyfriend were arrested on drug conspiracy charges. Gaines was wrongly accused, indicted, and sentenced to 19 years in a federal correctional facility. In the second instance, while attending Hampton University, Smith became involved with a charming young man whom she eventually realized was deeply involved in a drug ring. Over the course of their often abusive relationship, Smith never actually handled or sold drugs; yet she was convicted of drug conspiracy charges and sentenced to 24 years in federal prison. Both women regained their freedom after six years, with President Clinton's order of clemency in December 2000.

Since women are usually the primary caretakers, incarceration has a particularly devastating effect on their children, extended family, and spouses. These women fall further behind in developing the skills and abilities necessary to compete in society.

Regrettably, the juvenile justice system—which has grown exponentially in size and complexity—is no better. At the beginning of the 20th century, the founders of the juvenile court had great aspirations for the treatment of children and their families; more than a century later, their aspirations have regrettably not been realized. What began as a movement designed to correct errant youth through care and concern has lost sight of its original purpose, evolving into a system that now harms the very children it claims to protect. In 1967, in *In re Gault*, the U.S. Supreme Court first acknowledged that despite the rehabilitative rhetoric of the juvenile court, it "actually subjected offenders to more severe punishment while depriving them of the minimum legal protections given adult offenders."[4]

As a result of the coexistence of national antidrug efforts and "zero tolerance" campaigns—which reach into the schools and begin criminalizing Black children at a young age, more youth of color are being introduced to the juvenile justice system than ever before.[5] The striking racial disparities within the juvenile justice system corrode the notion of justice, particularly for youth who experience injustice first-hand. Furthermore, the racial disparity is discriminatory in its effect and impact. To reestablish integrity and fairness in the juvenile court system requires an emphasis on reducing racial disparities.

This *Covenant with Black America* represents a realization that there is a multiheaded, multitentacled monster out there devouring Blacks who live in certain neighborhoods. Incarceration is just one aspect of this menace, but it is an overwhelmingly damaging aspect. Our job, in working to achieve fairness and equity, is to sound the alarm about the unjust criminal justice system and demand that our leaders and those in power act now to halt this destructive, unfair treatment of our brothers and sisters, especially of our children.

This chapter provides a comprehensive game plan for community members, elected officials, and other stakeholders. Together we must challenge individuals, communities, cities, counties, regions, states, and the nation to be accountable for the outcomes of the justice systems at every level of government.

As we dedicate ourselves to this *Covenant,* we should be guided by the convictions of former First Lady Eleanor Roosevelt, who posited that universal rights of all humans begin "in small places, close to home."[6] Such are the places where men, women, and children seek equal justice, equal opportunity, and equal dignity.

To correct the system of unequal justice, we must challenge every decision-maker to be responsible for fairness and dignity toward others with measurable actions. In turn, we must use our collective voices to give voice to the voiceless. We must embrace the credo that every life counts, that every person—irrespective of station—deserves due process in a criminal justice system that is just, fair, and equitable.

As James Baldwin reminds, "If you can't be touched, you can't be changed. And if you can't be changed, you can't be alive."[7]

Be alive!

✛

JAMES BELL is Executive Director of the W. Haywood Burns Institute in San Francisco, California. Named for W. Haywood Burns— one of the founders of the National Conference of Black Lawyers, who cut his legal teeth as the first law clerk for the late District Court Judge Constance Baker Motley—the institute works intensively with local jurisdictions to reduce the overrepresentation of youth of color in their juvenile justice systems. For more information: http://www .burnsinstitute.org.

THE FACTS ON THE JUSTICE SYSTEM

- Of the 2.1 million inmates today, 910,000 are African American. Blacks make up 43.9 percent of the state and federal prison populations but only 12.3 percent of the U.S. population. Latinos constitute 12.6 percent of the country's population, and yet they are 18.3 percent of the prison population. Whites account for 69 percent of the U.S. population and 34.7 percent of those incarcerated.[8]

- One of every three Black males born today can expect to go to prison in his lifetime.[9]

- 1.4 million African American men, or 13 percent, have currently or permanently lost their right to vote as a result of a felony conviction—seven times the national average.[10]

- In five states that deny the vote to ex-offenders— Alabama, Florida, Iowa, Kentucky, and Virginia—one in four Black men is permanently disenfranchised.[11]

- In at least 15 states, Black men were sent to prison on drug charges at rates ranging from 20 to 57 times those of white men.[12]

- African Americans constitute 13 percent of all monthly drug users, but they represent 35 percent of arrests for drug possession, 55 percent of convictions, and 74 percent of prison sentences.[13]

- There were 98,000 African Americans incarcerated in 1954, and 288,800 in 1984, as compared to the 910,000 in prison or jail today. The Black prison population grew by 300 percent from 1954 to 1984; from 1954 to today, it has increased by a staggering 900 percent.[14]

- Black women born today are five times more likely to go to prison in their lifetimes than Black women born in 1974. [15]

- One in every 18 Black women born today can expect to go to jail in her lifetime; this is six times the rate for white women.[16]

- On any given day, 1 of every 14 Black children has a parent in prison.[17]

- Youth of all races sell and use drugs at similar rates, but African American youth represent 60–75 percent of drug arrests today.[18]

- Nationwide, young Black offenders are more than twice as likely to be transferred to adult court as their white counterparts.[19]

- While African Americans represent 15 percent of those below the age of 18, they are 26 percent of all the youths arrested, 46 percent of those detained in juvenile jails, and 58 percent of all juveniles sent to adult prison.[20]

What the Community Can Do

Reducing the high rates of incarceration is complex and must begin early. It is well established that getting a healthy start in life, identifying and treating problems with vision and hearing early, and doing well in school are all essential for keeping children out of trouble later in life. Making sure that children receive quality early education helps keep them engaged and successful throughout their school careers. Children who are frequently suspended or expelled from school, rather than provided with support, become vulnerable to ending up in serious trouble. These are often the children who grow up and become part of the incarcerated population that is the focus of this chapter.

Every child needs to be connected to a caring adult who can provide guidance, support, and connection to opportunities and pathways to a secure productive future. Parents, relatives, and adult caregivers have a tremendously important role to play in making sure that all precautions are taken to stop the high rates of Black incarceration.

What Every Individual Can Do Now:

- Encourage and help children in our families and neighborhoods to behave and do well in school.

- Plan family and neighborhood activities for children of all ages: movies, games, and outings.

- Form adult clubs in the neighborhood to plan activities, create safe houses where children can hang out when parents are not home, and tell parents when you see children misbehaving.

- Support children whose parents are incarcerated.

- Encourage religious institutions to provide support (jobs, counseling) for adults returning to the community from prison.

MOST OF ALL:

- Hold all leaders and elected officials responsible and demand that they change current policy.

What Works Now:

The Black community can also help to ensure children's safety and development, create awareness of the harsh realities of the criminal justice system, and reinforce citizens' rights. Churches, teachers, artists, and other advocates have come together to form a number of innovative programs that are making a difference, as illustrated in the following examples.

Charmaney Bayton: South Central's Mother Teresa

Charmaney Bayton lives in a one-bedroom apartment in the heart of South Central Los Angeles—an area that, with over 600 homicides last year, has been deemed one of the "Murder Capitals of the World."[21] She offers safe haven to 60 children who are running from gangs, dodging bullets, or seeking refuge from drug-addicted parents.

Bayton offers classes on ethics, preparing for college, and finding one's potential. She takes hurting children into her home, drives them to church, and nurtures them as they struggle with terror just around the corner. Some days she will encounter another needy family, and by the end of the week, she will have arranged for new shoes, school supplies, and a solid sampling of her home-cooked meals.

Seventeen-year-old Lamar was confronted by gangsters in front of his home and told to never return or he would be killed. Lamar has not slept in his own bed since then. Bayton let him stay in her home (his mother was deceased, and his 24-year-old sister was raising him and his brother). Within months, Lamar picked up his grade point average; excelling as a senior, he was next accepted at El Camino College as a stellar track and field sprinter.

Bayton's story illustrates just how powerful and possible change is on a family level. Her admirable work proves that children who have lost their parents to the criminal justice system or are at risk of entering into it themselves can be saved with a lot of love and dedication.

Rule of Law: Citizens' Rights in a Georgia Court of Law

The Prison & Jail Project of Americus and the Freedom Council of Blakely—citizens' rights advocacy organizations—were particularly concerned with and motivated by what they observed in the rural Southwest Georgia court system: Attorneys were almost never provided for persons charged with misdemeanor and low-level felonies. Unfair courtroom practices were evident everywhere. In 2002, they collaborated with The Sentencing Project to produce a manual that would help people understand how a court is supposed to operate and, particularly, the responsibilities of counsel during the sentencing phase.[22]

Released on the courthouse steps on Aug. 18, 2004, *Rule of Law: Citizens' Rights in a Georgia Court of Law is* an educational tool for defendants, families, and community members. Advocates in Southwest Georgia are using this booklet at training workshops for people who have to go to court or who are acting as volunteer "court watchers." The court watch aspect of the program trains volunteers to observe illegal behavior in court, including defendants' being invited into a judge's chambers to discuss their options—a situation in which they are often coerced into not going to trial and pleading guilty. Court watchers witness wrongdoings, and when the respective offending judges and other officials agree to listen, the court watchers report their findings; their actions have led to some judges changing the way they conduct business in their courtrooms.

The success of the document has been remarkable: results range from citizen awareness to the dismissal of unjust judges. The county in Georgia that is home to the central courthouse has a population of 12,000; 5,000 copies of *Rule of Law* were printed, meaning almost 50 percent of the residents have this bill of rights in their possession. Upon the document's release, representatives from the *Rule of Law* team made a presentation to the Nashville, Georgia, city council. After taking part in the discussion on citizens' rights in a court of law, the city council fired a judge whose practices were clearly unfair (the council is responsible for what goes on in the criminal justice system).

When designing the document, Pastor Cynthia Edwards of The Freedom Council insisted the cover be International Orange because she wanted to make sure that when judges look out into their courtrooms and see hundreds of citizens holding the small orange book, they can be sure that all defendants and their support networks know their rights. There is great power in *Rule of Law: Citizens' Rights in a Georgia Court of Law.*

Reentry National Media Outreach Campaign

The Reentry National Media Outreach Campaign is designed to support the work of community and faith-based organizations through offering media resources that will facilitate community discussion and decision-making about solution-based reentry programs.[23] Based on the belief that diverse media play an essential role in motivating and mobilizing community action, the campaign expands public awareness and partners with local organizations and initiatives to foster public safety and to support healthy communities.

A long-term initiative, the Reentry National Media Outreach Campaign is unique in that it incorporates several public television documentaries that span at least two years. The documentaries support a comprehensive campaign that should effectively reach multiple audiences. All productions incorporate the theme of reentry into family and community by individuals who were formerly incarcerated, which provides the title "Reentry" for this enhanced umbrella initiative.

Children Left Behind features interviews with adults who recall their experiences as the children of incarcerated parents. They discuss the trauma of their parents' arrests, their feelings of abandonment, and the sometimes humiliating treatment they experienced when visiting their parents in prison. The documentary next profiles community activities for children whose parents are incarcerated, featuring the views of experts and practitioners. Another documentary, *Girl Trouble,* follows the compelling personal stories of three teenagers entangled in San Francisco's juvenile justice system. The girls struggle with pregnancy, drug-selling and addiction, and homelessness as they actively strive to better their lives by working part time at the innovative Center for Young Women's Development. This is an organization run by young women who have faced similar challenges. Through these poignant stories, the filmmakers aspire to expose a system that fails to meet the needs of girls in trouble.

The series began broadcasting in June 2003 and is scheduled to end in the fall of 2006. The extended timeline allows for maximum exposure, awareness, and impact.

What Every Leader and Elected Official Can Do

- Reform drug policies.

- Overhaul mandatory sentencing programs to eliminate unfair treatment.

- Ensure adequate reentry and ex-offenders programs for adults and youth.

- Help women in prison to maintain family ties and improve parenting skills.

- Ensure that juvenile justice systems are accountable and effective.

- Restructure "zero tolerance" policies so that all children are treated fairly.

Reform Drug Policies

For the past 90 years, the federal government has pursued numerous policies attempting to prohibit and punish the use, possession, and/or sale of illegal substances with harsh laws, policies, and practices. These efforts have cost billions and billions of dollars but have not led to any significant decline in illegal drug use or availability since their inception in 1914.[24] The federal government spent $12 billion in 2004 alone, continuing its long string of failures to curb the flow

of these drugs.[25] African Americans are so vigorously and disproportionately arrested, convicted, and sentenced for drug-related offenses
that this effort is primarily responsible for the disproportionate incarceration of Blacks. The reform of drug policy, therefore, must be at
the top of the priority list to reduce disproportionate incarceration of
Black men, women, and children.

Vital to drug policy reform is eliminating federal sentencing
disparities for powder cocaine and crack cocaine. Crack cocaine is
derived from powder: It is made by cooking powder cocaine with
baking soda and water until it forms a hard rocky substance.[26] Even
though powder cocaine is a purer drug and a conviction for the sale
of 500 grams of it carries a five-year mandatory sentence, selling only
5 grams of crack cocaine garners the very same five-year sentence.
The punishment for the two substances has a 100:1 ratio.[27]

In the mid-1980s, crack cocaine exploded on the streets; because
of its cheap price, it was widely available for the first time. The media's
association of inner cities and uncontrollable violence by crack addicts
caused Congress to quickly pass shockingly unfair sentencing laws.[28]
Crack is often sold in small quantities on the street in low-income
neighborhoods, while powder cocaine is generally sold in larger
quantities in higher-income, suburban locations.[29] Since inner-city
neighborhoods—home to large numbers of low-income people of
color—are more heavily policed, those who live there are more susceptible to arrest.

To level the playing field for all cocaine-related crimes, the ratio
of drug weight to sentence must be the same for both powder and
crack cocaine. In addition, legislators must repeal the law that makes
crack the only drug that carries a mandatory prison sentence on an
individual's first offense. The Crack-Cocaine Equitable Sentencing Act
of 2005 is currently up for review; we need to urge our elected leaders
to support this bill.

Policy-makers must also increase and encourage the use of substance abuse treatment rather than incarceration. If the government
invested public dollars in drug rehabilitation, not only would incarceration rates decrease but ex-offenders would also become productive
members of our families and our communities.

Some states have begun to use drug courts in which addicted offenders are allowed to complete court-supervised substance abuse treatment instead of being sentenced to prison. Successful completion of the treatment program may result in dismissal of the charges, reduced sentences, lesser penalties, or a combination of these. Most importantly, recovering addicts work on gaining the tools they need to return to and successfully function in society.

Restructure Mandatory Sentencing

Mandatory minimum sentencing laws force the filling of prisons with individuals who have been convicted of minor offenses. Because of extreme poverty and desperate living conditions in inner cities as well as racial profiling, African Americans are arrested at exorbitant, disproportionate rates, thus forcing thousands of them into jails and prisons. Laws such as "Three Strikes" lead to an individual's serving a life sentence if convicted of theft for stealing something as insignificant as a slice of pizza. Such precariousness not only wastes taxpayers' dollars and crowds prisons; it psychologically damages those who are locked up and destroys Black families and communities in the process.

In those states choosing to amend their Three Strikes laws rather than doing away with them altogether, the decision has been made that all three felonies must be violent crimes or sexual offenses. California, the only state in which any felony offense can prompt a Three Strikes' sentence, reports 65 percent of those sentenced under the law are imprisoned for nonviolent offenses.[30] The original intent was to ensure that violent criminals be punished harshly and kept behind bars.

Lawmakers must also restore judges' freedom to sentence defendants based on the situation at hand. Judges are now prevented from considering other relevant factors such as a defendant's role in the offense, the likelihood of committing a future offense, or an individual's history. If criminal law is to be effective, the punishment should fit the crime.

Ensure Adequate Reentry for Ex-Offenders and Youth

Massive incarceration in the United States has created a challenge: the reintegration of numerous ex-offenders back into society
upon release from prison. In the midst of intense debate over sentencing and punishment policies in the United States, the issue of reentry
has been largely ignored. Unfortunately this oversight has dire consequences because the one rule of incarceration is that aside from those
who die in custody, "they all come back."[31]

Congress recently introduced legislation to address the need for
active reentry policies. The Second Chance Act of 2005 calls for federal
funding for programs and activities relating to the reentry of offenders into communities.[32] Services would include (1) providing structured
post-release and transitional housing, (2) employment training and
facilitated collaboration between the government and specific companies to promote the employment of people released from prison and
jail, and (3) the implementation of programs that support children of
incarcerated parents.

Support Women in the System

Although difficult, it is essential to focus on preserving families
despite incarceration.[33] In addition to the fathers missing from so many
African American households, mothers are also being incarcerated at
much higher rates than ever before. Policy-makers should strive to
tailor child welfare practices to ensure that women in prison have a
fair chance to demonstrate their ability to parent their children upon
release. This includes allowing incarcerated mothers to visit with their
children in an appropriate setting and providing parenting training/
family counseling in correctional facilities as well as upon release.[34]

Reintegrate Juvenile Ex-Offenders

To ensure the existence and success of future generations, we
must place special emphasis on juvenile offenders. Since the rate of

African American youth incarceration is growing as rapidly as that of adult offenders, it is crucial that policy-makers establish grants to states for improved workplace and community transition training for incarcerated youth. These juveniles need skills that give them the tools to survive in and contribute to society. Education, vocational training, emotional counseling, and drug treatment are among the services our states must provide. All young people deserve to live a quality adult life, including those who have been incarcerated and those who have never been caught up in the juvenile justice system. It is equally important for the government to fund projects that reach out to youth before they are incarcerated, including after-school programs, organized mentoring opportunities, and initiatives that provide juveniles in inner cities with esteem-building skills and alternatives to criminal activity.

The Improved Workplace and Community Transition Training for Incarcerated Youth Offenders Act of 2005 will provide grants to states for improved workplace and community transition training for incarcerated youth offenders.[35] It will amend the Higher Education Act, which delays or denies federal financial aid to anyone convicted of a state or federal drug offense. Because minority youth represent up to 75 percent of drug arrests today, thousands are ineligible for financial aid to pursue a secondary education even after they have completed their sentences.[36] This policy reform is key for African American youth at risk to progress and become productive.

Reform the Juvenile Justice System

While both violent and nonviolent youth crime rates have continually decreased since 1994 to their lowest level in 20 years, the decrease in rates has done little to roll back the legislative and prosecutorial measures that significantly increase punitive criminal justice sanctions for youth. More provisions and stricter legislation under the guise of "the best interest of the child" have expanded the definition of juvenile delinquency. This wide net is unjustifiably priming more children for a life of crime rather than weeding out a select few and serving as an effective intervention; it disproportionately impacts youth of color and ultimately weakens the juvenile justice system.

The juvenile justice system can and must be held accountable by requiring it to gather data, track recidivism, and monitor racial disparities. Additionally, we must demand that local justice systems partner with proven community alternatives to detention and corrections facilities.

Schools and Criminal Justice

The "Zero Tolerance" disciplinary policy was initiated in U.S. public schools in the late 1980s.[37] At its inception it required suspension or expulsion for a specified list of severe offenses, but it is now open to school officials' interpretation; punishment is left to their discretion. Students who commit nonviolent acts—tardiness, throwing spitballs, and engaging in verbal arguments—are subject to citations or arrests. Perceived violent offenses such as possession of imaginary or potential weapons and food fights are treated the same as criminal transgressions.[38] In addition, many students report visible reminders that schools are becoming more like prisons every day: drug sweeps, metal detectors, canine units, and police presence all serve to create a prison-like atmosphere.[39] Schools have gone too far and are using law-enforcement strategies that are needlessly steering students into the juvenile justice system.

Between the students who are simply exposed at a young age to the criminal justice system and those who are actually suspended, expelled, and/or locked up for school-related offenses, thousands of young people are being funneled from schools into correctional facilities.

To reverse this process and educate rather than incarcerate youth, policy-makers and school officials must limit suspensions, expulsions, and arrests to offenses that truly pose a serious threat to safety. School districts should also devise clear and concise disciplinary guidelines and review them with all parents and students throughout the year.[40] State governments must be responsible for funding school violence prevention and intervention programs and for hiring additional guidance counselors and social workers on school staffs to support students with behavioral and academic problems.

Trial and Incarceration

It is fundamentally unfair to prosecute children as adults because little allowance is made for the limited experience and understanding of an immature mind. Because the adult criminal court process is much more rigid and antagonistic, housing youthful offenders with adults compounds an already difficult situation.[41] Studies show that not only are many children in adult court unable to understand their legal rights and at a disadvantage that children in juvenile court do not experience, but also that they are actually disadvantaged in comparison to adults in the same courts.[42] While some public defenders' offices have adopted policies in which juvenile defendants must be tried in juvenile courts and served by multidisciplinary teams that have been trained to deal with children, this must become standard practice in all courtrooms across the nation.

Once a child has been tried in an adult court, he or she is often sentenced to serve time in an adult correctional facility. The Sentencing Project reports that "although youths transferred to the adult criminal justice system are more likely to be convicted and incarcerated, they are more likely to reoffend, [to] reoffend earlier, and to commit more serious subsequent offenses than those who remain in the juvenile system."[43] This is largely the result of the lack of rehabilitative programs adapted to children's specific needs in adult correctional systems and the high rates of abuse that occur while locked up.

Policy-makers must end the practice of placing juvenile and adult offenders in the same facilities in order to save the lives of and guarantee productive futures for African American at-risk youth.

A Final Word

If we encourage and help children in our families and neighborhoods to do well in school, participate in safe, engaging after-school activities, and if we hold our elected officials responsible for the rehabilitation and successful reentry of all ex-felons back into our communities, then we can start to correct the system of unequal justice.

CORRECTING
THE SYSTEM OF
UNEQUAL JUSTICE

In 2006 *The Covenant* described Black America as facing a "cradle-to-prison superhighway" comprising "a network of legislation, policy, practice, and structural racism that has fostered Black citizens being incarcerated at unconscionable rates."[1] The main on-ramp to that superhighway for the past 30-plus years has been America's "War on Drugs." More recently, lawmakers at the state and federal level, conceding the immense human and financial costs of America's mass incarceration effort, have begun to build some off-ramps. Republicans and Democrats are working to reform drug laws and a criminal justice system that have been particularly devastating to communities of color.

Whether this will prove to be, in the words of Attorney General Loretta Lynch, a "bipartisan moment"[2] that brings sweeping and lasting change is far from certain. Some current proposals in Congress failed on earlier attempts, and election-year effects on the political will for change are unpredictable, especially given the recent spike in violent crime and steady drumbeat of news stories about heroin ravaging the nation. Reform in the federal prisons, which currently house only 13.5 percent of total prisoners in the U.S. and where over 50 percent are serving time for drug crimes (many of them low-level and nonviolent offenders), will necessarily have limited impact; in the vast state prison system, over 50 percent of state male prisoners are serving time for violent offenses, and only 15.1 percent for drug crimes.[3]

Yet combined moral and fiscal imperatives seem to be building momentum for a nationwide shift toward laws that are racially equitable, fundamentally fair, and use sensible risk assessments to replace incarceration as much as possible with community corrections and rehabilitative programs. Contributing to this momentum are the Black Lives Matter movement and intensified focus on race and policing, which have emerged in the past 14 months following a series of African American deaths related to police encounters or custody. Even before these events, nearly 70 percent of Black Americans reported in a Pew Research Center survey their perceptions that police and the courts treated Black citizens less fairly than whites.[4]

And indeed, significant racial disparities remain in the criminal justice system since the original publication of *The Covenant*. While imprisonment rates have been falling overall the past few years, as of 2014 Black male imprisonment rates still far outpaced Black males as a percentage of the U.S. population and outstripped rates for prisoners of other races or Hispanic origin within all age groups. Black males ages 18–19 were 10 times more likely to be imprisoned than were whites of that age, and Black males ages 30–39 were three to six times more likely to be imprisoned than their Hispanic and white counterparts.[5] Black females were between 1.6 and 4.1 times more likely to be imprisoned than white females of any age group. In 2011–12, 84 percent of Black Americans convicted of a crime went to prison, as compared with 79 percent of white offenders.[6] Though Black and white citizens reported using marijuana at similar rates in 2010, a Black individual was nearly four times as likely as a white individual to be arrested for marijuana possession.[7] In 2009 African Americans served longer sentences for almost every type of offense.[8]

Yet change is underway, and reforms in drug law and policy top the list of positive steps taken toward achieving equal justice since *The Covenant's* 2006 publication. By 2007, only 13 states had any disparity in crack and powder cocaine sentencing rules, and currently only three states—Missouri, Arizona, and New Hampshire—have ratios above 10:1.[9] Between 2009 and 2013, 40 states reduced drug penalties in various ways and enhanced the use of drug courts and other alternatives to the standard criminal justice system.[10] Four states and the District of Columbia have legalized marijuana for recreational use and 19 states for medical use, and 20 have decriminalized the possession of small amounts for personal use.[11] Though marijuana remains illegal under federal law, the Justice Department has allowed states to experiment, while reserving the right to crack down on distribution to minors, "drugged driving," involvement of gangs or weapons, diversion to non-legalizing states, and other similar concerns.[12]

In 2010 Congress finally responded to long-standing calls from advocates and experts—including four separate reports by the U.S. Sentencing Commission—to fix the disparities in federal crack and powder cocaine sentencing. The Fair Sentencing Act (FSA), a bipartisan compromise, increased the quantities of crack that triggered 5- and 10-year mandatory minimum sentences, replacing the 100:1 powder-to-crack cocaine drug-weight ratio for calculating sentences with an 18:1 ratio. The FSA also repealed the mandatory minimum sentence for simple possession of crack cocaine—the first repeal of a mandatory minimum in 40 years.[13]

Congress did not make the ratio 1:1 as many social justice advocates had demanded, nor did Congress make these changes retroactive.[14] This means that thousands of Black Americans are serving sentences they would not have received under the new law and that were imposed originally based on since-discredited theories about much greater harms associated with crack.[15] Federal appeals courts have rejected claims that the FSA provides for—or that Constitutional rights demand—retroactivity.[16] The Supreme Court has let those decisions lie, although in 2012 it provided partial relief by holding that judges must apply the FSA's new rules to all sentences imposed after

August 3, 2010 (the law's effective date), even if the offense occurred earlier.[17]

The U.S. Sentencing Commission also provided partial relief, revising its guidelines to reduce drug sentences in 2007, 2010 (to reflect the FSA's 18:1 ratio), and 2014, and making the revisions retroactive. These changes have allowed prisoners to seek reductions in their current sentences as long as they do not go below the pre-FSA mandatory minimums. In December 2014, the Commission reported that over 6,600 Black prisoners convicted on crack charges had received reduced sentences, with reductions (across all races and jurisdictions) averaging 20 percent of original sentence length.[18] In late 2015 roughly 6,000 federal inmates will be released, 34 percent of whom are Black men primarily serving pre-FSA sentences for crack convictions. The Commission estimates that up to 40,000 more of the roughly 100,000 drug offenders in federal prison may qualify for sentence reduction and release.[19]

The Justice Department has also eased the burden of mandatory sentences; the DOJ announced in 2013 it will not seek mandatory minimum sentences for low-level nonviolent drug offenders without connections to gangs or cartels, and President Obama has in fact commuted the sentences of some offenders who were serving lengthy pre-FSA terms.[20] And Congress has reentered the arena; companion bills in the House and Senate were introduced in early October with strong bipartisan support and would, among other things, reduce several mandatory minimum sentences and make them and the FSA retroactive, provide broader "safety valves" that allow nonviolent drug offenders with minimal criminal history to avoid mandatory minimums, and replace life imprisonment under federal "three strikes" laws with a 25-year sentence that would apply retroactively.[21]

Critically, the Senate bill also supports risk-based assignment of inmates to educational, drug rehabilitation, job training, and other recidivism-reduction programs, and crediting their completion toward early release or transfer to home confinement or a halfway house.[22] Data from the Sentencing Commission showing no higher recidivism rates among those serving shortened sentences[23] have not entirely eased concerns about early release efforts, and solid reentry programs are vital to making large-scale prisoner release work. The Bureau of Prisons can greatly influence how federal prisons approach such programs and all aspects of prison reform.[24]

Successful reentry requires tackling the "collateral consequences" of felony convictions—the restrictions imposed by civil law as a result of a criminal conviction, including a conviction resulting (as most do) from a guilty plea. Since defendants often accept plea deals to avoid the severe risk posed by prosecutors' current ability to seek lengthy mandatory minimum sentences,[25] it is particularly troubling to impose further "invisible punishments"[26] that can include disqualification from public jobs, business licenses, and education and housing benefits, as well as loss of voting rights and jury participation. While some restrictions reflect legitimate public-safety concerns (for instance, keeping guns from violent offenders), others unduly obstruct reentry into society, limit civic engagement—felony disenfranchisement laws ban 2.2 million Black citizens, or one in 13 Black adults nationally, from voting[27]—increase the risk of recidivism, and trap many Black Americans in what Michelle Alexander called in *The New Jim Crow: Mass Incarceration in the Age of Color Blindness* "a racial caste system."[28]

In 2010, the U.S. Supreme Court raised awareness of collateral consequences when it held in *Padilla v. Kentucky*[29] that noncitizen residents have a Sixth Amendment right to be advised that pleading guilty to most drug offenses carries the risk of deportation. *Padilla* did not address what if any advice on other collateral consequences is constitutionally required, and all lower courts considering the issue have rejected such a requirement.[30] Because collateral consequences "mushroomed" over the past 20 years and are scattered among federal, state, local, and territorial codes, it has been hard for anyone—defendants, counsel, courts, lawmakers, and advocates—to know the true, lifelong impact of conviction.[31] The chronic shortage of defense counsel for the poor[32] exacerbates the problem, though the American Bar Association is helping to fix that issue. In 2012 the ABA launched a federally funded, publicly accessible, and user-friendly National Inventory of the Collateral Consequences of Conviction (NICCC),[33] which allows people to find and assess the restrictions imposed on ex-offenders at the federal, state, and territorial levels. This should enable better decisions about pleading and sentencing, and make it easier for lawmakers, advocates, and the public to pursue change in the underlying laws.

Some change has come already. Since *The Covenant*'s original publication, several states have eliminated lifetime voting bans and "waiting periods" after release from prison[34] and passed laws to modify felony bans on public benefits and ease other burdens of reentry, like waiving fees for replacement IDs and driver's licenses.[35] Yet having a criminal record continues to shut many out of public and private jobs because employers (and insurers) fear that they will re-offend and generate liability.[36] Research shows that employment substantially decreases recidivism,[37] and the Equal Employment Opportunity Commission has suggested that indiscriminate rejection of job candidates based on prior convictions may itself expose employers to liability under Title VII.[38]

Accordingly, momentum is building among states and localities to "ban the box"—to remove the criminal conviction history question on job applications and delay the background check inquiry until after a conditional hire offer so that employers fully consider an applicant's qualifications instead of reflexively tossing the application based on the prior conviction. Since *The Covenant*'s original publication, 18 states and over 100 cities and counties have banned the box, and 7 states have banned it for private employers as well.[39] The National Employment Law Project (NELP) has developed and published a "Ban the Box Toolkit" that advocates can use to pursue "fair chance" hiring nationwide,[40] and in January 2015 NELP and others urged President Obama—whose My Brother's Keeper initiative supports fair-chance hiring—to use executive action to apply these principles to federal hiring and contractors.[41]

Education and retraining programs, critical to job success, are also getting renewed attention and support. The U.S. Department of Education announced in July 2015 the Second Chance Pell Pilot Program, which reinstates Pell Grant eligibility for those serving time and aims to "help these individuals successfully transition out of prison and back into the classroom or the workforce."[42] A 2014 study conducted by the nonprofit RAND Corporation's Justice, Infrastructure, and Environment found that, for adults, on average "[f]or every dollar spent on correctional education, five dollars are saved on three-year re-incarceration costs.[43]

For juveniles the evidence is less clear, but RAND identified two promising programs: "Read 180," a blended reading curriculum that combines face-to-face instruction with computer-enhanced, self-paced instruction; and the Avon Park Youth Academy in Florida, which combines personalized academic instruction with intensive mentoring by the same parole officer while jail time is served and after release.[44] To support efforts like these, in 2014 Congress passed the Workforce Innovation and Opportunity Act and authorized grants to states of between $802 million and $964 million annually in 2015–2020 for investment in the out-of-school (including incarcerated) youth workforce.[45] This funding supersedes the earlier program mentioned in the original *Covenant,* which gave states between $17 million and $22.7 million annually for ten years to fund transition training programs for incarcerated youth and adults.[46]

Helping youth offenders reenter school and the workforce is critical, but keeping youth out of the criminal justice system—particularly the adult system—to begin with is better. Some progress has been made on two of *The Covenant's* recommendations—ending the "zero tolerance" disciplinary policies that help create a school-to-prison pipeline, and not prosecuting children as adults. While zero-tolerance policies remain prevalent in schools, and school shootings have made many in schools anxious and risk averse in dealing with potential dangers,[47] research has underscored how much suspension and expulsion continue to disproportionately affect Black children and how often they are used for minor, nonviolent infractions.[48] In 2014 the U.S. Department of Education and Justice Department responded by jointly releasing a "Supportive School Discipline Project" and corresponding toolkit aimed at keeping kids in school and in a safe and productive environment.[49] The toolkit offers tools, data, and resources regarding the impact of suspension and expulsion and emphasizes identifying at-risk students and matching tiered support and interventions to students' individualized needs.[50]

Several states and school districts are heeding the call for reform and trying new approaches like restorative justice, which use reflection and conversation to identify the root causes of misbehavior and reconcile those engaged in and harmed by it.[51] In 2014, California passed the first statewide limit on expulsion for minor school disruption, such as talking back and violating dress codes, and eliminated suspension for K–3 children for such violations.[52] In 2014, Chicago Public Schools, the nation's third largest school district, replaced its zero-tolerance policy with a new discipline code and Suspension and Expulsion Reduction Plan aimed at preventing and de-escalating misconduct, building social and emotional skills, and addressing the root causes of behavioral problems. CPS trained thousands of staff, added positions to support school efforts to keep students in school and engaged, and scaled back mandatory police notification to only drug and firearm possession.[53] These efforts resulted in a 60 percent reduction in suspensions and 69 percent reduction in expulsions between fall 2014 and spring 2015.[54]

For youth who do encounter the criminal justice system, some reforms have reduced the prospect of their being handled like adults. Through a trio of cases decided between 2005 and 2012, the Supreme Court declared that both the death penalty and mandatory life sentences without parole are unconstitutional for juvenile offenders.[55] Two state supreme courts have since made the elimination of mandatory life without parole retroactive.[56] In recent years almost half of the states have taken steps to keep more juveniles out of the adult system. For example, four states have raised the age at which juveniles enter the adult system,[57] and in 2012 Colorado amended its "direct file" law, which previously gave prosecutors unbridled discretion to file charges against certain 14–17-year-olds in adult court. The new law narrows the age and crime ranges for direct filing, allows the accused to request before a judge a "reverse transfer hearing" to go to juvenile court, and limits mandatory and adult sentencing.[58]

Fifteen states still let prosecutors decide whether to try youth offenders as juveniles or adults, and many states still automatically transfer youth to adult court based on the category of crime charged or prior interaction with the adult system.[59] Given the evidence that community-based programs and individualized treatment are cheaper and more effective than imprisonment in transforming youth, state reform efforts should continue to emphasize judicial discretion and individualized assessment and provide the resources to support this.[60]

Overall, while the picture is improving somewhat for Black Americans, much remains to be done to correct the system of unequal justice of which *The Covenant* spoke ten years ago, and—as noted elsewhere in this edition—to address the persistent racial disparities in policing and access to good housing, education, jobs, and health care, all of which greatly contribute to Black Americans disproportionately encountering the criminal justice system.

—Prepared by Beth Cate, J.D., Associate Professor, School of Public and Environmental Affairs, Indiana University; Andrea Need, J.D., Lecturer and Deputy Director, Master of Public Affairs Program, Indiana University, Bloomington, Indiana

✣ ✣

IV.

FOSTERING ACCOUNTABLE COMMUNITY-CENTERED POLICING

Introductory Essay by Maya Harris

I have long since forgotten the name of the song or the rap artist who performed it—it has been over ten years since I saw the music video flickering across my TV screen—but I will never forget the vivid images I saw. Thousands of Black people—men, women, children, young, old, healthy, and sick—all being corralled into huge, outdoor camps fenced off by barbed razor wire. Guarding the locked cages were white men in military garb, armed with rifles and snarling German shepherds, the dogs' breath hanging as mist in the cold, nighttime air when they barked. Bright lights pierced the darkness; frightened men and women were marshaled into different caged areas, separated from their children and from each other, concentration-camp style. Overhead, a helicopter spotlight beamed down to ensure no one would escape this wholesale incarceration of an entire group of people.

It was a scene supposedly set in the future, but at the time it felt all too real to me, then a law student becoming increasingly aware of the disproportionate incarceration of Black people in a criminal justice system hobbled by racial bias.

Now, more than a decade later, I know that rap video was as much an omen as it was a description of a reality in which the African American community is increasingly finding itself.

The mass incarceration of Black people in America is a real and present danger. About one in every 265 whites is incarcerated in local, state, or federal prison. By contrast, of the 36 million African Americans in this nation, almost one million of them are in prison; that is about one in every 36 Black people who is behind bars somewhere in America. African Americans represent 44 percent of all incarcerated people in state and federal prison cells, yet account for only 13 percent of the American population. Something is clearly wrong when the government's most effective affirmative action program is the preference people of color receive when entering not college, but the criminal justice system.[1]

How did we get here? And, given the current trend, can we change direction?

Racial bias in our criminal justice system has many causes—historical, political, and economic—but we know that any solution to the growing crisis of mass Black incarceration must begin with focusing on how our communities, especially our youth, are policed. Police are the entry point, the gatekeepers, of the criminal justice system. They make discretionary decisions every day about who is likely to commit a crime and who should be targeted by the criminal justice system; about who should be stopped, questioned, searched, and arrested. These decisions are made on the basis of individual police officers' life experiences—their training, their instincts, their prejudices and biases. And all too often, they are decisions informed by race.

Racial Profiling

Several years ago, ABC News broadcast a story in which it pulled together two groups of young men. Each group was the same size and comprised of men about the same age. The groups were separated by race—one group white, the other Black—and the network mapped out a route for each group to drive through the streets of Los Angeles. The route was the same for each group; both drove the same car at the same speed on successive nights.

The result? The car filled with young Black men was stopped repeatedly by the police during their drive, yet the white group was not stopped once. Even though the white group reported that it saw police cars in its immediate area at least 16 times during its drive, no one pulled the car over. When the story aired, many people were surprised because either they did not know about "racial profiling" or did not believe it really existed.

But whenever I tell that story to African American audiences, they are not surprised at all. In fact, the nods of assent I see throughout the audience are a reminder that, to our communities, racial profiling is nothing new. It is something that law-abiding African Americans quietly endure on a daily basis across the country: Repeated stops; pointed questioning; humiliating searches at the hands of law enforcement on the way to work or school or the grocery store or, painfully, in front of our children or parents. For too many of us, "Driving While Black" is simply a fact of life.

As the nation undertook the "War on Drugs," racial profiling became more acute. Officers in state highway patrol agencies nationwide were trained to use minor traffic violations as an excuse to pull people over and attempt to search their cars for drugs, based on a racially biased drug-courier profile. Studies across the country began to show that African Americans were two to three times more likely to be pulled over and searched, yet no more likely to be engaged in any criminal activity than white Americans.

At the same time, because police look for drugs primarily among African Americans and in Black communities, a disproportionate number of Blacks are arrested, prosecuted, convicted, and incarcerated.

This leads to more African Americans in jails and prisons, a fact that only serves to reinforce the false perception that Blacks are primarily responsible for the drug and overall crime problem in this country. This perception persists even though studies have documented that whites constitute the vast majority of drug users and—in direct contradiction to the popular myth—whites are the majority of *crack* users.[2]

Social Attitudes and the Media

Does this mean that all police are racist? Hardly. These days, racial bias is often not intentional; it is unconscious. Unfortunately, racial stereotypes are a part of our culture and our collective history as a nation, which is why Black police officers have not only been racially profiled, but can racially profile, too. You do not have to be a racist to racially profile; you simply have to be susceptible to prevailing notions about who is more likely to be dangerous. And more often than not, these views are colored by race.

These views are reinforced, justified, rationalized, and dramatized by an electronic media that feeds us a steady diet of ratings-rich crime coverage, which, more often than not, has a Black face.

Even though white-collar corporate crime may affect far more lives (think of all those people who lost everything when Enron collapsed because of fraud), it is the Crime in the Hood that most Americans think of when they support lengthy mandatory prison sentences and "tough on crime" policies.

Politicians, too, recognize that the (irrational) fear of the mythical young, Black male "super-predator" strikes a chord deep within the American psyche. It is the same fear that compelled Louisiana Governor Kathleen Blanco, in the face of massive African American suffering during Hurricane Katrina, to warn sternly that National Guard troops were under her orders to "shoot and kill" in order to prevent looting—never mind that for many, "looting" meant ensuring diapers and baby formula for a child or bottled water for a loved one.

In the face of such stereotypes, images, and fear, it is not surprising that most Americans incorrectly believe that Blacks commit most crimes and most Black men are criminals.

"Zero Tolerance" Policing and Criminalizing Youth

The fear of escalating crime, even as crime rates were steadily declining, has led the public to embrace a series of "get tough," "zero tolerance" law enforcement policies—from laws on the books like "Three Strikes" and mandatory minimum sentences to police practices on the streets like aggressive stops-and-frisks and random street sweeps. America's assault on crime over the past decade has exacted a high price, mostly paid by the African American community and frequently impacting law-abiding citizens. These overbroad, in-your-face tactics not only create tension and resentment in the community, they have also resulted in avoidable, tragic consequences.

Some of the harshest policing policies have been directed at youth. In many areas, it is a crime for African American kids to simply congregate. Youth hanging out at the mall are photographed and cited for loitering and trespass. If you wear baggy jeans, Nike tennis shoes, and a baseball cap, and you live in a high-crime neighborhood, you can be labeled a gang member whether you are part of a gang or not. Getting caught outside after dark can result in arrest for a curfew violation. Just like our prisons and jails, gang databases and curfew arrests are overwhelmingly Black and brown. In some California counties, over 90 percent of those in the gang database were kids of color, even though the majority of young people in that area were white. In other parts of California, Black kids were being arrested for curfew violations at two, three, even seven times the rate of whites.[3]

And police are now becoming an increasing presence in our schools. Schools are spending millions of dollars to hire their own police forces or contracting with local authorities. Kids are searched before being allowed into the building, under surveillance by video cameras in hallways, and subjected to random searches of their backpacks and lockers. Behavior that used to warrant a trip to the

efforts focused on police practices and the abolition of the death penalty. Before joining the ACLU, the former law school dean (Lincoln Law School of San Jose) was a Senior Associate at PolicyLink, where she authored two national publications: a report highlighting community-centered policing practices nationwide and an advocacy manual for police reform. For more information: http://www.aclunc.org.

THE FACTS ON COMMUNITY POLICING

RACIAL PROFILING

- Across the United States, over 10 percent of Black drivers stopped by police were likely to be searched or have their vehicle searched, as opposed to 3.5 percent of white drivers stopped by police.[4]

- A study of racial profiling on the New Jersey turnpike found that while only 13.5 percent of the cars on the road had a Black driver or passenger, 73.2 percent of motorists stopped and then arrested were Black.[5]

- In Maryland, white and Black drivers seem to violate traffic codes at equal rates, and yet 72 percent of the people who were stopped and searched by police were African American.[6]

COMMUNITY POLICING

- There are a reported 72 citizen-oversight boards across the country, but close to 13,500 state and local law enforcement agencies. This means only 0.5 percent of police departments are regularly monitored by the community.[7]

- Fifty-seven percent of Black officers believe that police officers are more likely to use physical violence against African Americans than against white people, while only 5 percent of white law enforcement officers agree.[8]

- In local police departments, 11.7 percent of full-time sworn police personnel are African American, 77.4

percent are white. Black officers make up 20.1 percent of large city police departments (population served of 250,000 or greater).[9]

- Black women are just 2.7 percent of full-time sworn police personnel in large city police departments.[10]

POLICE BRUTALITY

- A national study shows close to 65 percent of African American officers, as opposed to 49 percent of white officers, believe that community-oriented policing has the power to reduce the number of incidents involving police use of excessive force.[11]

- From 1995 to 2000, there were almost 10,000 cases of police use of excessive force reported in the United States; African Americans made up 47.5 percent of them.[12]

- Of the 4,318 incidents of police violence on African Americans, 3,622—or 84 percent—were committed by white officers.[13]

What the Community Can Do

The data in the preceding section vividly illustrate the racial disparities present in the criminal justice system. Mass rates of incarceration can be linked to many other pressing issues in the African American community. One of them is clearly the relationship between police accountability and arrest rates. The hyper and hostile police presence in Black communities causes many young people to get caught up at early ages. It also leads to the rearrest of numerous ex-offenders who may commit minor parole violations. One way to remedy this is to place great emphasis on the hiring, training, oversight, and accountability of police officers.

"Police accountability means that police officers will be held responsible for all of their actions and treat all citizens [regardless of race or ethnicity] in a respectful and lawful manner. In particular, police officers will not abuse their power and use more force than necessary, nor will they exhibit bias against any group of persons."[14] If law enforcement departments are truly accountable, it also means that they will "maintain policies and procedures to effectively ensure that their officers meet the highest standards of professionalism."[15]

The policy recommendations offered in this chapter combined with significant community effort would provide for a system in which police departments are more effective and responsive, tensions between police and the public are decreased, a mutual respect is created between the police and the communities they serve, and communities are safer overall.

What Every Individual Can Do Now:

- Get to know the police officers who patrol your neighborhood.

- Ask your local city council representative to host a neighborhood meeting to discuss local policy/ community relations.

- Talk to young people about how to conduct themselves if they are stopped or confronted by police officers: even if police officers do not respect your rights, be respectful of theirs, so as not to escalate the situation.

- Encourage your local high school to invite police in to get to know the students.

- If there is an incident of alleged police brutality in your community, join with neighbors and community leaders in demanding an investigation and appropriate action.

MOST OF ALL:
- Hold all leaders and elected officials responsible and demand that they change current policy.

What Works Now:

Turning around and refocusing a nonsupportive police department can be accomplished using a multitude of strategies, as the following examples attest.

Bullets in the Hood: A Bed-Stuy Story

Terrence Fisher, a teen living in a housing project in Bedford-Stuyvesant, Brooklyn, had seven of his friends shot and killed by a gun.[16] In trying to figure out what to do to stop gun violence in Bed-Stuy before losing another friend, or his own life, Terrence and a fellow teen filmmaker, Daniel Howard, decided to pick up a camera and create awareness by telling their stories.

Then, a few months into the production, Terrence tragically lost another friend. In this case, Terrence watched a police officer shoot and kill Timothy Stansbury, his best friend of close to 10 years. Terrence, Timothy, and another friend were on the roof of Terrence's building when they were met by a bullet fired by an officer who was on a regular rooftop patrol.

Terrence was severely scarred by this incident, while the Bed-Stuy residents were outraged by the killing of an innocent teen. The grand jury decided that the shooting was a tragic accident and no indictment was issued against the officer, despite the police commissioner's assessment that the killing was "unjustified." Terrence and his friends were furious. Uncontrollable anger and pain were eating Terrence alive, but he knew that violent retaliation was not the answer. Terrence, Daniel, and their friends took the path of organizing protests, creating tribute music for Timothy, and completing the documentary so that their story would spread to the world outside Bed-Stuy.

The young men subsequently won an Honorable Mention Student Emmy® as well as the 2005 Sundance Film Festival Special Jury Award for Short Filmmaking. When faced with immense grief and immeasurable frustration with the system, Terrence and Daniel chose to direct their energy into a creative project that proved to be educational, healing, and inspirational for all.

Bay Area PoliceWatch

Bay Area PoliceWatch is a program of the Ella Baker Center for Human Rights, which has a three-part objective: to document, expose, and challenge human rights abuses in the United States criminal justice system; to build power in communities most harmed by government-sanctioned violence; and to develop and advocate for proactive, community-based solutions to systemic "criminal injustice."[17] PoliceWatch fulfills this mission by working to protect citizens from corrupt and abusive police officers.

Since the program's inception in 1995, it has "policed the police" by engaging in grassroots mobilizing and media activism while offering a combination of social and legal services. PoliceWatch is unique in that it has a helpline, abuse documentation center, and state bar–certified lawyer referral service.[18] The helpline offers information about civil rights and instructions for reporting abuse. Trained counselors document reported abuse and advise callers on how to get an offending officer disciplined, demoted, or fired. The documentation center has a highly developed database that makes it easy to track problem officers, precincts, and practices.[19] Callers may also inquire about how to file a lawsuit. Helpline counselors fortunately have the resources to refer callers with strong legal claims to PoliceWatch's state bar–certified lawyer referral panel.

When it is necessary and appropriate, Bay Area PoliceWatch strives to create public awareness of police misconduct cases. If community advocates do not force or persuade the media to tell the truth about these kinds of cases, the victims are often blamed.[20] In some situations, PoliceWatch may engage in high-profile mobilization campaigns to get justice for victims or their families.[21]

A few examples of its aggressive advocacy include participating in a broad community campaign to remove two repeatedly abusive officers in the African American community from the Oakland police force. PoliceWatch is also currently campaigning to get both the San Francisco and the Oakland police departments to significantly upgrade the mental health crisis training they provide for their officers. Oftentimes, cops are not equipped with the skills to deal with mentally ill citizens, and confrontations with them end too frequently in violence.[22]

Most people are not informed well enough to deal with the legal system, so Bay Area PoliceWatch serves as protector, educator, and advocate.

Berkeley Police Review Commission

Communities can be proactive; they must demand that their local police departments have a community oversight model that has adequate resources, policy-making capacity, independent and representative appointments, and broad investigative authority. The Berkeley Civilian Police Review Board, created in 1973, was the first oversight agency to have full independent authority to investigate complaints.[23]

The Berkeley Police Review Commission has a broad mandate with regard to policy recommendations. The city ordinance empowers the commission to "review and make recommendations concerning all written and unwritten policies, practices, and procedures of whatever kind and without limitations, in relation to the Berkeley Police Department."[24] This pertains to a number of different areas, including treatment of sexual assault victims, use of weapons, recruitment, hiring and training, and police relationships with communities of color.[25]

Unlike some cities where the mayor appoints most, if not all, of the community oversight representatives, the Berkeley ordinance establishing the Police Review Commission provides that it "shall consist of 9 members. Each Councilmember shall appoint 1 member to the Commission. All members shall be residents of the City of Berkeley. No officer or employee of the city shall be appointed to the Commission."[26] Berkeley's appointment process appears to have reduced the unbalanced nature of community oversight appointments found in some other cities. With district elections for city council members, there is some accountability to different communities for the choices made about their community oversight representative.[27]

The Police Review Commission of Berkeley also has independent investigative authority supported by subpoena power.[28] It is authorized to receive, and responsible for receiving, complaints against officers and the police department and thoroughly investigating these claims.[29] While this power may not be fully exercised often, it is still a necessary tool.[30]

What Every Leader and Elected Official Can Do

- Recruit and hire community-conscious personnel.
- Adequately train all officers in cultural sensitivity, racial profiling, and excessive force policies.
- Proactively maintain diverse and effective police departments.
- Create efficient oversight mechanisms.
- Eliminate barriers to citizens' filing complaints against police.
- Ensure a fair and thorough investigation of accused police officers.
- Collect, compile, and publish relevant statistical data on police abuse.

Getting and Keeping the Right People

Recruitment and Hiring

For police departments to be effective, they must be representative of the communities they serve. A large, diverse applicant pool should be the ultimate goal of any recruitment effort, and this can only be achieved through a committed, continuous, proactive, targeted, and community-engaged process. Successful recruiting efforts require adequate resources, both money and officers, and time dedicated to developing a strategic recruiting plan. The participation of officers from underrepresented groups is particularly important. When interested applicants see officers that look like them, they are more likely to complete the application process.[31]

Police departments often focus their recruiting efforts around advertising in the few months prior to administering a police exam. To ensure a wide range of applicants, continuous, fully funded outreach efforts throughout the year, and over time, are necessary.[32] Departments must also be proactive and aggressive in delivering the message that they are "working vigorously to ensure that the personnel of [their agencies] do not, in their daily contact with members of the minority community, discriminate against them."[33] It must be apparent to the community and to possible recruits that a police administrator is actively trying to improve African American representation in their respective departments.

Recruitment efforts must be tailored to particular audiences, recognizing that diverse ethnic groups may respond differently to various messages and may frequent different locations.[34] In targeting prospective Black officers, a police department may host an "African Americans and Policing Career Fair" or develop fliers, billboards, and brochures that feature African American officers.

It is also important to engage the community in staffing efforts. Members of the Black community can be very helpful in developing and implementing strategic, targeted recruiting plans.[35] Some city police departments have invited people from surrounding neighborhoods to participate in focus groups to evaluate the people's needs and different slogans, images, and approaches. Group members also actively participate in distributing materials and sponsoring officer presentations.[36] This involvement presents an opportunity to create a respectful bond between African American communities and their respective police departments.

Once a diverse body of applicants has been approved, it is important to engage practices other than pencil and paper and physical exams in the hiring process. Bilingual language skills, problem-solving ability, and community connection must all be considered when hiring new officers.[37] Language skills are integral to effective policing and all departments should offer monetary bonuses to those who are bi- or multilingual. In addition, residency requirements and incentives affirm the connection between officers and the communities they serve and should be implemented nationwide.[38]

Training

It is proven that "the quality of police service depends on an officer's knowledge of the specific neighborhood he polices—its values and customs . . . The presence of increased numbers of minority police officers . . . and the interrelationships which it fosters can be the most effective means the agency has [of training]."[39] While it may be true that no academy training is as effective as consistent "contact among peers to break down the barriers and hostilities between different cultures,"[40] there are certain topics that must be addressed formally.

Currently, most academy training emphasizes the technical, tactical aspects of policing, devoting far less time to the service-, people-oriented aspects, although studies have shown that police officers spend more time engaged in service activities than crime fighting.[41] More time and greater emphasis must be placed on developing community-oriented skills and knowledge. Interactive learning tactics such as required research reports on different ethnic communities force officers to emotionally engage themselves in the process. Also, spending time at victim-based nonprofit organizations, mental hospitals, and domestic violence centers allows police personnel to gain a greater understanding of the communities they serve.

Cultural sensitivity, use of force, racial profiling, community policing, language training, homelessness, and hate crimes are all issues that police departments must not only cover with their rookie officers, but also consistently review with veteran members. As times change, so do citizens and communities; police policy and response must always adapt.

Retention

Retention of good employees, especially women and people of color, is a significant challenge that requires conscious efforts.[42] Police administrators and high-level officers must frequently and publicly affirm the contribution of African Americans, women, and other officers of color while also refusing to accept any harassment or discrimination in the workplace. This creates a culture of inclusion and tolerance and makes for a desirable and supportive workplace.[43]

Formal mentoring programs for newly hired officers have also proved successful and are widely regarded as promoting cohesion and peer support while enhancing professional development.[44]

Maintaining Oversight and Accountability

Effective External and Internal Mechanisms

Because city officials are almost always responsible for appointing independent auditors or members of community review boards, they must encourage their active development. Currently most oversight mechanisms do not have sufficient investigative or disciplinary powers. For them to be most effective, subpoena power must be granted. (In this context, this refers to the power of an oversight agency to compel the testimony of police officers or other persons and/or to compel the production of other evidence.)[45] "Citizen oversight contributes to accountability by providing an independent citizen perspective on the complaint process, police department policies, and practices that give rise to citizen complaints."[46]

Because Internal Affairs is responsible for police misconduct investigations in some departments, all police officials should construct a national uniform policy on the use of excessive force. In addition, internal bureaus must employ an early warning system to identify potential problem officers. A data-based management system for reviewing police officer performance and identifying officers with recurring problems such as citizen complaints would prepare internal reviewers to provide interventions designed to correct officers' performance before it is too late.[47]

It is critical for both individual and group civilian oversight units to have adequate and credible funding, training, and staff, as well as adequate outreach and the full extent of investigative authority and powers.[48]

Complaint Process

To ensure an unbiased and a transparent complaint process, citizens need to be given simple forms with clear instructions and a telephone contact for follow-up purposes when they want to file a complaint against a police officer, whether with a citizen review agency or a police department official. No review agency or police officer should ever attempt to dissuade or intimidate an individual making a complaint; anyone who attempts to do so must be punished appropriately. In addition, filed complaints should never be removed from an officer's file—even after a substantial amount of time has passed.[49]

Ensure Fair and Thorough Investigation of Police Officers

Federal, state, and city governments must work to remove all barriers to the fair and thorough investigation and, where appropriate, prosecution of civil rights abuses committed by police officers.[50] In many cases, there are not adequate resources to carry out police misconduct investigations. Federal funds must be allocated to see all worthwhile cases through to resolution.

Each state ought to appoint an independent prosecutor to handle only police misconduct cases. Currently, because district and county attorneys rely heavily on the support and cooperation of police departments for their other cases, there is a conflict of interest, and thus they are ineffective in most police misconduct cases.

Federal law must also be amended to ensure the just trial of police officers. Presently, a police officer may be prosecuted for official misconduct only if an attorney can prove that he or she acted with the "specific intent" to abuse a citizen's civil rights. It should be enough that a police officer intentionally and unjustifiably disrespected, beat, or killed a victim.[51] Elected officials must remove this requirement of the civil rights statutes. In some cases against police officers, prosecutors do not seek criminal remedies, but rather professional consequences or suspension. As with all other alleged violent criminals, if there is sufficient evidence to support the charges, police officers should receive the appropriate punishment.

Access to Information

Governments at all levels should compile and publish relevant statistical data on police abuse and racial profiling. This is necessary to inform policy-making, oversee data collection, and make required monitoring by all law enforcement agencies possible.[52] Full access to police misconduct information keeps citizens aware and police accountable.

"The collection of racial profiling data is also needed to examine the extent of its use, to enact legislation to prosecute those who utilize it, and to realize the total elimination of this practice in law enforcement."[53]

A Final Word

If we familiarize ourselves and our children with our rights and with local police personnel, and if we hold our elected officials responsible for adequately recruiting, hiring, and training community-conscious personnel and creating efficient police oversight mechanisms, then we can foster community-centered policing.

FOSTERING ACCOUNTABLE COMMUNITY-CENTERED POLICING

Racial Profiling and Bias-Based Policing

A decade after the original publication of this book, the term *racial profiling* is more prominent than ever in contemporary discussions of police-community relationships. While an abundance of research has verified that people of color are stopped more often than whites, to use this particular term undermines the breadth of issues involving police and minority communities. "Bias-based policing" more appropriately encompasses the broader notion of police bias and its implications for communities of color across a vast array of police-citizen encounters.

Interactions between minorities and police extend from traffic stops to street stops, use of force, arrests, and a range of officer discretionary behaviors. Research has established the differential treatment of minority citizens across officer decisions to search individuals and use force when enacting an arrest. These officer decisions have been shown to differ significantly across individuals of color as well as communities of color. A discussion to remedy police discretion with Black citizens must extend beyond "driving while Black" to encompass a more holistic view of police and their commitment to communities.

It's Called "Community Policing," Not "Policing the Community"

Research has shown that crime concentrates in microplaces, or "hot spots," in a city. These areas of high crime concentration are predominantly comprised of minority citizens—largely African American.[1] This correlation should not be interpreted as "Black people are criminal," but the result of a culmination of sociological factors over time that have left Black communities without equal access to economic, educational, health, and safety opportunities. These neighborhood conditions generate crime and disorder and undermine the ability of communities to protect themselves. The relationship between serious crime and conditions of unemployment, poverty, truancy, education attrition, teen pregnancy, housing segregation, inadequate health care, crowded and unsanitary housing, homelessness, underfinanced public services, and a lack of civic amenities are undeniable.[2] Unfortunately, societal progress pertaining to these issues has not resulted in a demonstrable change to improve the quality of life for many Black communities, nor the ability for police to properly serve these communities. Today, as C. D. Robinson said 40 years ago, police can only "perform a holding operation until other institutions attack such problems with an array of resources."[3]

While the concentration of crime lends itself to crime-prevention benefits through tailored police interventions, the police must be sensitive to community relationships in order for the intervention strategies they choose to have a benign impact. If police simply allocate officers to these microplaces of crime via directed patrols without remaining cognizant of community perceptions and positive engagement, the relationship between police and the communities are likely to further erode. This is especially true if police opt to employ more severe and less thoughtful approaches, concentrating intensive enforcement efforts or zero-tolerance policies in Black neighborhoods.

Evidence has shown that minorities living in distressed neighborhoods routinely report high levels of dissatisfaction with, and skepticism of, the police. Police executives and city managers sometimes point to elevated crime rates to justify officers' use of aggressive policing initiatives in poor Black neighborhoods. Minority perspectives of aggressive policing, coupled with occasional disrespectful treatment at the hands of officers, further reinforces Black citizens' negative views of the police. Because African Americans constitute a substantial portion of victims and witnesses in high-crime areas, citizens' distrust of police may compromise crime-control efforts in their communities.[4]

More appropriately, police departments could adopt crime-prevention strategies that actively engage members of the community to be positive agents of change in their neighborhoods. This approach mirrors a recent movement for police to reimagine themselves as "community guardians" as opposed to "community warriors."[5] Put simply, this approach seeks to reinforce positive, engagement-oriented community-policing principles that enhance police service, procedural justice, and community satisfaction with the police.

Though community policing has long been considered a staple of policing, departments nationwide have begun to invest more firmly in developing actionable community-policing practices. From 2007 to 2013, police departments nationwide increased community policing in mission statements (13 percent), required academy training (5 percent), and in-service training (28 percent).[6] In addition, one-third of all police departments have a formal partnership with local organizations to facilitate connections with the community—a percentage that increases to 67 percent of agencies when serving a population of 250,000 or more.[7]

Police departments are currently at the crossroads of balancing positive community engagement and effective public-safety tactics. "Stop and frisk" practices (also known as *Terry Stops*),[8] although once commonly upheld by the courts as a lawful and legitimate practice by law enforcement, are now more often being questioned. Officers are not necessarily aware of, nor comply with, the limitations of Terry stops, as many stops fail to meet the criteria of a lawful search.[9] Such aggressive policing tactics have been argued to be an Achilles' heel of community policing; and the same can be said for zero-tolerance policies that target juveniles. An emphasis on the formal sanctioning of minor offenses to deter future offending has resulted in a more aggressive and targeted style of policing that operates inverse of community-policing principles.

What Can Be Done

Community-centered policing involves forming both formal and informal partnerships with community organizations and citizens, prioritizing transparency, actively pursuing feedback, and establishing programs that allow police to engage with residents outside of the law-enforcement arena. At its best, the practice allows community members to feel heard, respected, and empowered to help police control crime in their neighborhoods. Police should actively engage youth from minority and challenged neighborhoods. Research has shown that developing positive perceptions of the police from an early age helps to promote trust and legitimacy later in life. Improved oversight and accountability of police can be obtained in many ways. The city government should solicit the public's views of police performance through regularly occurring independent surveys. The city should support and publish regular independent surveys of police officers to get a firm sense of officer morale and the pressures of the job. Citizens should demand ongoing independent audits of critical police functions, including crime reports, enforcement actions, and responses to 911 calls.

Police in the U.S. do many things well, even many things great, but unfortunately serving communities of color is not one of them. Effective reform requires an articulated plan, commitment to actionable progress, and accountability for change. The multifaceted "Campaign Zero" proposed by We the Protestors[10] is a model for such reform. This policy agenda, illustrated in the figure below, focuses on improving police service through limitations on aggressive tactics, improved training and accountability mechanisms, more diversity in police personnel and oversight bodies, and video technology.

The movement started by activist organizations such as We the Protestors and Black Lives Matter has shown a demonstrable influence on contemporary policy and garnered the attention of 2016 presidential candidates, chiefs of police, and community members nationwide. This is a movement that is positioned to leave a mark on the next era of police reform. Moreover, the focal areas of Campaign Zero are not simply the demands of Black citizens, but are widely agreed upon and supported by police executives and scholars. Police departments nationwide have begun to recognize their failure to effectively serve Black citizens and communities, thus resulting in progress toward change.

Progress Toward Change

Following the deaths of Eric Garner, Michael Brown, Tamir Rice, Walter Scott, and Antonio Zambrano-Montes (to name a few), the Police Executive Research Forum (PERF) gathered a meeting of police chiefs from across the U.S. to address the issue of how police are trained (or, perhaps, not trained) to best manage situations involving minorities. This 2015 gathering yielded a number of insightful conclusions from police leaders.[11] Most notably, the training currently provided to new recruits and experienced officers in most departments is inadequate; the extent to which use of force can be minimized requires more improved training as well as a shift in police culture. Such change is currently underway in many cities in the United States.

Police in Kansas City, Missouri, are receiving training in tactical disengagement while Los Angeles officers are receiving training on the "preservation of life." The Seattle Police Department won praise from the U.S. Justice Department for its department-wide tactical de-escalation training program. Oakland, California, is overhauling its use-of-force training to emphasize de-escalation skills; officers' management of stress during threatening situations; assessment of officers in realistic, scenario-based exercises; and procedural justice. Police in San Diego have implemented a number of changes in their training of officers, including an emphasis on emotional intelligence that teaches officers how to manage their emotions during intense and unruly encounters with citizens. Spokane, Washington, experienced a decline in use-of-force incidents of 22 percent between 2013 and 2014 that is attributed to a series of reform efforts, including 40 hours of de-escalation and crisis-intervention training, the hiring of a more diversified police force, and a requirement for officers to spend time on foot patrols in challenged communities.[12]

The Facts—Ten Years Later:

- Black citizens are 1.5 times more likely to be searched for discretionary reasons compared to white citizens. Citizens with a criminal history (actual criminal history, not perceived criminality) are 4.7 times more likely to be searched in discretionary searches compared to citizens without a criminal history, independent of other factors. This research indicates race is mediated by consideration of criminal history.[13]

- Regardless of the reason for the traffic stop, Black drivers (67 percent) are less likely than white drivers (84 percent) to believe the reason for the stop is legitimate. A greater percentage of Black (7 percent) and Hispanic (6 percent) drivers are ticketed than white drivers (5 percent). Among Black and Hispanic stopped drivers, a similar percentage of ticketed and not ticketed drivers believe the police behaved properly during the traffic stop.[14]

- Both Black males and Black females are 2.5 times more likely to report that white police officers stopped them for an illegitimate reason.[15]

- Statistics from New York City's "Stop and Frisk" policy show that officers frisked white suspects slightly less frequently than they did similarly situated nonwhites (29 percent of stops versus 33 percent of stops). Black suspects are slightly likelier to have been frisked than white suspects stopped in circumstances similar to Black suspects (46 percent versus 42 percent). While there is a gap, this difference is much smaller than what the aggregate statistics indicated. Arrest rates for white suspects are slightly lower than those for similarly situated nonwhites (4.8 percent versus 5.1 percent). Officers were slightly less likely to use force against white suspects than they were to use it against similarly situated nonwhites (15 percent versus 16 percent). Officers recovered contraband (such as weapons, illegal drugs, or stolen property) in 6.4 percent of the stops of white suspects. The contraband recovery rate was

5.7 percent for similarly situated Black suspects and 5.4 percent for similarly situated Hispanic suspects.[16]

- Police departments in the United States are 14 percent less racially diverse than the communities they serve.[17]

—Prepared by Jeremy G. Carter, Ph.D., Assistant Professor, School of Public and Environmental Affairs, Indiana University–Purdue University, Indianapolis, Indiana

✛ ✛

V.

ENSURING BROAD ACCESS TO AFFORDABLE NEIGHBORHOODS THAT CONNECT TO OPPORTUNITY

INTRODUCTORY ESSAY
BY ANGELA GLOVER BLACKWELL

I grew up in a segregated St. Louis, Missouri, in the late 1950s and early 1960s. I know from reading and talking to my parents that, during this period, racism there was harsh. Yet as a child, I was surrounded by a web of caring adults who were determined to raise bold, proud, intellectually curious children, shielded from the sting of discrimination. My family must have been a powerful Black family because within two years of our moving into the 4900 block of Terry, our presence forced nearly all the existing white residents to move off the block. We were the second Black family to move in—the first having moved in the day before. Though we lived in segregated neighborhoods and attended segregated schools, my parents, and the other Black adults who were the stalwarts of the community, created a rich, nurturing environment for us that was full of activity and adventure. I remember fondly the Sunday school picnics, the volunteering at local homes for the elderly, well-chaperoned Saturday-night dances, and the usual holiday activities. These adults also braved cold stares to expose us to museums, parks, the symphony, the city zoo.

While we may have been locked out of the mainstream, we refused to be locked into a narrow world. These ingenious adults may have suffered indignities as they sought to shop, buy homes, and work in a city filled with racism, but they built a community that protected their children that emphasized one message: "You can do and be whatever you want in this world." In effect, community was the scaffolding that allowed us to thrive under even the most oppressive circumstances.

Much has changed since my childhood in St. Louis. In the 1970s and 1980s, it became more and more painful to return home and see deteriorating neighborhoods that were being steadily neglected by the city power structure and to watch young people trying to survive in a hostile world, without the benefit of the kind of community life I had known as a child. Ironically, the decline came in the wake of one of the most dramatic and courageous chapters of our history, as grassroots civil rights activism swept across the small towns and cities of the United States. Responding to this legal and social progress, my hometown, as did many other cities, weathered tremendous loss—most starkly, over half its population. In the 1950s, St. Louis was the ninth-largest city in the nation, with nearly 900,000 residents; today, only 334,000 people remain. St. Louis has fallen not only out of the top 10 largest cities, but also out of the top 50, replaced by rapidly growing "sunbelt" cities—Las Vegas, Austin, and Phoenix. And despite the gains of the civil rights movement, for Black people, gaining access to opportunity is as hard as, if not harder than, ever.

On the heels of the civil rights movement, whites—fearful of school integration—continued their outward march, this time to the suburbs; and middle-class African Americans embraced newly opened opportunities to find housing outside of the traditional

Black community. The ripple effect of these changes left abandoned inner-city neighborhoods of extreme poverty characterized by failing schools, few businesses to provide jobs, high crime and tense relationships with police, and declining retail presence, such as supermarkets and drugstores.

It's a familiar story, unfolding in metropolitan regions across the country, and a story of contradictions. As central cities struggled with poverty, urban disinvestment, and an exodus of residents, services, and jobs, the surrounding suburbs reaped the benefit of this urban flight, with new employment opportunities, a robust tax base, increased political clout, and dramatic growth. *Brown v. Board of Education* marked a transformative moment in American history, yet more than 50 years later, many public school districts are in effect resegregating based on housing patterns—locking many low-income children of color in failing, overcrowded schools with woefully limited resources. Even "inner ring" suburbs (those closest to the central city)—once symbols of prosperity and idyllic middle-class life—increasingly find themselves facing urban problems of blight, unemployment, poverty, and crime, as resources and sprawling, unchecked development leap-frog from city to ever-more distant suburbs and "exurbs."

In the United States today, where you live literally determines access to opportunity. Your address dictates whether you will have access to good schools and jobs, grocery stores, parks, and other important amenities. The availability of affordable housing in neighborhoods of rich opportunity, therefore, has become the next battleground in the fight for Black people to fully participate and thrive. Many opportunity-rich neighborhoods are not accessible to African Americans because of policies and practices that are exclusionary. For example, despite laws against housing discrimination, it is still quite prevalent and most likely to be practiced against Black people. Too many neighborhoods with good schools and desirable amenities are too expensive and do not allow renters. Some communities present so much hostility toward Blacks who do move there that Black people are discouraged from attempting to even move into those neighborhoods. Achieving access to affordable housing in communities that can provide opportunity is difficult for too many African American families.

Equally important is access to public transit. Proportionately Black people are less likely to own cars and much more dependent on public transit than are whites. Plus, because so many new jobs are in suburban communities, Black people must rely on public transit to get to these jobs. Fair and equitable transportation strategies could effectively link African Americans to opportunity throughout the region. But most transportation spending goes to support continued sprawl by building more and more highways, not to increasing public transit, such as buses, light rail, and subways.

Sprawling suburbs and the inadequacy of public transit in many communities evolved not by accident, but through specific policy choices—government loan programs that encouraged suburban home-buying but initially excluded African Americans, for example, or transportation funding that overwhelmingly favored highway construction at the expense of deteriorating public transit systems. Low-income communities and communities of color bear the brunt of decades of inequitable policy decisions and sprawling metropolitan development patterns. Throughout America's urban centers, an entire generation of young people has grown up isolated from the opportunities that stable, mixed-income neighborhoods can provide, while many older African Americans have been disheartened to watch their vibrant, nurturing childhood communities slide into blight and decline. African Americans are moving to the suburbs in record numbers; in fact, African Americans and Latinos are the fastest-growing residents in suburbs. Often, though, the areas to which we are moving begin to suffer from "white flight," disinvestment, failing schools, and disappearing jobs.

At the same time, this is an exciting moment for some of America's cities. We are witnessing a revival of urban life, as young professionals and suburban residents return to central-city neighborhoods, drawn to the convenience, bustling sidewalks, and cultural amenities many revitalized downtown areas now offer. Even some of the most blighted neighborhoods have experienced rapid, stunning reinvestment and rejuvenation over the past several years. Yet there is a troubling flip side to this renaissance: longtime residents—often lower-income and working-class African Americans—with deep community ties often struggle to remain in the neighborhoods they have advocated for and organized so diligently to improve. Tenants risk displacement as market-rate rents rise along with neighborhood improvement; increasing housing values can be a double-edged sword, offering a wealth-building opportunity for some homeowners, but forcing out lower- or fixed-income owners vulnerable to drastic property tax hikes. Our challenge as advocates, policy-makers, journalists, faith leaders, community activists, and local residents and business people is to ensure urban revitalization works for African Americans and low-income people of color; neighborhood reinvestment must not displace and further isolate low-income communities of color, but rather *connect* them to good jobs, educational opportunities, high-quality affordable housing, comprehensive public transit systems, parks, and cultural amenities essential to living a healthy, productive life.

Just as policy decisions have fostered economic and social disparities in our metropolitan regions, policy is the key to creating more equitable regions for low-income people of color and for *all* Americans. To do this, we need a new generation of policies, guided by the belief that those closest to the nation's challenges are central to the search for solutions and based on the wisdom, voice, and experience of local constituencies. We must also recognize that creating opportunity for *people* in low-income communities of color is as critical as the physical revitalization of these communities. Revitalizing cities and neighborhoods must ultimately focus on rebuilding "community," that scaffolding that engaged, empowered, thriving residents provide for each other and our future generations.

It is not a foregone conclusion that America must continue along a path toward greater disparities in wealth, health, and well-being. By strengthening neighborhoods and holding our leaders accountable to ensure that *all* communities are communities of opportunity, we can build cities, regions, and an entire nation where *everyone* can participate and prosper.

✢

ANGELA GLOVER BLACKWELL is Founder and Chief Executive Officer of PolicyLink, a national nonprofit research, communications, capacity building, and advocacy organization based in Oakland, California, dedicated to advancing policies to achieve economic and social equity. A renowned community building activist and advocate, Blackwell served as senior vice president of the Rockefeller Foundation, where she oversaw its domestic and cultural divisions. A lawyer by training, she gained national recognition as founder of the Oakland Urban Strategies Council, where she pioneered new approaches to neighborhood revitalization. For more information: http://www.policylink.org.

THE FACTS ON OUR NEIGHBORHOODS

RACIAL SEGREGATION AND JOBS MISMATCH

- Seventy-five percent of citizens who receive welfare live in central cities or rural areas, but 66 percent of entry-level job growth is in the suburbs.[1]

- Our federal government continues to segregate low-income African Americans; its biggest funding source for affordable housing builds nearly 60 percent of low-income housing in central-city neighborhoods that are mostly low-income and African American.[2]

- Of people in Detroit who receive income assistance from the government, 42 percent of whites live in neighborhoods with above-average access to jobs, while only 13 percent of Blacks live in job-rich areas and are therefore much less likely to exit income-assistance programs.[3]

QUALITY AFFORDABLE HOUSING

- African Americans are more likely to be told that housing in predominantly white neighborhoods is not available or they are directed to predominantly Black neighborhoods.[4]

- Black renters are 20 times more likely to get less information and help than whites with similar economic backgrounds when inquiring about advertised housing.

- Landlords tell them about fewer apartments on the market and do not show them everything that is available.[5]

- African Americans have the lowest homeownership rate in the nation, at 49 percent, compared to 76 percent for whites.[6]

- Nationally, the average rent for a two-bedroom apartment requires full-time earnings of $15.37 an hour. On average, African Americans make less than $12 an hour.[7]

- Basic housing is out of reach for the more than 24 percent of African Americans who live in poverty. A full-time worker making minimum wage could afford a typical one-bedroom apartment in only four out of all 3,066 counties in the United States.[8]

- Forty-nine percent of the nation's homeless population is African American.[9]

- In interactions between real estate brokers and minorities trying to buy or rent a home, discrimination occurred 46–59 percent of the time and was most often against African Americans.[10]

RACIAL DISCRIMINATION IN OUR TRANSPORTATION SYSTEMS

- African Americans tend to live farther from job opportunities than whites but have less access to cars and are more dependent on public transit. Only 7 percent of white households do not own a car, while nearly 25 percent of African American households do not.[11]

- African Americans make approximately six times more trips by public transit than whites, and African Americans and Latinos together comprise 54 percent of public transportation users (62 percent of all bus riders) in cities. Yet only 12 percent of the U.S. Department of Transportation's approximately $60 billion budget goes to public transit, while nearly 60 percent is spent on highways, which serve white suburban commuters.[12]

What the Community Can Do

For many African Americans, few decent jobs exist in the neighborhoods where we live, and public transportation linking our communities to areas of greater opportunity is often inadequate, underfunded, or unsafe. There are direct links among where we work, where we live, how many resources (both time and money) are spent on transit and on housing, and our opportunities. Although public transit is often seen as the domain of state and federal governments, communities of color play a crucial role in advocating for more and better transportation options. The Black community must band together if we are to end the systemic discrimination that persists by isolating affordable housing choices far from good schools and jobs; charging us more for mortgages and loans; and underinvesting in public transit choices that would connect us to opportunities in the region.

What Every Individual Can Do Now:

- Join a self-help housing project such as Habitat for Humanity and build your family or another family a home.

- Start an Individual Development Account (IDA) to save money for a down payment. IDAs will match your contributions. (See "Support Individual Development Accounts" in Covenant VIII or go to www.Cfed.org for more information.)

- Ask your employer about establishing a home loan program that helps lower the cost of a mortgage.

- Ask your banker to compare a loan offer with the best rates the institution is offering. Ask for an explanation if your terms are less favorable. Shop and compare among financial institutions.

- Find multiple ways to get home or to work—walk, bike, ride public transit, or carpool, and teach your kids to do the same. Carpool with neighbors or co-workers, and arrange for carpools or school buses to take your children to school.

- Organize neighborhood groups to advocate for expanded and better public transit services, as well as safe pedestrian walkways and public transit stations. Let your voice be heard by your transit authority: attend meetings regarding transit lines that are closing or opening.

MOST OF ALL:

- Hold all leaders and elected officials responsible and demand that they change current policy.

What Works Now:

Abdul Hafiz

Abdul Hafiz resides in a disadvantaged area of Clifton Staten Island, New York. In May of 2000 Abdul's life changed forever: His 16-month-old brother, Ibrahim, accidentally crawled out his window onto the fire escape and fell to his death. Immediately after the accident, Abdul and his classmates focused their energy on helping to save all children, in memory of little Ibrahim. They created their own website and started a campaign to obtain safety gates on fire escape windows, which would open in an event of a fire but would prevent a toddler from accidentally falling through.

Abdul and his classmates met with the heads of the U.S. Housing and Urban Development (HUD) Department and obtained a grant for one-half-million dollars to install safety gates, security cameras, and two computer labs to reduce crime in their neighborhood housing complex. His group still did not feel it had done enough, so it pushed for legislation to mandate these safety gates for the entire city, state, and nation, obtaining thousands of petition signatures and regularly meeting with legislators and commissioners. It even helped pass resolutions with the New York State NAACP and Business and Professional Women's Clubs in support of the campaign.

In addition to working on the safety gates campaign, Abdul and his group have become youth advocates in their community, volunteering at events and rallies to improve the community. They recently worked on a project to save a local hospital and to bring additional safety agents and crossing guards to schools. The group often volunteers at local nature parks. For example, it has helped transform Eibs Pond Park from an illegal dumping ground to a beautiful oasis. The group acts locally but has committed to acting globally as well. A new project now involves assisting in a humanitarian effort to collect and send goods—toys, school and medical supplies—to Liberia.

Abdul and his group have learned how to transform a tragedy into a catalyst for positive change. His causes have built bridges to all in a unique way. Not only does he excel in the community, but Abdul also has consistently earned a position in the high honor roll in school. He has received numerous academic awards and was the valedictorian at his graduation. He received honors for Outstanding Community Service from local elected officials, New York's governor, and the mayor of New York City. At just 12 years of age, Abdul has already touched the hearts of the city, state, and nation.[13]

Bethel New Life

Bethel New Life in Chicago, Illinois, has fused affordable housing, commercial development, and community facilities into a single complex, bringing a valuable neighborhood asset to the Lake-Pulaski station in Chicago. A neighborhood congregation, Bethel New Life first had to fight to keep its transit line open. It then demonstrated that transit-oriented development in this working-class community could provide social returns to the neighborhood and economic returns to the investors. Public transit is often an underutilized asset in African American and low-income communities. By tying it to housing and other community services, it can open up opportunity and increase mobility.

In addition, Bethel New Life strives to develop quality, affordable, energy-efficient housing and commercial space. In just one year, it built, sold, and closed on 12 single-family homes, provided home-ownership workshops and individual counseling to over 600 people, and began the predevelopment phase on Parkside Estates II—66 new condo units; Douglas Villa rehab and conversion to 24 affordable condos; and Keystone homes—seven new homes in partnership with Keystone Baptist Church.[14] As an organization, Bethel New Life builds "on the strengths and capacities of the people and the place, starting with what we have, with what people know and want. [They] turn liabilities into opportunities for 'smart growth.' "[15]

East San Francisco Bay Area Bus Riders

In response to the ever-widening gap between the branches of the "separate and unequal" public transit system in San Francisco's East Bay and the Metropolitan Transportation Commission's (MTC) lack of response to public critique, AC Transit bus riders have come together, organized, and rallied civil rights and labor groups to take MTC to federal court for its racially discriminatory planning and fund-ing practices.[16]

The MTC of the San Francisco Bay Area has long been criticized for failing to meet the needs of minorities, blue-collar workers, and residents living in the urban areas of the East Bay. In recent years, MTC's rail system—consisting of Caltrain and BART, which serve predominantly white and relatively wealthy commuters—has been expanding. Meanwhile, its bus system—AC Transit, which serves a population that is nearly 80 percent people of color, many of them low-income—has suffered more and more drastic cuts in service and funding. This means that African Americans and low-income Bay Area residents who are dependent on buses to get around often have to wait hours for a bus; switch buses several times; and walk long dis-tances to work, school, child-care centers, grocery stores, and health clinics. This harsh reality often makes them late, leaves women and children in unsafe situations, and forces many African Americans to turn down employment opportunities.

The East Bay bus riders allege that MTC's funding practices are prejudiced. For example, passengers receive public subsidies totaling $6.14 per BART trip, and Caltrain passengers receive $13.79, while AC Transit riders receive only $2.78. In April of 2005, MTC received more than $100 million in federal funds, 20 percent of which went to public transit. Yet all of that money went to its rail lines, rather than to the already underfunded bus system.[17]

This case illustrates how crucial the participation of public transit riders is in bringing large public entities to task for unjust practices. With the help of other community groups and law firms concerned with civil rights, the African American community in the San Francisco Bay Area is on the right track to make the area's public transportation system start doing what it should have been doing all along: taking us where we need to go.

What Every Leader and Elected Official Can Do

- Expand affordable housing choices in opportunity-rich neighborhoods.

- Increase African American homeownership.

- Fund and support fair housing enforcement to eliminate unfair treatment.

- Ensure diverse housing choices in job-growth areas.

- Prioritize public transit over highways in all transportation funding.

- Ensure African American representation on transportation planning bodies.

- Build more mixed-income housing near public transit.

Expand Affordable Housing Choices
in Opportunity-Rich Neighborhoods

While 2004 marked the 50th anniversary of the *Brown v. Board of Education* decision by the U.S. Supreme Court, opening the door to inclusion in education, voting, employment, and housing, the persistence of housing segregation continues to limit advancement in the arenas of education and employment opportunity. In metropolitan Boston, for example, seven in 10 white students attend schools in the outer suburbs that are over 90 percent white, while almost eight in 10 African American and Latino students attend schools in the City of Boston or one or its urbanized satellite cities.[18] Numerous policies have exacerbated the continuing trends toward housing segregation.

The Federal Housing Administration (FHA) historically restricted loans on a racial basis, supporting and encouraging the movement of middle-class white households to the suburbs. Limiting investment in African American neighborhoods lowered the property values of individuals' homes, creating a generational "asset divide" between whites, whose homes appreciated, and Blacks, whose homes largely stagnated or depreciated. Decreasing property values also limited the budgets of the cities Blacks lived in, resulting in fewer services than their surrounding suburbs. While civil rights laws helped change those earlier FHA lending practices, today's housing segregation patterns are exacerbated by newer federal housing investment practices, by local land use laws, and by private lending practices.

Low Income Housing Tax Credits (LIHTCs)—the largest source of money for the construction and rehabilitation of affordable housing—go largely to central-city neighborhoods with disproportionate shares of Black residents (58 percent of LIHTC units are in these neighborhoods),[19] making racial and economic segregation worse. Because the program is administered by the U.S. Treasury Department, and not the U.S. Housing and Urban Development (HUD) Department, the projects are not subject to HUD guidelines that call for being located outside areas of high minority and poverty concentration. These tax credits are allocated to states, which set their own allocation criteria. Federal and state policy-makers can set criteria that require LIHTC developments be located in opportunity-rich, mixed-income neighborhoods. Giving priority to tax credit housing in job-growth areas, near public transit and near high-achieving schools, would strengthen African American residents' access to other opportunities.

Local and state officials can make a huge difference in creating housing opportunity by ensuring that every jurisdiction builds a variety of housing types. A study of 1,100 jurisdictions in the 25 largest metropolitan areas shows that low-density zoning reduces the availability of rental housing or multifamily ownership housing such as condominiums. Land use laws that require large lot sizes or large square footage single-family houses drive up the cost, raising the bar too high for lower-cost multifamily developments. The resulting shortage of such housing limits the number of African Americans in those communities.[20] States can enact fair-share housing policies that require every jurisdiction to plan for and build a portion of their housing to serve low- and modest-income families; or they can pass a minimum requirement for a percentage of every town or city's housing stock to be affordable. California's Housing Element law and Massachusetts' Anti-Snob Zoning law have contributed substantially to the development of more modest-cost housing in those states.

Local officials can use the most promising mixed-income housing tool, "inclusionary zoning," requiring a portion of every new market development to include a percentage of affordable houses.[21] By tying the development of lower-cost housing to market-rate housing, hundreds of cities and towns across America have developed tens of thousands of affordable houses in new mixed-income communities. Lower-income families benefit by securing housing in opportunity-rich neighborhoods, and developers benefit by getting to build more houses on a piece of land than they would without the affordable units. Montgomery County, Maryland, has the oldest inclusionary housing program in the country, producing over 12,000 affordable houses in market-rate developments across the county. Today, no school in the county has more than 15 percent low-income students—helping make them all high-performing schools.

A key way to finance new housing development is the creation of housing trust funds at the local, state, and national levels. Thirty-seven states have housing trusts that dedicate revenue to housing development, rehabilitation, and mortgage subsidy. Vermont, Florida, and the District of Columbia dedicate over $20 per capita annually to their funds and have robust housing development. And a proposal is currently before Congress to support a national housing trust that could jump-start more housing in all 50 states.

Increase African American Homeownership

Owning a home is how most Americans build wealth. Yet significant racial disparities exist in homeownership rates, with African American ownership standing at 48 percent, compared to 76 percent for whites.[22] Local, state, and federal leaders can systematically increase ownership for African Americans by creating housing capital pools that affirmatively market to underrepresented communities and that offer mortgage subsidy, down-payment assistance, and credit counseling. Florida's 1992 Affordable Housing Act created the largest state housing trust fund that channels approximately $300 million annually to affordable housing and has produced over 150,000 affordable houses.[23] In 2001, 41 percent of the funds went to African American households, helping Florida raise its Black homeownership rate to 52 percent.

Local first-time homebuyers programs can also further this goal. Establishing credit counseling for these new homeowners is a key component of both local and state programs' success. Local and state leaders that establish these trust funds can identify goals to increase Black ownership every year for 10 years until parity with whites is reached.

Fund and Support Fair Housing Enforcement to Eliminate Unfair Treatment

In 1968, Congress passed the Fair Housing Act, outlawing discrimination in housing on the basis of race and ethnicity. And in the 1970s, the passage of the Home Mortgage Disclosure Act and the

Community Reinvestment Act were meant to eradicate racial discrimination in mortgage lending. Yet today, African Americans still cannot count on getting the same information as comparable white home seekers when they contact realtors, landlords, or financial institutions.

African Americans and Hispanics are likely to be told about fewer available homes than whites; to be steered to neighborhoods with larger minority populations and lower house values; to be given less assistance with the complexities of mortgage financing;[24] and to be given less favorable credit terms than white home buyers with comparable incomes and assets. A survey of metropolitan Boston found that an overwhelming 85 percent of African Americans said that members of their group miss out on good housing because they fear they will not be welcome in a particular community.[25] In fact, African Americans are the most segregated group from whites in communities across America.[26] High residential segregation for African Americans seriously limits other opportunities, such as access to jobs, good schools, grocery stores, and open space.

A nonprofit or state-run Fair Housing Program can be used to detect discrimination in the rental, sales, and lending markets, while also providing education regarding current laws. Federal lawmakers can adequately fund HUD fair-housing enforcement activities and ask HUD to build the capacity of local, state, and federal civil rights agencies to conduct widespread, ongoing audits that test for discrimination in both rental and homeownership markets. Testing—sending Blacks and whites separately to the same residential properties to see if they are treated the same—remains the most effective way to combat discrimination within housing; education, too, is key. State and local lawmakers can make sure these programs are operating in your home communities, and you can be active spokespeople by highlighting those who are fair and inclusive and ensuring sanctions for those who discriminate.

Sweeping changes have transformed the mortgage banking industry from small thrifts and savings institutions to the new financial services giants backed by the secondary mortgage market. While these changes were accompanied by a positive increase in lending to lower-income and minority borrowers during the 1990s, three distinct mortgage markets emerged, two of which had a negative impact on African American borrowers: the prime market (best interest rates); the legitimate subprime market (higher rates for higher-risk borrowers); and the predatory subprime market (generally targeting borrowers who are disconnected from credit markets and vulnerable to having their equity stripped). For low-income African Americans, 18 to 42 percent of home purchase and refinance loans from 1993 to 2001 were subprime,[27] bleeding resources from the community most in need of building ownership equity. Local, state, and federal lawmakers can pass new regulatory rules that prohibit the worst aspects of predatory loans: balloon payments, prepayment penalties, and stripping the cash value of a borrower's equity in the home; and they can require counseling for high-cost home loan borrowers prior to loan closing.

Ensure Connectivity to Job-Growth Areas

A relatively recent trend is the isolation of African American residents from new job growth centers. As of 1996, less than 16 percent of jobs nationwide were within three miles of central business districts.[28] A study of welfare recipients in Detroit showed that 42 percent of white welfare recipients live in neighborhoods with above-average access to jobs, and only 13 percent of Black welfare recipients live in job-rich areas and are thus less likely to exit welfare than whites.[29]

Three key avenues for reconnecting people to jobs include building new affordable housing choices in suburban job-growth areas; providing convenient transportation from transit-dependent communities to job centers; and planning for future growth that creates better jobs-to-housing balance. In 2002, when the Association of Bay Area Governments wanted to plan for future growth, it identified areas of job concentration to plan for how to locate new housing near that asset. A community-based, workforce-training consortium in Los Angeles keeps a consistent focus on transportation allocations to create transit connectivity between job corridors and African American and new immigrant communities. And the Unity Council in Oakland created childcare services at its local light rail station to integrate workers' transportation and childcare needs.

Change Transportation Funding Priorities

Nationally, spending on highways far outweighs spending on public transportation systems. And, in many metropolitan areas, the federal and state dollars earmarked for public transit often go to commuter rail lines that serve affluent, white, suburban commuters rather than low-income African Americans and inner-city residents who are often dependent on buses. Balanced or increased spending on public transit is crucial to providing African Americans with access to jobs. Local and state leaders can focus their policy attention on these transit-dependent communities and ensure better service to these neighborhoods.

In addition, benchmarks for increased funding and expanded services should be reflective of target populations utilizing transit. For example, in Boston, increased ridership is a marker of success that prioritizes where new transit money is invested. This criterion ignores public transit-dependent communities where people are waiting long hours to ride overcrowded buses to work and school; though a relatively low number of new riders may be added, increased funding is clearly needed.

Ensure Minority Representation on Planning Organizations and Regional Transportation Authorities

To increase funding for public transit and to ensure that regional transportation authority decisions more accurately and fairly meet the needs of all the people they serve, Metropolitan Planning Organizations (MPOs) should seek equal representation from urban areas and communities of color. In many metropolitan areas, suburban, affluent, or white communities are overrepresented on the boards of their MPOs. According to a 1994 Federal Highway Administration analysis, 68 of 74 MPOs around the country had significant central-city underrepresentation.[30] Leading the charge for more balanced MPO representation is a crucial way to provide the African American community with mobility and pathways to opportunity. In Detroit in 2003, for example, a faith-based community organization called MOSES teamed with the City of Ferndale, an inner suburb of Detroit, to sue their MPO for imbalanced membership and discriminatory funding practices. The executive committee of the Detroit region MPO, which represents 147 local governments and controls approximately $1 billion in annual federal, state, and local transportation funds, is comprised of mostly new suburban representatives. With population of greater than 900,000, Detroit has three votes on SEMCOG's executive committee, while suburban Monroe and Livingston counties both contain less than a quarter of Detroit's population, yet each has four votes on the executive committee. Livingston, Monroe, and other area counties have African American populations of between one and three percent, while central Detroit is over 80 percent African American.

Build More Mixed-Income Housing Near Public Transit

For the African American community to more readily access good jobs and affordable housing, our leaders must push for inclusionary zoning and dense mixed-income housing near transit stops—a strategy known as transit-oriented development. As limited land resources are exhausted, many states are beginning to investigate the possibilities of transit-oriented development—increased density and development near existing transit—as a way to promote effective growth and community development. Done properly, this approach encourages pedestrian activity, improves local environmental conditions (by reducing congestion), and connects residents to economic opportunities throughout the region. Done improperly, it can lead to gentrification and the displacement of lower-income and working-class residents in a community, many of whom are African American.

It is pivotal that our communities participate in these discussions, so that there can be shared benefit from the growth and neighborhood improvement that often results from this type of development. A case in point: The historic West Oakland African American community paired nonprofit developers and low-income housing tax credits to build hundreds of new apartments and affordable condominiums near the light rail station that is *one stop* from downtown San Francisco!

A Final Word

Building reasonably priced housing near good jobs with convenient, accessible public transit; enforcing fair housing laws already on the books; and including African Americans and low-income people of color in every step of the transit and housing policy-making conversation are the requisite scaffolding to ensure that all Americans can have access to livable, affordable neighborhoods.

ENSURING BROAD ACCESS TO AFFORDABLE NEIGHBORHOODS THAT CONNECT TO OPPORTUNITY

Having access to economically viable and secure communities remains a natural desire of all Americans. In addition to their proximity to employment centers, such communities also tie in to the ability to own a home and, presumably, build wealth through that investment. Both elected officials and community development practitioners may agree that the development of communities is a long-term endeavor that should be equitable and inclusive, but the rhetoric does not match the reality. Homeownership is one indicator that demonstrates rapidly expanding losses in economic equality and wealth for Black America, and the pattern for the foreseeable future does not look favorable for the Black community.

For as long as records have been kept in America, the nation's housing stock and the level of homeownership have been stratified by race and ethnicity. This phenomenon not only has not changed since the first edition of this book was published, but the gap between Black America and white America in terms of housing availability and ownership has widened. The Great Recession that began in the mid- to late-2000s further exacerbated this trend. In addition, the location of housing has also been stratified, leading to differences in access to wealth, jobs, and security across race and ethnicity. As noted earlier in this chapter, where one lives determines access to economic opportunities.

As recently reported in the journal *Social Problems*: "[W]idening economic inequalities that disproportionately affect minority families combined with the racialized context of the foreclosure crisis raise concerns not only about the possibility of closing persistent ownership gaps, but also about the ability of minority homeowners to reap the long-term benefits of homeownership."[1] Even as most Americans have recovered from the economic crisis (i.e., total personal wealth is back to pre-recession levels), Black America has not. Indeed, the leading indicators of economic attainment, housing being one of them, demonstrate definitively that the prosperity of Black individuals and families trails the rest of America. Overall, from 2007 to 2010, wealth for Black citizens declined by an average of 31 percent (whites 11 percent), home equity by an average of 28 percent (whites 24 percent), and retirement savings by an average of 35 percent (whites gained 9 percent).[2]

Many working class Black Americans struggle to obtain affordable housing. Seasonally adjusted homeownership rates for all Americans are still below what they were in 1995, and have continued to drop precipitously since 2006 and the effects of the housing boom of the mid-2000s. In 2005, more than 69 percent of all Americans owned a home; in 2015, approximately 63 percent of Americans owned a home. Indeed, during that same time frame, white ownership dropped as well, from approximately 76 percent in 2005 to 73 percent in 2015. In addition, the rate for whites stopped falling in 2013. For Black fellow citizens, the drop in homeownership fell at a much higher rate than for whites: from approximately 50 percent during the housing bubble to 43 percent in 2015.[3]

Looking at these data differently, we can discern that well more than one-half of African Americans rent (compared to just 25 percent of whites). While there are some economic and geographical advantages to renting a home, the price of rental units since the Great Recession has increased dramatically. Since 2006, the median price of rental units has increased from around $600 to over $800 in 2015, which is an increase of more than 33 percent and nearly twice the rate of inflation over that same time period.[4] That fact, coupled with inflation-adjusted stagnating wages,[5] means that Black Americans have, in the aggregate, a larger percentage of their income going to housing today than in 2006. Furthermore, while mortgage rates for new homes have been historically low since the economic recovery, nearly 60 percent of Black renters now spend more than the recommended 30 percent of their household income on rent. In 2005, that figure was closer to just one-half. Finally, even for Black homeowners, the percentage of households spending more than 30 percent of their income on housing increased from 40 percent to nearly 44 percent during the same time period. Although this is lower than it is for renters, it is still higher than the national average of 34 percent.[6]

In addition to the losses incurred due to the Great Recession, Black Americans also face housing and lending discrimination. The U.S. does have many policies in place, ostensibly to assist the Black prospective house buyer, including the Fair Housing Act of 1968, the Equal Credit Opportunity Act of 1974, and the Community Reinvestment Act of 1977. All of these laws are designed to ban discrimination in lending and home sales based on race and national origin. However, the housing boom over the past few decades, encouraged by Clinton and Bush administrations that created programs to widen home buying, also brought about a practice known as "reverse redlining" —or steering residents of minority neighborhoods into high-cost mortgages—which led to a flood of foreclosures when the market crashed.[7] More than 25 percent of loan applications by Black applicants in the U.S. are denied, compared with 10 percent of their white counterparts.[8] Many Americans lost their houses to foreclosure in the aftermath of the Great Recession, but the brunt of the losses was particularly felt in the Black community. Also, even with the protections of the Fair Housing Act, discrimination complaints are still filed each year through nonprofit fair-housing agencies, the U.S. Department of Housing and Urban Development (HUD), the U.S. Department of Justice, and state and local government agencies.[9] Even HUD acknowledges the rampant racial discrimination that exists in the housing and lending market, and announced in the fall of 2015 that it was awarding more than $38 million under HUD's Fair Housing Initiatives Program (FHIP) to more than 100 groups across the nation to fight housing discrimination. The funding provided through the competitive grants will help to support a range of fair housing enforcement efforts, including fair housing testing, as well as activities that help educate the public about current federal law.[10]

Finally, there is an epidemic of homelessness among Black Americans. The overrepresentation of Black fellow citizens in homeless shelters is staggering. One in 141 Black family members stays in a homeless shelter, a rate 7 times higher than for white families. Black people in families make up 12.1 percent of the U.S. family population, but represent 38.8 percent of sheltered people in families in 2010. In comparison, 65.8 percent of people in families in the general population are white, while white family members occupied only 28.6 percent of family shelter beds in 2010. Homelessness is primarily a poverty issue.[11] In 2010, more than one-quarter (26.2 percent) of African Americans lived in poverty, two-and-one-half times the rate of whites (10.1 percent). And there is more to it than that. Understanding why Black Americans are overrepresented in homeless shelters requires an examination of the long-standing and interrelated social and structural issues facing the Black community. A report by the Institute for Children, Poverty, and Homelessness (ICPH) concludes that this overrepresentation demonstrates that "[B]lacks continue to face prejudice and substantial access barriers to decent employment, education, health care, and housing not experienced by whites."[12]

In conclusion, it is obvious that the bifurcation between Black and white in homeownership is a function of a number of socioeconomic and demographic factors. Nevertheless, it is also true that strides should and can be made through a persistent government agenda that improves the economic situation for millions of Black Americans. The HUD program in 2015 is one effort to do just that, but small sums of money will not come close to addressing the structural issues that prevent Black America from engaging in a housing market that is more equitable, open, and accessible, and which leads to greater prosperity.

—*Prepared by Michael McGuire, Ph.D., Executive Associate Dean, School of Public and Environmental Affairs, Indiana University, Bloomington, Indiana*

✧ ✧

VI.

CLAIMING OUR
DEMOCRACY

INTRODUCTORY ESSAY
BY WADE HENDERSON

Prior to the Civil War, African Americans were almost totally disenfranchised throughout the states. Even after enactment of the 15th Amendment to the Constitution, in 1870, which gave all men— regardless of race, color, or previous condition of servitude—the right to vote, many states continued to use various methods to prevent African Americans from voting, including literacy tests, poll taxes, the disenfranchisement of former inmates, intimidation, threats, and even violence. Until 1965, federal laws did not challenge the authority of states and localities to establish and administer their own voting requirements. The Voting Rights Act of 1965 was a new beginning for African American citizens. For the first time, the federal government would require states to comply with the 15th Amendment.

And the Voting Rights Act has worked. African American registration and turnout rates have risen dramatically since 1965, when there were only five Black representatives in Congress. Today, there are 43 members of the Congressional Black Caucus.

Despite this progress, African Americans have yet to achieve full equality in our democracy. While it is true that in many communities

Black registration has increased significantly, real democracy is not just about being able to have equal physical access to the polls. Real democracy means the ability of minority voters to cast an "effective" ballot. What good is the right to cast a ballot, if the district in which you live is so racially gerrymandered that your candidate of choice will never have a chance to win? What good is the right to cast a ballot, if your polling place has been moved to an inaccessible location for the minority community? What good is the right to cast a ballot, when the electoral system has been rigged against you?

In recent elections we have seen partisan challenges targeting African American and Latino voters, as well as attempts to rig the election system against minority voter empowerment through the use of at-large election systems, discriminatory annexations, draconian photo ID requirements, and the like. In places such as South Dakota, with large Native American populations, there have been overt racial appeals, egregious attempts to intimidate minority voters, and other tactics reminiscent of the Deep South in the 1950s. From Texas to Georgia to New York, we continue to see attempts by states and counties to implement voting practices that would diminish the impact of the minority vote.

The Voting Rights Act (VRA), and its special provisions, is the best and most effective way to address these problems.

In 2005, we marked the 40th anniversary of the Voting Rights Act of 1965, often cited as the most successful civil rights statute ever enacted. What accounts for this success? The answer lies, in part, with one of the provisions that is due to expire in August 2007: the federal preclearance provision, commonly referred to as "Section 5."

In 1965 Congress knew that in the past, whenever one type of discrimination had been blocked, another had sprung up to take its place, sometimes within 24 hours. Section 5 was Congress's answer to this problem. It simply provided that in places with a long history of institutionalized racial discrimination in voting, no change in any voting law or procedure could be enforced until the change had been "preapproved" as nondiscriminatory by the federal government. In this way, as Congress and the courts put it, the burden of proof and the burden of inertia were shifted from the longtime victims of discrimination to those who sought to enact the change.

In August 2007, three key provisions of the Voting Rights Act will expire unless they are renewed by Congress, including the federal preclearance provision (Section 5), the minority language provisions (Sections 203 and 4(f) (4)), and the federal observer and examiner provisions (Sections 6 and 8), which authorize the federal government to send federal election examiners and observers to certain jurisdictions covered by Section 5 where there is evidence of attempts to intimidate minority voters at the polls.

As the debate around the reauthorization of these provisions begins, some have asked whether we still need Section 5 or the minority language assistance provisions. Blacks and Latinos now register and vote in numbers comparable to whites. There are no sheriffs at the polling place doors. But dig a little deeper, and you will see that our work is not finished.

In recent years, highlighted by the controversies surrounding the 2000 and 2004 presidential elections, our nation has been confronted with an election system that is far from perfect. There are many problems that need solving for the sake of our democracy. But even if we successfully address the variety of problems related to electronic voting machines, hanging chads, confused poll workers, and provisional ballots, we will still be left with America's oldest problem: the problem of racial and ethnic discrimination.

For the electoral system to work for all Americans, the Voting Rights Act must be reauthorized and strengthened. Our old problems of race and ethnicity have gotten better, but they have not gone away. As a colleague of mine, Armand Derfner, recently stated in his testimony before the House Judiciary Committee, "when you have a bad infection, your doctor always advises that you keep taking the antibiotic, long after the most obvious symptoms have abated."[1]

As we go forward in this fight, we should be comfortable debating issues of right and wrong—or, to use a phrase that is now fashionable, "moral issues"—because morality ultimately depends upon doing right by our fellow human beings and especially, as the Scripture says, "the least among us."

In many of his speeches, Martin Luther King used to say, "The moral arc of the universe is long, but it bends towards justice." Together, we can move America closer to the day we dream of, when justice and morality are the norm, instead of just an aspiration for the future.

As we prepare for the impending reauthorization, we celebrate the ways in which the sacrifices of many brave Americans forced our nation to live up to its promises of democracy and equality. Without question, America is a better place today than it was in 1965 because of the Voting Rights Act. But discrimination against minority voters still exists.

For example, the Department of Justice (DOJ) recently objected to a proposed annexation by the Town of North in Orangeburg County, South Carolina, because it concluded that the town did not provide equal access to the annexation process for white and Black persons. In its Sept. 16, 2003, objection letter, the department stated that "race appears to be an overriding factor in how the town responds to annexation requests."

In August 2002, DOJ objected to a proposal by the City of Free-port in Brazoria County, Texas, to return to using an at-large system of electing members to its city council, after Hispanic voters succeeded in electing their candidates of choice utilizing a court-ordered single-member district system. A return to at-large council elections, DOJ concluded, "would result in a retrogression of the ability of minorities to exercise the electoral franchise that they enjoy currently."[2]

And despite requirements under Section 203 of the Voting Rights Act, no bilingual assistance was made available to Vietnamese voters in Harris County, Texas, for the 2003 election. As a result, local Asian advocacy groups worked with the Department of Justice to ensure that the county was meeting its legal obligations under the VRA for future elections. This pressure resulted in an agreement among the county, the groups, and DOJ that the county would (1) hire a full-time employee to coordinate the Vietnamese election program for all elections within the county; (2) establish an advisory group to assist and participate in the Vietnamese language program; and (3) require, in most cases, a bilingual poll worker where a polling place has more than 50 Vietnamese-surnamed registered voters at the time of an election. In the wake of these changes, the November 2004 election saw a Vietnamese candidate, Hubert Vo, win a legislative seat in Harris County.

As we look forward to the legislative battle around reauthorization, we are concerned that opponents of the Voting Rights Act will emphasize how far we have come without acknowledging how far we need to go, and the need to reauthorize and strengthen the law in order to get there. We know that the Georgia of 1965 is not the Georgia of 2005. But we also know of the continued persistence of racially polarized voting in states and communities across the country. We also know that language minorities in communities across America are often denied the bilingual assistance that they need in order to cast an informed vote.

We have not reached our goal of equal opportunity until every voter has an equal opportunity to determine the distribution of political power. We can see that America, but we are not there yet.

Today, at a time of bipartisan support for creating a multiethnic democracy in Iraq and across the globe, we need bipartisan support for a multiethnic democracy at home.

✛

WADE HENDERSON, Esq., is the Executive Director of the Leadership Conference on Civil Rights (LCCR), Counsel to the LCCR Education Fund (LCCREF), and the Joseph L. Rauh, Jr., Professor of Public Interest Law at the David A. Clarke School of Law, University of the District of Columbia, Washington, DC. LCCR is the nation's premier civil and human rights coalition created to promote the passage and implementation of civil rights laws designed to end discrimination and to achieve equal opportunity for all Americans. Before joining LCCR, Henderson was the Washington Bureau Director of the NAACP; before that, he was the Associate Director of the Washington National Office of the ACLU, where he began his career as a legislative counsel. For more information: http://www.civilrights.org.

THE FACTS ON OUR DEMOCRACY

- The United States is one of 11 nations in the world that do not provide an explicit right to vote in its Constitution.[3]

- In the 2004 election, voters in low-income, high-minority districts were significantly more likely to have their votes discarded than voters in affluent, low-minority districts.[4] For example, in Georgia, 5.2 percent of the votes in low-income, high-minority districts were uncounted, while only 1.9 percent of the votes for president were uncounted in an affluent, low-minority district.[5]

- Racially polarized voting is persistent in many parts of the country, particularly in areas of concentrated minority populations in the South and Southwest. For example, in 2004, a federal appellate court found that voting in Charleston County, South Carolina, county council elections was "severely and characteristically polarized along racial lines."[6]

- In Louisiana, African Americans are five times less likely to have a photo ID—a requirement for voting—than whites.[7]

- More than one million African American men, or 13 percent, have currently or permanently lost their right to vote as a result of a felony conviction—seven times the national average.[8]

- In the November 2004 election, minorities and students experienced higher levels of voter intimidation and harassment than other groups.[9]

- While African Americans make up 13 percent of our population, they occupy less than 4 percent of elected offices in the United States.[10]

- On a national level, while there are 435 members of the U.S. House of Representatives, only 42 of them are Black; the U.S. Senate is composed of 100 legislators, with only one being African American.[11]

What the Community Can Do

The notion of democracy is familiar yet still not a reality for the majority of African Americans. Many members of the Black community are increasingly disenfranchised and alienated from the electoral and legislative processes. It is crucial for our survival as a people to take back the right to vote for all citizens. With education, empowerment activities, and leadership training, we can uplift all African Americans, young and old, male and female, felons and free citizens.

What Every Individual Can Do Now:

- Register to vote, and then make sure to vote in all elections.

- Teach children about the importance of voting by introducing them to the civil rights struggle to earn the right to vote.

- Support all legislation to promote and ensure civil rights for all, including:

    - The reauthorization and strengthening of the Voting Rights Act;

    - A constitutional amendment to secure a federal right to vote for all American citizens;

    - Measures to reform local laws restricting the right to vote of ex-felons; and

    - Efforts to secure voting rights for all residents of the District of Columbia

MOST OF ALL:

- Hold all leaders and elected officials responsible and demand that they change current policy.

What Works Now:

Kemba Smith

While attending Hampton University, Kemba Smith became involved with a man whom she eventually realized was deeply involved in a drug ring. Over the course of their often-abusive relationship, Smith never actually handled or sold drugs; yet she was convicted of drug conspiracy charges and sentenced to 24 years in federal prison. With President Clinton's order of clemency in December 2000, Smith regained her freedom after six years. She established the Kemba Smith Foundation and is actively engaged in the fight for community education, civil rights, and prisoner reentry. Since her release, Smith has graduated from Virginia Union University with a bachelor's degree in social work and applied to law school.

But Smith is still unable to vote, as Virginia law does not grant automatic restoration of certain rights to felons released from prison.[12] She is actively involved in the crucial battle to help eligible felons regain their right to vote in Virginia. Activists are busy informing thousands of ex-felons across the commonwealth about how they can regain several rights, including serving on a jury and running for public office, as well as voting.[13]

Smith and thousands of other ex-felons have paid their dues, "but [the restoration of rights] has nothing to do with crime," she points out.

African American Ministers in Action

The mission of African American Ministers in Action—based in 20 states and the District of Columbia—is to "share an understanding that grace gives [them] both the responsibility and the courage to challenge systems of injustice that prevent God's children from reaching their potential. [They] believe in speaking truth to power on behalf of the powerless."[14] Their mission continues: to "raise [their] voices in pursuit of the broad justice vision championed by Martin Luther King,

Jr., . . . [advocating] for public policies that support vision, including advocacy for and against specific local, state, and federal legislative proposals."[15]

AAMIA's work includes organizing around a host of civil rights issues: affirmative action, class size, DC vouchers, education, election reform, and the Real ID Act. They are involved in the effort to restore voting rights to felons, currently focusing on reenfranchisement in Texas and Florida.

While their struggle is ongoing, they have savored victories along the way. Less than two weeks before Election Day 2004, a court decision was upheld that blocked a controversial state law from taking effect that would have dramatically restricted the types of photo identification that may be used when voting. Thus, African Americans were allowed to vote with a range of photo IDs—not just a driver's license.[16]

Hip-Hop Summit Action Network

Founded in 2001, the Hip-Hop Summit Action Network (HSAN) is dedicated to harnessing the cultural relevance of hip-hop music to serve as a catalyst for education advocacy and other societal concerns fundamental to the well-being of at-risk youth throughout the United States.[17] It seeks "to foster initiatives aimed at engaging the hip-hop generation in community development issues related to equal access to high-quality public education and literacy, freedom of speech, voter education, economic advancement, and youth leadership development.

The network was established as a means to fulfill the commitments made after the first National Hip-Hop Summit, themed "Taking Back Responsibility," held in June 2001 in New York City. Since that time, HSAN has been on the forefront of initiatives that have tested and affirmed that its efforts are timely and effective.[18]

Headed by business mogul Russell Simmons, the group of activists, artists, and entertainers set out to register 2 million youth voters for the 2004 election. Their success was tremendous: in the time leading up to the Hip-Hop Summit action day, 114,000 new youth voters registered in the state of Missouri. In one day alone, the Philadelphia Hip-Hop Summit registered over 11,000 voters, the largest number of young new voters ever registered at a single hip-hop event in the United States.[19]

These hip-hop activists recognize that youth hold the key to the nation's future. If they are educated and empowered, then we can count on them to effect necessary change.

What Every Leader and Elected Official Can Do

- Reauthorize and strengthen the Voting Rights Act.

- Restore the right to vote for former felons.

- Ensure that all residents of the District of Columbia have voting representation in Congress.

- Modify voter identification requirements.

- Do away with all voter suppression and intimidation.

Reauthorize and Strengthen the Voting Rights Act

The federal government must guarantee all citizens the right to vote. Prior to the 2000 presidential election, most Americans believed that we had a right to vote in our national constitution. The U.S. Supreme Court's decision in *Bush v. Gore* was a wake-up call that we do not. While the 15th Amendment to the U.S. Constitution guarantees nondiscrimination in voting based on race ("the right of citizens of the United States to vote shall not be denied or abridged by the United States or any state on account of race, color, or previous condition of servitude"), nowhere does the constitution provide a federal right to vote for all its citizens. What does this mean for Black America?

Under our current system, states control voting policies and procedures. As a result, we operate under a variety of voting systems, run by 50 states, 3,067 counties, and over 12,000 voting districts.

Historically, when decisions about voter access have been left up to the states, those systems have not worked to the advantage of Black voters. With no federal guarantee of the right to vote, states are free to erect barriers to voting that often disproportionately impact Black voters. While these systems can be challenged under the Voting Rights Act, such litigation is often costly and difficult to win. Thus, millions of U.S. citizens are being denied the right to vote because of voter registration processing errors, lost or miscounted votes, language barriers, felony convictions, and targeted voter disenfranchisement.

Elected officials must demand that American citizens are implicitly guaranteed a right to vote in the federal constitution; it could have a direct impact on the voting rights of former felons, the right of citizens of the District of Columbia to gain voting representation in Congress, and the problems associated with disparate ballot access rules that disproportionately harm African American and other minority voters.

Restore Voting Rights for Ex-Felons

The right to vote is the most basic constitutive act of citizenship; regaining that right reintegrates ex-offenders into free society. Denying this right undermines one's attempt to return to the community as a responsible, contributing member and quiets the political voice of African American communities nationwide.

Disenfranchisement, or having the right to vote revoked, is in fact a consequence of a criminal sentence; it is not a part of the criminal justice system. For all free citizens to live consistent with the democratic principles on which the United States was founded, states must reform their felony disenfranchisement laws.

In 2005 a number of bills were presented to Congress concerning civil liberties, among them, the Count Every Vote Act and the Civic Participation and Rehabilitation Act. Both assert that unless an individual is serving a felony sentence in a correctional institution at the time of an election, he or she should not be denied the right to vote for federal officials. While a number of representatives support these measures, it is crucial that the initiatives are passed. On the state level, some voting rights have been restored, but in comparison with the number of persons disenfranchised, there is still much work to do. There is growing support for repealing permanent disenfranchisement laws, and as states consider adopting new policies, they should eliminate waiting periods for restoration and aid eligible ex-felons in the restoration and registration process.

At least 500,000 citizens have been reenfranchised in the last five years because of policy changes; this is hopeful, but not good enough, considering that close to 2 million African Americans have lost the right to vote. We must press our elected officials to take action. The government must take a proactive stance until there is a complete separation of state election rules from the criminal justice system.

Endorse and Fight for DC Voting Rights

United States citizens who are residents of the District of Columbia have no voting representative in Congress—not in the House of Representatives, not in the Senate. These citizens, 60 percent of whom are African American, pay federal taxes, serve in the military in large numbers, and otherwise share the burdens of citizenship, without the benefit of self-governance; or, as their DC license plates attest, "Taxation without representation."

Congress freely exercises its powers under the District Clause of Article 1, Section 8 of the Constitution to review every line of the District's local budget, frequently vetoing how District residents choose to raise and spend local tax revenues. Would Omaha, Nebraska, accept such extensive federal intrusions into local issues? Would Congress tell them "not only are we going to decide how much your city health department can spend on public health, but when we vote, your Congressmen and both Senators are also going to be told to sit this one out?" Of course they would not accept it! And Americans from every other state would consider it an outrage.

The right to vote is nothing short of the definition of democracy. It is a fundamental civil and human right and a focal point of America's efforts to promote freedom throughout the world. Yet our failure to provide this basic right to the citizens of our nation's capital saps the strength of our call for human rights abroad. It is a hypocrisy that can give others an excuse to ignore us when we try to spread democracy and promote human rights and other ideals of democracy globally.

Voting is the language of our democracy. Without it, the half-million-plus citizens of the District of Columbia, the majority of whom are African American, are the silent voice in the wilderness, spectators to democracy, literally in the very shadows of the governing institutions that serve as a shining beacon to the rest of the world. The very notion of having two distinct classes of citizens—those of the 50 states who have full voting rights and those of the District of Columbia who do not—is anathema to our own principles of democracy. No other democratic nation in the world denies the residents of its capital representation in the national legislature. It is an embarrassment before the world and undermines American leadership and our moral authority.

Modify Voter Identification Requirements

The struggle for equality in voting rights for African Americans has often been a battle for access: access to the registration rolls, access to polling places, and access to political power. Opponents of full political empowerment for African Americans have long argued that while they support access, they are concerned about fraud. The debates about voter fraud are often a mask for debates about how to make sure that voting is difficult, expensive, inconvenient, and thus underutilized by vulnerable populations.

While our nation has taken steps to increase access to voter registration in recent years, principally with the enactment of the National Voter Registration Act (NVRA, or "motor voter" law) in 1995, the backlash against this enhanced access has been a recent movement by state legislatures to enact onerous voter ID requirements. Advocates of these policies generally allege that they are necessary to combat voter fraud. However, according to numerous reports, including one by the Commission on Federal Election Reform (the "Carter-Baker

Commission") in September 2005, there is no evidence of extensive fraud in U.S. elections or of multiple voting.

The impact of these voter ID requirements is felt most heavily by African American, poor, and elderly voters. For example, in Louisiana, Blacks are five times less likely to have a photo ID than whites. These new requirements are, in short, an effort to keep minority and elderly participation at low levels by requiring that voters jump through more hoops to participate in the democratic process.

The most extreme example of this regressive trend toward requiring voter IDs took place in Georgia in 2005, when the state legislature enacted one of the strictest measures in the United States for screening voters. It requires voters to present one of six forms of government-issued photo identification at the polls. Under the old law, Georgia voters were allowed to present any of 17 forms of identification, including bank statements and utility bills, which contain no photos.

Sponsors of Georgia's voter identification bill assert that the legislation is intended to prevent fraud and enhance confidence in election results. However, supporters of the bill have yet to make a convincing case that existing methods of discouraging and punishing fraud are insufficient. Thus, while the case has not been made for the need for this new requirement, the case has been made that its impact is to disproportionately shut Black Georgians out of the political process.

Eliminate Voter Suppression and Intimidation

In every national election, voters—especially African Americans and other minorities—have faced efforts aimed at reducing turnout. While the violence of the post–Civil War voter suppression tactics, poll taxes, and literacy tests of the Jim Crow era may be behind us, more subtle and creative tactics are taking their place.

We now see efforts to diminish turnout through the use of misleading public information campaigns, such as flyers distributed in minority neighborhoods reminding voters to get out and vote on Wednesday, November 4, for example, instead of Tuesday, November

3, or through so-called "ballot integrity" initiatives that use poll challengers (or even law enforcement officers) to slow things down at polling places and drive potential voters away.

For example, in Florida, the state Republican Party announced in 2004 that it would use the infamous felon challenge purge list that the state created—and withdrew—to target challenges. Despite knowing that the state's list was tainted by racial discrimination, the Republicans decided to use it anyway. In Wisconsin, the GOP went even further, conducting background checks on newly registered voters. This is voter suppression, 21st-century style.

In recent elections, we have also seen new methods of disenfranchisement such as unfamiliar voting machines, insufficient deployment of voting machines in minority neighborhoods, and erroneous voter purging. Other deleterious examples: flyers distributed on official-looking letterhead targeting African Americans and other racial, ethnic, and minority communities telling voters, for example, that (1) a citizen would be ineligible to vote in a presidential election if he or she had already voted in some other election that year or (2) a voter would not be permitted to vote if he or she or any other family member had ever been found guilty of a crime, including a traffic ticket.

These tactics, and others like them, have no place in our democracy. Equality of voting rights and claiming our democracy should mean an end to targeted intimidation and discriminatory barriers to the franchise.

A Final Word

We will reach our goal of equal opportunity when every voter has an equal opportunity to determine the distribution of political power. We can visualize that America, but we are not there yet. Today, at a time of bipartisan support for creating a multiethnic democracy in Iraq and across the globe, we need bipartisan support for multiethnic democracy at home.

CLAIMING OUR DEMOCRACY

In 2008, the United States elected its first African American President, Barack Hussein Obama, and then reelected him to a second term in 2012. These historic events gave some hope that the nation had finally emerged from its long history of racism. Voting rates rose for Black Americans, surpassing the rates for non-Hispanic white Americans in the 2012 presidential election.[1]

However, since 2006 there have been massive changes in law placing our democracy in jeopardy. In *Citizens United v. Federal Election Commission*, 558 U.S. 310 (2010), the U.S Supreme Court held that the First Amendment prohibited limits on campaign spending by nonprofit organizations. This opened the floodgates to massive unregulated spending; at the time of this writing, just 158 families, "overwhelmingly white, rich, older and male," have been the source of half of all campaign contributions toward the 2016 presidential election.[2]

In *Shelby County v. Holder*, 570 U.S. __ (2013), the U.S. Supreme Court struck down Section 4(b) of the Voting Rights Act of 1965 (VRA, 42 U.S.C. Sec. 1973, et seq.) as an unconstitutional coverage formula for Section 5's requirements that certain states and local governments obtain preclearance from the U.S. Department of Justice before making changes to state election law. This effectively released states to adopt new laws that had previously been forbidden through preclearance under the VRA (the Fannie Lou Hamer, Rosa Parks, Coretta Scott King, Cesar E. Chavez, Barbara C. Jordan, William C. Velasquez, and Dr. Hector P. Garcia Voting Rights Reauthorization and Amendments Act of 2006, 52 U.S.C. 10101, et seq.).

Without preclearance, voters must go through the time and the expense of litigation after these laws that reduce voting rights have already gone into effect. Studies show that ballot access restrictions such as reduced early voting hours, voter ID laws, and laws affecting the time and method for voter registration have a disparate impact based on race, ethnicity, and national origin.[3] Since *Shelby*, a number of states, mostly those with Republican majorities in state legislatures, have modified election laws.[4]

- Texas implemented a photo ID law that had previously been blocked by the Department of Justice and a federal court under Section 5.[5] After *Shelby*, Texas implemented the law, which affected voters in local elections and the March 2014 primaries.[6]

- North Carolina passed a law that imposed strict photo ID requirements, reduced early voting, and reduced a registration window used disproportionately by African American voters to both register and vote on the same day. The legislature waited for the Supreme Court's *Shelby* decision, then passed a more restrictive version of the bill, as it no longer had to seek preclearance.[7]

- Alabama passed a voter ID law in 2011 that was able to take effect in 2014 without getting preclearance, due to *Shelby*. Alabama also recently targeted for closure 31 Department of Motor Vehicles offices, which would leave eight out of the ten counties with the highest percentage of non-white registered voters without a

DMV to obtain the photo identification that is now
required for them to vote.[8]

Since *Shelby*, one study reported ten voting changes in seven states that have raised concerns about voting discrimination.[9] Because there is no longer central recordkeeping for preclearance, it is both difficult to track the changes and to stop them; each is individually subject to challenge in litigation after the fact under Section 2. Some states are pushing back. In 2015, California enacted a state law that automatically registers to vote all eligible people when they obtain or renew a driver's license or state ID, unless they opt out.[10] California is only the second state, after Oregon, to introduce automatic voter registration.

Election and voting developments are exacerbating an existing inequity in descriptive representation (representation by someone of the same race) by elected officials that the VRA was intended in part to address. Despite an increase in the diversity of Congress—resulting in the most diverse Congress in history (with 17 percent non-white members)—the Pew Research Center notes that only 35 percent of Black Americans are represented by someone of the same race.[11]

Underrepresentation occurs at the local level, too.[12] African Americans could see better local representation with more district (rather than at-large) local elections and elections held in tandem with national elections. Instead, there is minority-vote dilution through at-large elections and *cracking,* or splitting a single heavily majority-minority district (a district in which minorities compose most of the population) into two or more districts that are barely or no longer majority-minority districts, and thus make it hard to convert voting power into wins. There is also *packing,* which is overconcentrating minorities into a single district to reduce their number of representatives.[13] State and local laws that require at-large voting instead of voting by district, and redistricting or gerrymandering that either gathers all Black voters into a single district (packing) or divides them so as to preclude an effective majority that can elect a Black representative (cracking), mean that African Americans are statistically significantly underrepresented in state or local legislative bodies.

The results of underrepresentation include systemic racist practices in policing, prosecutorial, and judicial functions as illustrated in Ferguson, Missouri.[14] Ferguson's system created an incentive for police to arrest for minor traffic infractions that generated fees and fines when the predominately poor Black residents of Ferguson received a ticket or failed to show up in municipal court. Arrests turned into contempt of court and what some term "debtors prison" practices. The Department of Justice is also looking into the disparate impact based on race of a public-school discipline system that feeds young Black males into juvenile justice and criminal justice systems, ultimately resulting in voting disenfranchisement upon conviction of a felony.[15]

There is some mixed evidence on restoring the right to vote to convicted felons. Felon disenfranchisement is still a problem: 2010 estimates show 5.85 million disenfranchised, 2.5 percent of voting-age population (about 1 out of 40 adults).[16] Only about one quarter are currently incarcerated; so roughly four million people who are out of prison are disenfranchised. Of these, one million are African Americans. One in thirteen voting-age African Americans are disenfranchised, or about 7.7 percent of Black adults compared to 1.8 percent of others. The Koch brothers, unlikely champions, are working with progressive groups like the ACLU to seek prison reform and to address overcriminalization and mass incarceration.[17]

In response to growing evidence of systemic bias in the criminal justice system and absence of effective voice in the political system, what some have called a "new civil rights movement" has arisen. Born when the unarmed teen Trayvon Martin was shot dead and that shooting upheld by a predominately white jury who found it justified by Florida's "stand your ground" law, the movement spread through social media as Black Lives Matter.[18] Smartphone recordings of police shootings or killings of unarmed Black men have become common; the speed at which the video travels through social media, and the resulting protests, have been steadily increasing. As the beatings in Selma on Bloody Sunday galvanized a nation to support passage of the VRA, so too do the organizers of Black Lives Matter hope to generate public support for legislative and electoral change.

Increasingly, the prospect of litigation is prompting local governments both to discipline police for excessive use of force and to reach financial settlements with grieving families. However, the practices are so pervasive that commentators say it will take a sea change in police training to alter what is perceived as acceptable use of force.

There has been no substantial progress in passing an amendment that would formalize a constitutional right to vote.[19] Two Democrats proposed a constitutional amendment in 2015.[20] The Democratic National Committee also announced its support. Similarly, despite two different proposals that alternately passed the House and Senate, there has been no progress in empowering residents of the District of Columbia (which is still a majority African American city) to participate in our national democracy.[21]

In sum, while there have been historic achievements in the election of President Obama and the most diverse Congress in history, there have also been deeply troubling developments. *Citizens United* gives the rich and white disproportionate financial influence in the electoral system. State election laws with documented disparate impact based on race are making their way through state legislatures and prompting litigation under VRA Section 2 in the absence of effective preclearance limits under Section 5. African Americans are underrepresented in state and local elective office. A disproportionate number of Black voters remain disenfranchised through the criminal justice system and by living in the District of Columbia. And no citizen in the United States has an express constitutional right to vote.

—*Prepared by Lisa Blomgren Amsler, J.D., Keller-Runden Professor of Public Service, School of Public and Environmental Affairs, Indiana University, Bloomington, Indiana*

✢ ✢

VII.

STRENGTHENING
OUR RURAL ROOTS

INTRODUCTORY ESSAY
BY OLETA GARRETT FITZGERALD
AND SARAH BOBROW-WILLIAMS

America, often called a "nation of immigrants," heralds the contributions of those who, fortified only by culture and family, created
something from nothing; those inspiring immigrants demonstrating
integrity and perseverance in the pursuit of the American dream.
However, Black Americans—namely, African slaves and their descendants—are perceptually excluded from the American immigrant legacy. Perhaps this is one reason for the gross lack of coverage given to
the immense contributions to the nation's development made by Black
Americans, particularly the development of the colonial economy.

The original Black settlers, West African slaves and Caribbean
and Mexican migrants beginning as early as the 1500s, brought with
them advanced agricultural and environmental knowledge. From the
healing properties of plants to elaborate agricultural systems that
formed the foundation of the plantation economy and enabled it to
thrive, these Black Americans and their ancestors made significant and
long-lasting contributions to the cultural and economic enrichment

of this country. Their highly developed family and social networks and cultural dynamics have influenced every aspect of American life.[1]

During the 100-year period between the abolition of slavery and the end of Jim Crowism (1865–1965), hundreds of "land based institutions" were established to meet the critical needs of Black American communities in the South. These institutions were often the sole providers of academic, vocational, and agricultural education, demonstration, and outreach to land-based cultures.

America's rural South is a reservoir of African and Black American cultural roots and history. African influences passed on through centuries can be found in everyday rituals and routines, from preparing natural remedies and family recipes to more renowned "American" traditions, including community-based education, sustainable agriculture, folk art, regional cuisines, family reunions, fabric and fashion trends, the blues, gospel, spirituals, regional dialects, agricultural cooperatives, credit unions, sororities, fraternities, and the list goes on.

Black Americans are a land-based people. Most of us who were born in this country have Southern rural roots. Some may be generations removed and not even realize their relationship to the land, and that is a great loss. The rural South is where we suffered most and accomplished much toward those freedoms we now enjoy. It is the relationship of man to the universe, the understanding on a daily basis of how small we are and how big God is. It is the draw and sometimes the anathema we feel toward the area. Blacks who do not live in or experience rural areas sometimes feel that people who do live here are "country," unexposed, and somehow inferior. They do not understand that we live here by choice. We are comforted by the ability to visit the city when we wish and to return home to our rural roots.

Born in the rural South, we grew up in a time and place where rural was mostly all we knew. Yet we have lived and influenced life in all the major cities—Boston, Atlanta, Chicago, Detroit, New York, Washington, DC, Milwaukee, Los Angeles, the Bay Area, and even Alaska; all over this world, we have gone and made names for ourselves. But we come back. We find solace, comfort, and peace in the slow pace and sacredness of being close to the land. We cannot escape it: the land remains sacred, respected, and accommodated.

"Strengthening Our Rural Roots" is very important to any covenant with Black America. We must realize that our rural ancestors represent the strength of our race. It is in the rural South where movements for social and economic justice have their roots. Blacks who remained in the rural South stayed, fought, and experienced victories that influenced the rest of the country. Rural Black America has been the front line of the fight against injustice and inequity. Leaders of social movements around the world continue to be influenced by what has happened in these rural communities.

Rural areas are undergoing tremendous social and cultural changes that threaten the existence of their unique and important Black American culture as well as the natural environment and ecology. Large-scale agricultural consolidation and the urbanization of rural towns—industrial development, population increases, rapidly growing suburbs, and precarious development—have caused escalating Black land loss and locked "indigenous" residents into the bottom of an economic system in low-wage jobs. Rural areas are under attack by powerful influences both within and outside the United States.

In addition to land loss, rural Black people also face the same racial challenges of urban Blacks—crumbling education systems, globalization and lack of alternative economic development strategies, and the growing number of single-women heads of households. In the face of unrelenting systemic, institutionalized discrimination and abuse, Southern rural Black women have held together the Black American family and community for generations. While tremendously resourceful, creative, and hardworking, they must have help to advance community-centered and culturally affirming economic and asset development strategies that will allow them the health care, schools, and other services needed by their children, youth, and the elderly.

For many Black Americans our "country within the country" is the rural South. It can be argued that the loss of land and rural life in general cuts deeply into the foundation of Black American sustenance and identity, as did the loss of land-based institutions that emphasized cultural exploration and learning. There is a synergy that can and must be developed between rural Black people and Blacks in urban and suburban areas. Urban, suburban, and rural Black Americans must work together to reclaim, strengthen, and sustain our rural roots; it is the basis of our history—good and bad—in this country.

✛

OLETA GARRETT FITZGERALD is Southern Regional Director for the Children's Defense Fund (CDF). **SARAH BOBROW-WILLIAMS** is Asset and Finance Development Officer of CDF's Southern Regional Office, based in Jackson, Mississippi. Both women are principals in the Southern Rural Black Women's Initiative for Economic and Social Justice (SRBWI), which works with women in 77 rural counties in the Black Belt of Alabama and Georgia and the Mississippi Delta. Headquartered in Washington, DC, CDF's mission is to Leave No Child Behind® and to ensure every child a Healthy Start, a Head Start, a Fair Start, a Safe Start, and a Moral Start in life and successful passage to adulthood with the help of caring families and communities. For more information: http://www.childrensdefense.org; http://www .cdf-sro.org.

THE FACTS ON OUR RURAL ROOTS

QUALITY OF LIFE

- Nearly 11 percent (10.8 percent) of African Americans living in rural communities have managerial/professional jobs as opposed to 23.6 percent of whites.[2]

- Eighty-one percent of white rural residents have health insurance compared with 64 percent of African Americans.[3]

- More than 40 percent of Black families in rural communities live below the poverty line, while 29.6 percent of Black urban families live below the poverty line. Of white Americans, 12.5 percent of those in rural neighborhoods live below the poverty line, compared with 7.2 percent who live in metropolitan areas.[4]

- Nearly 40 percent of Black rural residents do not have a high school degree, as opposed to 20.2 percent of whites.[5]

- Rural whites are at least two times as likely to have a college degree as rural African Americans. [6]

- Black residents in urban areas are more than two times as likely to hold a college degree as Black rural residents; this is the largest attainment gap among all races.[7]

- Fifty-five percent of the nation's African American population lives in the South; 12.5 percent of these residents live in rural communities.[8]

LAND OWNERSHIP

- There are 98 percent fewer Black farmers today than there were in 1920.[9]

- African American, Latino, and Asian farmers are now going out of business 3.25 times more frequently than white farmers.[10]

- Of the estimated 10,000 Black farmers left in the United States, fewer than 200 are younger than 65. Opportunities for African American youth to be exposed to the principles and practices of sustainable agriculture in the Southeast are rare; roots communities are disintegrating.[11]

- The U.S. Department of Agriculture denied payment to 86 percent of African American farmers who came forward seeking restitution, after a multimillion-dollar discrimination settlement in their favor.[12]

What the Community Can Do

No matter where we live now, most African Americans are descendants of the slave plantation system of the South. Black landownership represents an asset and a wealth creation vehicle. African American leadership should embrace the opportunity that landownership presents to Blacks and create an environment encouraging cooperation among the estimated 500,000 affected Black landowners who could aggregate their six million acres, leveraging other capital for housing, mixed-use development, and job creation. Such an environment would go a very long way in improving the overall quality of their lives.

Landownership for African Americans has served and can still serve as a psychological and transformative mechanism. Landownership for African Americans conveys a sense of pride, power, place, self, family, and community.

What Every Individual Can Do Now:

- Support and contribute to existing African American institutions devoted to assisting African American landowners to acquire, retain, and develop land.

- Work with your neighbors and local grocers to organize a farmers' market to connect with Black farmers in your area. If there is already one in your community, shop there frequently, and take your children with you.

- Find out if your family owns land in the South and reach out to other family members to develop a strategy to hold on to that land.

- Consider developing or joining a cooperative to save money and build community if you are a Black farmer family.

- Demand that institutions that support farmers provide fair and equitable opportunities, resources, and allocation of resources to Black farmers.

- Educate yourself about the issues impacting Black rural residents and speak out about these issues at every opportunity—at town council meetings, before the media, and to other outlets.

MOST OF ALL:

- Hold all leaders and elected officials responsible and demand that they change current policy.

What Works Now:

Mandela Farmers' Market

In 2001, a group of concerned residents, community-based organizations, and social service agencies formed the West Oakland Food Collaborative (WOFC) to increase access to nutritious and affordable food while stimulating community economic development. Their planning process resulted in the identification of five priority areas: a thriving farmers' market, small business development, a cooperative marketplace, liquor store "conversion," and community green space. The cornerstone of their effort is the Mandela Farmers' Market, which opened in April 2003.[13]

One of the ideas behind the market is to connect Black farmers—who suffer greatly from the displacement of small family farms from large industrial producers—to the community, which has a rich history of being a center for Black culture. Every Saturday, farmers sell fresh, mainly organic produce, and local residents sell jams, baked goods, jewelry, and other items. The collaborative provides ongoing support, providing the farmers and vendors with equipment, training, resources, and technical assistance. WOFC also helps residents get to the market, operating a free, weekly shuttle bus service that stops at senior residential facilities, the West Oakland Health Center, and other neighborhood locations with limited public transportation access. The group plans to add benefits screening and application services at the farmers' market to help residents apply for public benefits such as food stamps and Medi-Cal.

The market is doing well and turnout is increasing, with about 200 customers a week. Nearly 70 percent of the customers are local residents. The prices are excellent: A survey found that Mandela

Farmers' Market offered the lowest prices of the 90 Bay Area farmers' markets. WOFC hopes that the market will be self-sustaining within three years. In the meantime, the group continues to work on its other priority areas to ensure a "food secure" West Oakland: developing community-owned gardens and increasing access to other green space; persuading corner stores to sell healthier products; helping small businesses by developing a food distribution and delivery system and providing access to a commercial kitchen; and developing a locally owned food cooperative.

Southern Rural Black Women's Initiative

The Southern Rural Black Women's Initiative (SRBWI) aims to eradicate historical race, class, cultural, religious, and gender barriers that are experienced by Southern Black women.[14]

SRBWI held its first Young Women's Leadership Development Institute in July 2005 at Tougaloo College, Tougaloo, Mississippi. The Institute uses a human rights agenda to acquaint young women of color with the significant social movement that took place in the South and to build an awareness of what is needed to assure social and economic justice for women today. Art, culture, and spirituality are all integrated into the agenda. Many young women living in the rural South are unaware of how much of what has been gained in human rights came from the region where they live. Participants, ages 13 to 24, have an opportunity to study the contributions of their ancestors and to learn advocacy and public policy skills.

The Initiative works in 77 counties across the Black Belts of Alabama, in Southwest Georgia, and in the Mississippi Delta. These counties are some of the poorest in the rural South, and SRBWI helps women who live in them to secure employment and acquire skills necessary to support themselves and their families, while engaging them in advocacy and policy initiatives that will better their communities.[15]

Federation of Southern
Cooperatives Land Assistance Fund

The Federation of Southern Cooperatives Land Assistance Fund (FSCLAF) was founded in 1967 with a charge to strive toward developing self-supporting communities with programs that increase income and enhance other opportunities.[16] It also makes every effort to assist in land retention and development, especially for African Americans, but essentially for all family farmers.[17]

The Fund aids low-income people with molding their communities into more humane and livable ones through education and outreach strategies. It also assists in developing cooperatives and credit unions as a collective strategy to create economic self-sufficiency.

Extended membership includes 12,000 Black farm families, who individually own small acreage, but collectively own over one-half million acres; FSCLAF works through 35 agricultural cooperatives to purchase supplies, provide technical assistance, and market their crops. It also includes 10,000 small savers in 19 community development credit unions that have accumulated over $5 million in savings and made over $52 million in loans since its inception.[18]

FSCLAF is the only organization in the Southeast United States that has as its primary objectives the retention of Black-owned land and the use of cooperatives for land-based economic development.

What Every Leader and Elected Official Can Do

- Improve the overall rural quality of life, including in education and in health care.

- Ensure that small-scale farmers can sell directly to local markets.

- Provide necessary credit to sustain farms.

- Guarantee funding of the 1997 class action lawsuit to provide technical assistance to disadvantaged farmers.

- Offer adequate and affordable legal assistance to all farmers.

- Support the organization and existence of cooperatives.

- Implement a national agriculture education program.

Improve the Quality of Rural Life

Rural America is often left out of advocacy and policy reform discussions, but as is true throughout the rest of the country, elected officials must help it to secure a better quality of life, particularly with regard to basic rights such as education and health care.

Schools in rural communities need very specific attention. Even though "half of the nation's public schools and about 40 percent of the nation's students are in rural and small-town areas, only 22 percent of the total education budget goes to schools in rural and small towns."[19] Government at both the state and federal levels must ensure that all rural schools are fully funded. Higher salaries and full benefits for teachers should also be part of educational reform for them to be most productive. Schools must also offer opportunities for teachers to enhance their skills: Rural educators have less education than their urban counterparts;[20] it is in our children's best interest to not only encourage but also demand ongoing professional development.

For those living in nonmetropolitan parts of the country, there are specific, acute health issues and concerns. As we insist on universal health-care access and coverage, we must also address the particular needs of rural residents. Emergency services need to be greatly expanded and to service adequately residents that might fall victim to farming accidents or other rural work-related injuries. Paramedics and fire departments must be close enough to all residents to ensure appropriate emergency response time. While this might come at a greater federal cost, it is still a necessity. Officials have to open more clinics and medical care facilities so as to overcome the current lack of available medical services to rural residents.

Ensure That Small-Scale Farmers Can Sell Directly to Local Markets

Small-scale farmers are the foundation of our food system, but that fact is often forgotten because consumers are so disconnected from healthy food production. Local and state branches of government must make it legal and simple for small-scale farmers to sell their produce directly to local markets such as grocery stores, schools, and hospitals. Because food production and processing are dominated by big business, most of the nation's produce and meat are grown and distributed by large-scale or corporate farms. Our leaders need to look out for small-scale, localized farmers, ensuring that money will be invested in their local economy and that consumers will end up with healthier, fresher products.

Local officials must also establish and support farmers' market associations, which can connect farmers with existing markets, arrange for them to share costs for transportation and storage, provide technical assistance on establishing new markets in low-income communities, and offer additional benefits—all while bringing nutritious food to local residents who do not have easy access to fresh fare themselves.[21]

Provide Credit to Sustain Farms

Federal officials should guarantee that the full range of available farm loan and benefit programs are available to Black farmers. Government-subsidized loans and grants are designed to support the small farmers and to provide vital resources to this important segment of the farming industry. For this system to operate effectively, it must operate equitably.[22]

The credit application process should be quick, painless, and efficient. Mandatory customer service training for all state and local agricultural employees will underscore the importance of timely loan processing. The sooner farmers can get a decision, the sooner they can continue to plan the development of their farms.

Credit eligibility standards must also be considered when approving a federal loan or grant. If officials can be flexible when it comes to each individual financing case, there is a greater chance that they will approve the loans. Considering the history of landownership discrimination and institutionalized racism in America, Black farmers may not meet the same qualifications as whites.

The federal government should ensure adequate outreach with regards to financial assistance programs for Black farmers by creating information centers and creditor referral services. All farmers must be familiar with the financing options available to them; they should be informed enough so that they can make wise decisions about the future of their land and understand how the application and review process is conducted.

Guarantee Funding of 1997 Class-Action Lawsuit

A landmark class-action civil-rights suit was recently settled between the U.S. Department of Agriculture (USDA) and Black farmers, ruling that a great number of the farmers had been wrongly denied loans. Powerful as the decision was, most of the farmers who were due thousands of dollars in reparations have yet to receive their money. More disturbingly, the federal government has stopped the paybacks because its stated deadline has passed.

The majority of Black farmers who were not compensated turned in their paperwork too late or were never aware or notified of the suit. Congress should order USDA to provide full compensation to the nearly 9,000 farmers who were denied relief after being accepted into the settlement class. The USDA must also reevaluate the merits of the nearly 64,000 farmers' claims shut out because of the lack of notice of the settlement. All African American farmers who meet the preliminary requirements should receive the $50,000 payment and debt relief the settlement provides.[23]

Federal officials must hold the USDA accountable for monitoring and enforcing all civil rights standards throughout the agency. We have to demand that the USDA complies with all applicable statutes and regulations prohibiting discrimination.[24]

Offer Legal Assistance to All Farmers

When it comes to current land laws, African American farmers and rural landowners are particularly disadvantaged because of the lack of qualified, informed attorneys. The federal government should make adequate and affordable legal assistance readily available to all.

Currently, private community organizations attempt to provide this service for as many citizens as possible, but the federal government must assume responsibility. These public legal service centers should specifically focus on real estate, land issues, wills, and real estate titles for legal protection. Without legal knowledge about the land, African Americans are much more apt to lose their farms. They must be adequately prepared to fight for maintaining what is rightfully theirs.

Support Cooperatives

Cooperatives are owned by the members who use their products and services. Members decide how the co-op is run; its goals are offering services to and for members as well as enhancing their financial well-being. Savings and benefits are passed on to members, depending on the amount of business they do with the co-op. Local government officials should advocate for and assist community members with forming cooperatives in rural communities, including providing whatever initial resources are needed to establish the co-op.

Types of cooperatives include credit unions, farmer co-ops, and consumer co-ops. Not only do cooperatives give people a way to keep the money they make in their own community; when they begin to control their own businesses, they will also be able to have some control over what happens in their neighborhoods.

Implement a National Agriculture Education Program

Federal officials must develop and implement a national agriculture education program. In addition to "the law" as discussed above, farmers should be educated about or trained in: (a) their rights as landowners, (b) financial analysis of farming, (c) technical assistance in setting individual farm goals, (d) technical assistance in farm management, (e) assistance in debt restructuring, and (f) alternative crop analysis.[25] If farmers are not kept up to date with agricultural and business management techniques, they will be unable to maintain their own land.

Just as important as teaching African American farmers how to manage their property is teaching children skills that will enable them to remain members of the rural community. In addition to math, science, English, and history, rural elementary and high schools should teach youth the principles and benefits of agriculture and family farming. We cannot let Black farmers become extinct with these last few generations.

Finally, the history of Black land farming and ownership must be shared with *all* Americans. We cannot allow our rural elders to be a forgotten population. Local officials should commemorate farmers' history, make their products available to all consumers, and publicize their stories.

A Final Word

If we connect with Black farmers in our communities and advocate on behalf of institutions devoted to retaining African American land, and if we hold elected leaders and officials responsible for providing substantial monetary, legal, and technical assistance and support; then and only then will we strengthen our rural roots and preserve and conserve a most precious part of our history in America.

STRENGTHENING

OUR RURAL ROOTS

Many Americans still hold visions of rural communities as being idyllic locations with space to roam, clean air to breathe, neighborly inhabitants, and lower crime rates. Rural towns, it is often thought, are self-sustaining and self-contained, and perfect for living a quiet life. Although less than 20 percent of the American population live in rural, nonmetropolitan regions, this romantic view of rural life still pervades American culture. Yet real life in rural America challenges this notion.

In general, the U.S. economy is still recovering after the Great Recession. Employment in most regions in 2014 exceeded pre-recession levels at the same time that a slight decline in poverty was occurring nationally. Indeed, urban employment rose by 5 percent between 2010 and 2014. Rural employment, on the other hand, remains well below its 2007 peak. Over the same four-year period, employment grew by just 1.1 percent in rural America, and it remained more than 3 percent below pre-recession levels as of mid-2014. One recent study found that 86 percent of U.S. counties experiencing persistent poverty over the past few decades are in rural areas.[1] Employment losses persisted in many rural areas, including much of the South and in Appalachia.[2]

Living in rural areas is even more difficult for African Americans. Although the rural roots of Black America run deep, the stories of economic hardship for Black citizens in these areas are disheartening, even as the rest of America finds its way out of the recession. Moreover, these roots have been planted for generations, primarily in the Deep South. Rural Black citizens compose just around 2 percent of the rural population, but the Black population in the Deep South is now nearly 17 percent of the total population in this region, which is a much higher ratio than we see for Black Americans across the country as a whole. In addition, the Deep South includes some of the most destitute and impoverished regions in the U.S. Fully one third of Black Americans residing in rural locations live in poverty. For example, whereas approximately 10–11 percent of white Americans in Deep South states are living below the poverty line, more than 40 percent of Black residents in Mississippi and Tennessee are impoverished. The Black share of the poverty burden in rural communities thus is wildly disproportionate. Whether one compares Black rural inhabitants to white rural residents, or even Black rural residents to Black urban residents, the reality is clear: Black rural communities in the Deep South still are home to the poorest and most disadvantaged people in the U.S.[3] ten years after the original publication of *The Covenant*.

One group of the population in the Deep South that is particularly affected by poverty is Black women, girls, and children. These residents suffer in some of the most difficult conditions known to American culture. As one recent study of "Black Belt" counties in Mississippi, Alabama, and Georgia noted, "On nearly every social indicator of well-being . . . Black women, girls, and children in the rural South rank low or last."[4] What they found were living conditions that would be unacceptable for any region of the world. As much as 95 percent of African American women in seven counties from those states lived in poverty.[5] Women, girls, and children suffered with poverty rates of 56 to 60 percent in two other counties. The unemployment rate for Black women was four times higher than that of white women in the same counties, and those who did have jobs earned nearly a third less than white women.[6] The unemployment rate for the poorest county in the U.S., located in the rural Deep South, was approximately 2 percent for whites and more than 36 percent for

Black inhabitants.[7] And these conditions are not recently emerging. The counties studied were those that have been impoverished since at least the early 1980s, which indicates that females have been living in poverty for multiple generations and remain in such conditions almost permanently. Therefore, it is not simply that "Black women and their children live in abject poverty in the rural South, but the gap between their status and the conditions faced by other poor and non-poor people in rural areas is so huge, stark, and distressing."[8]

Because of low employment and high poverty, rural Black Americans also face serious health disparities compared to other segments of the U.S. population. Such disparities are demonstrated by looking at differences in health status when compared to the general population, often characterized by indicators such as higher incidence of disease, disability, increased mortality rates, lower life expectancies, and higher rates of pain and suffering.[9] Even the status of rurality is markedly different from urban dwellers. Rural adults are more likely than their urban counterparts to smoke, abuse alcohol, be physically inactive and thus overweight, and have limited access to healthy food options.[10] Rural residents are older, poorer, and have fewer physicians to care for them. The findings of one study conducted in 2014 offers a bleak look at this urban-rural and Black-white divide in health status. It concludes that rural minorities, particularly Black Americans residing in rural areas, suffer from health disparities that are rarely addressed in the national conversation about health care. The study indicates that (1) rural Black Americans have extremely high rates of obesity compared to rural whites; (2) rural Black Americans have much higher rates of diabetes compared to whites, urban dwellers, or any other minorities; (3) rural Black Americans are more likely to defer getting care due to high costs for a health condition than are rural whites; and (4) rural Black adults are less likely to report a dental cleaning compared to rural white adults.[11]

High unemployment, high rates of poverty, and severe health disparities characterize the rural Black experience. Decades of federal and state government programs have only prevented conditions from becoming worse, but positive action that turns around destitute rural conditions is limited. Such programs seek to ameliorate destitute living conditions for rural Black Americans, but changes are slow to result.

Civil society organizations are much less likely to donate money and time to rural Black cities and towns. "With the exception of support in the wake of Hurricane Katrina or other natural disasters, philanthropic investments do not flow easily to rural communities and programs in the South. The paucity of funding for rural nonprofits and institutions located in the Deep South means they must work harder and with fewer resources to meet the needs of low-income individuals and families with significant barriers to economic security and overall well-being."[12] The associated inequities are apparent. Rural Black Americans are disadvantaged in labor markets in rural locations, and the "labor market" in the rural Deep South is sometimes nonexistent. Pay discrimination is rampant for Black men, particularly in rural areas. Education in rural communities is less effective when compared to urban or suburban areas, and that condition is much more pronounced among rural Black Americans.

In the face of largely ineffective investment in the rural Deep South, what can be done to help Black fellow citizens in that region of the country? Many of the solutions raised by advocacy groups are based in job training, business investment, enterprise development, links to a viable labor market, and targeted tax incentives. Such business-based action is necessary, but not sufficient. Indeed, tax incentives, for example, are shortsighted, if it is believed that the tax code can be used to lift up rural Black Americans. Major government and philanthropic investments must be made in the infrastructure, such as increased Internet access, better roads, training in and better access to healthy eating, and in programs that maintain the cultural heritage of rurality and recognize that Black culture is not the problem. Black citizens in rural areas need to be lifted up with large and targeted activities such as those that guided the American Recovery and Reinvestment Act of 2009. Without such a dedication of resources, the lives of rural Black Americans will continue to be rendered invisible. Until a solid commitment is made, Black people growing up in rural communities may suffer the same fate as their ancestors, trying to navigate lives where their vulnerabilities outnumber their possibilities.

—*Prepared by Michael McGuire, Ph.D., Executive Associate Dean, School of Public and Environmental Affairs, Indiana University, Bloomington, Indiana*

✛ ✛

VIII.

ACCESSING GOOD
JOBS, WEALTH, AND
ECONOMIC PROSPERITY

INTRODUCTORY ESSAY BY MARC H. MORIAL

"If you can't stand the heat, get out of the kitchen," so it has been said. But for Black America, what if it is hot in every room?

There is no hiding place from the realities, hardships, and challenges that reflect the complexity of Black economic progress since the civil rights movement 50 years ago. At that time, many assumed that the hard-fought victories for voting rights, access to education, and economic opportunity would become the gateway to economic parity and the elimination of urban poverty. However, as the painful images of Hurricane Katrina have revealed, there remains a significant wealth gap between Blacks and whites in this nation—one that must be closed if America is to thrive in the 21st century.

In economic terms, what is the state of Black America today? How much progress has actually been made? More importantly, what must be done to reverse the economic stagnation that continues to plague African American families?

Forty years ago, we were at the height of the civil rights movement. On a cold January night in Selma, Alabama, six months after the Civil Rights Act was signed into law but only two months away from the bloody showdown on the Edmund Pettus Bridge, Dr. Martin Luther King, Jr., inspired a crowd one thousand strong to keep the faith and the fight alive. No matter what gains they had made, he told them, when it came to the full economic equality they dreamed of, there was still a "long, long way to go."

Forty years later, we can look around and take some comfort in the gains we have made since that day. The Black middle class has quadrupled, the African American poverty rate has been cut in half, and there are more African American doctors, lawyers, business owners, and elected officials than ever before in our nation's history. There are more African American corporate executives in board rooms than ever before, and three of America's largest Fortune 500 companies are headed by African Americans: Richard Parsons at Time Warner, E. Stanley O'Neal at Merrill Lynch, and Kenneth Chenault at American Express—a feat never dreamed of by our civil rights forefathers and foremothers. By 2003, *Black Enterprise* magazine's top 100 list counted its largest company with revenues of over one billion dollars, more than 20 times the size of the largest Black-owned firm just 30 years ago.

But when we look more closely at where we are today, as Dr. King would say, we still have a long, long way to go. In the past two years, the "Equality Index" in the National Urban League's annual publication, *The State of Black America,* measured the disparities or "equality gaps" that exist between Blacks and whites in education, economics, health and quality of life, civic engagement, and social justice. The latest index found that the overall status of Blacks is 73 percent that of whites. More troubling is the fact that the economic status of Blacks is much worse, just 56 percent when compared with their white counterparts.[1]

In 1999–2000, the Black unemployment rate fell to record lows, while African Americans as a group enjoyed record gains in income. But the years following the post-9/11 recession have been marked by economic stagnation. For example:

- More than one in ten African Americans are now unemployed—more than twice the number of unemployed whites.[2]

- In cities such as New York and Chicago, some estimates put the number of unemployed Black males at 50 percent.[3]

- Long-term African American unemployment is now at a 20-year high.[4]

The fact is almost every indicator available shows that economic progress for Black America is stagnant and starting to fall behind. In *The State of Black America 2004: the Complexity of Black Progress,* Dr. Samuel Myers' essay, "African American Economic Well-Being During the Boom and Bust," revealed that while the income gap between Blacks and whites narrowed in the 1990s, the wealth gap actually increased during that same period.

"Whereas income is a flow, wealth is in stock. Measured in real 2001 dollars, mean net worth exploded from $280,500 in 1992 to $395,500 in 2001. The net worth of white, non-Hispanic families grew on average from $274,800 to $482,900. Average nonwhite wealth increased from only $95,800 to $115,500. The mean wealth of African American families increased from $59,400 to $75,700 between 1992 and 2001. Therefore during this period, the wealth gap—far larger than the income gap—widened while the household income gap narrowed. Black net worth plunged from nearly 22 percent of white net worth to barely 16 percent of white net worth in 2001."[5]

Further, in *The State of Black America 2005: Prescriptions for Change,* Thomas M. Shapiro's essay, "The Racial Wealth Gap," discusses how severe the racial wealth gap is really becoming. After the last recession, when white families still saw their wealth grow slowly, Black families lost a fourth of theirs. When white families rode out the bumps in the stock market, Black families saw their stock and mutual funds decline by an astounding two-thirds!

"By 2002 over one in four Hispanic and African American families were asset poor, having no liquid financial assets, compared to six percent of whites. Families with small amounts or a moderate amount of wealth drew down their meager stockpile of savings to use as private safety nets."[6]

What this means is that without the wealth and equity of home-ownership and sound investments to fall back on, African Americans stand on shaky ground. In hard economic times, as the saying goes, when white America gets a cold, Black America gets pneumonia. And now that the recession is over and the rising tide is once again lifting the boats of many, that tide is pushing the boats of Black families further and further out to sea.

America must wake up.

The growing wealth gap is not just leaving behind Black America; it is leaving behind middle-class America and urban America, rural America and Hispanic America, too. When one community in America suffers, our entire economy suffers. W. E. B. Du Bois identified the color line as the great challenge of the 20th century;[7] our great challenge in the 21st century is the economic line between Blacks and whites; rich and poor; the haves, have-nots, and have-mores.

Black people and our organizations, including the Urban League, must rise to meet this great civil rights challenge. Our government must rise to meet this challenge. And our entire nation must rise to meet this challenge because a productive, working America with a strong middle class is the only way we can compete globally in the 21st-century economy.

Why is closing this wealth gap crucial to America's future?

In a word, diversity. Between now and the year 2050, America will become a nation without a majority ethnic group. The African American population will grow from 37 million to 61 million, and the Hispanic population will grow even more. If the economic and educational disparities continue to exist as they do today, who will be the consumers of American products in the future? Who will be the producers and manufacturers of the nation's products to the world? More business leaders and corporate CEOs recognize this fact: that closing the equality gap is not merely a challenge for Black Americans and other people of color; it is also a challenge for the nation if we are to maintain our position as the economic and moral leader of the world.

How do we get there?

The most powerful tool we have to make our voices heard is the vote. With the vote, we can start electing leaders such as Georgia Congressman John Lewis, who is committed to closing this gap. Forty years ago, student activist John Lewis walked toward violence and hate on the Edmund Pettus Bridge because he had the courage to believe that freedom and the right to vote were waiting on the other side. Four decades later, Russell Simmons, Sean "Diddy" Combs, and many other activist-entertainers helped to energize the hip-hop generation to participate in the political process, resulting in a record Black voter turnout across America.

Washington must change its priorities. For too long, there has been too much partisan bickering in the nation's capital and too few problems being solved. With a massive wealth gap that is growing ever wider and a long-term unemployment rate that is growing ever greater, the conversation must be about how to eliminate joblessness and the wealth gap, not how to eliminate the job training programs and opportunities people count on to get ahead.

It is time for us to face the great civil rights challenge of this new century head-on. As former National Urban League President Whitney M. Young said in his Inaugural Address to this organization more than 40 years ago, ours is a "crusade for justice, for decency, for morality . . . a crusade to put into operational framework on a day-to-day, person-to-person basis the American creed and democratic promise." And this is a crusade not just for ourselves, but also "a responsibility to all America as it faces its greatest hour of challenge."

This is our hour: We have seen the challenges ahead of us and know that we have a long way to go. We have also seen that our economic progress sometimes stands on shaky ground. But, our resolve must be solid as a rock. We must take ownership of our own economic destiny as well as urge our leaders to develop policies to help working families. In the pages that follow, you will read about the multitude of specific measures you can take to stabilize your and your community's economic future.

Let our generation's commitment to equality and economic opportunity be our guiding force. We must stand together—steadfast and unmovable—in this new century to become an America that truly reflects justice, equality, and opportunity for all people and for generations to come.

✣

MARC H. MORIAL is the eighth President and Chief Executive Officer of the New York-based National Urban League, the venerable civil rights and community-based organization. Since his appointment in 2003, Morial has worked to reenergize the organization's diverse constituencies by building on the strengths of its nearly century-old legacy and increasing its profile both locally and nationally. Prior to his League appointment, Morial served two terms as the Mayor of New Orleans; during his last two years in office, he also served as President of the U.S. Conference of Mayors. For more information: http://www.nul.org.

THE FACTS ON JOBS AND ECONOMY

WAGE DISPARITY

- The median weekly wage earned by African Americans in 2004 was $523; for white workers, it was $677 a week.[8]

- One out of four (25.7 percent) African Americans is employed as a nursing or home health-care worker, cook, janitor, maid, cashier, salesperson, customer service representative, secretary, truck driver, or laborer. Annual salaries for these professions range from $29,020 to $10,335.[9]

UNION ALLIANCES

- Twenty years ago, one in every four Black workers was a union member; now just one in seven belongs to a union.[10]

- The number of African Americans in unions has fallen by 14.4 percent since 2000, while white membership is down 5.4 percent.[11]

EMPLOYMENT PATTERNS

- The unemployment rate for Black people nationwide is twice that for whites.[12]

- Eighteen percent of Black workers are uninsured.[13]

- Employment rates continue to be higher for white youth, at 62 percent, than for African American youth, at 42 percent. When employed, African American youth are more likely to earn lower wages than white youth.[14]

- Twenty-three percent of African Americans ages 18–19 are "disconnected"—not in school and not working, compared with 10 percent of whites within the same age range.[15]

NET WORTH

- African Americans have a median net worth of $5,998, compared to $88,651 for whites. Even more alarming, 32 percent of African Americans have a zero or negative net worth.[16]

- Although African Americans are more than 13 percent of the nation's population, their total net worth is only 1.2 percent of the total net worth of the nation. This number has not changed since the end of the Civil War in 1865.[17]

HOMEOWNERSHIP AND BORROWING POWER

- Fewer than 50 percent of Black families own their own homes, compared with more than 75 percent of whites.[18]

- African Americans are 3.6 times as likely as whites to receive a home purchase loan from a subprime lender and 4.1 times as likely as whites to receive a refinance loan from a subprime lender.[19] Subprime lending is usually one to six points over the prime rate and is reserved for lending to businesses that do not qualify for "prime" rates.[20]

- In neighborhoods where at least 80 percent of the population is African American, borrowers are 2.2 times as likely as borrowers in the nation as a whole to refinance with a subprime lender. Perhaps more revealing, upper-income borrowers living in predominately African American neighborhoods are twice as likely as low-income white borrowers to have subprime loans.[21]

What the Community Can Do

We, as a people, must fight for good jobs, not just entry-level jobs, but also career-making jobs. To build wealth, African Americans need to energize our focus on savings, investing, and estate planning through stronger financial education and a commitment to long-term economic self-sufficiency.

It is also crucial to urge corporate America to recognize that the promise of equal opportunity and diversity extends not only to jobs, but also to procurement opportunities for urban entrepreneurs and the boardroom.

What Every Individual Can Do Now:

- Open and maintain a savings account, no matter what your family's income is.

- Encourage your children to save.

- Create neighborhood job clubs to share information about available jobs and support (such as transportation) for employment.

- Shop at Black-owned businesses.

- Make sure that schools teach children about checking and savings accounts.

MOST OF ALL:

- Hold all leaders and elected officials responsible and demand that they change current policy.

What Works Now:

Following are examples of what some folks are doing now—or have done—to assure good jobs, wealth, and economic prosperity.

Farrah Gray

Farrah Gray—20-year-old entrepreneur, venture capitalist, and self-made millionaire—was raised in the projects of East Chicago.[22] "People tell me, 'Boy, you were just born yesterday.' I always say, 'Yes, but I stayed up all night,'" asserts Gray, the author of *Reallionaire: Nine Steps to Becoming Rich From the Inside Out.*

Gray brings this clear-cut, frontal perspective to everything he does. His list of accomplishments is truly incredible. Shuttling between offices in New York and Las Vegas, he manages businesses in both cities. He publishes *Inner City* magazine, owned by Inner City Broadcasting Corp. (ICBC), parent company to radio station WBLS. He sits on the advisory board of the Las Vegas Chamber of Commerce (he was the youngest person ever to do so) and the National Association of Realtors. In addition, he heads the Farrah Gray Foundation, which he funds to support community initiatives and to provide seed money for youth entrepreneurial projects. Through it all, he maintains a healthy social life.

"I believe there is a recipe for success," Gray points out. For him, that means wanting change. "Comfort is the enemy of achievement," he maintains. "I was just familiar with struggle. The ghetto life makes everybody uptight."

His first venture came at age six, when he created his own blend of body lotion by mixing the remains of near-empty bottles he found in his bathroom. He renamed the product FG Enterprises and sold it door to door for $1.50. That earned him $9. To celebrate, he took his mom out for Chinese food. "In the 'hood, there's not much. We don't lack brain power. We lack [the funds] and the resources," he says. "We don't have any rich relatives, and if we did, they've moved out."

Using homemade business cards he began carrying at age seven that read "Farrah Gray, 21st century CEO," he approached local business people about supporting UNEEC (Urban Neighborhood Economic Enterprise Club), a club in which he and his friends could learn about business and entrepreneurship. Guests became mentors and future business contacts. "My friends were getting arrested for taking stuff from the store. I decided . . . I wasn't. I figured the same knowledge I would have of being a drug dealer is the same knowledge I would have of buying wholesale and selling retail," he observes.

Shortly after forming UNEEC, Gray persuaded some local businesspeople to lend the group money to invest. They made $15,000. "In the 'hood, we wanted entrepreneurship just as much as we needed it," he explains. Gray believes you must know your market. That's why at 13 he began his first company, FarrOut Foods, where he sold his grandmother's strawberry-vanilla maple syrup. "My grandmother used to make all of our syrup from scratch because we couldn't afford it," he recalls. That netted him his first million dollars. At the same time, he funded the Farrah Gray Foundation with company profits. Other successful business ventures have included Kidzel calling cards (prepaid calling cards that allow children to phone home for free from anywhere in the world) with telecommunications giant WorldTel.

Figueroa Corridor Coalition For Economic Justice

The Figueroa Corridor Coalition for Economic Justice proves that communities can use their voice effectively to advocate that public investments be accountable to communities and provide community benefits.[23]

More than 300 residents from neighborhoods adjacent to the site of the new Staples Center in Los Angeles advocated for—and got—a Community Benefits Agreement that will respond to the needs of those who have been displaced by the construction and those who will continue to live in the community. The coalition established a connection between public subsidies and community voice: the entertainment and sports complex was getting an estimated $70 million in public subsidies with no built-in expectation to meet a double bottom-line goal—providing benefits to the community as well.

Upon completion targeted for 2008, the complex will be a $1 billion sports and entertainment facility in Los Angeles. The Community Benefits Agreement includes a goal of 70 percent of new jobs at the officially recognized living wage; a hiring program to give local residents and those displaced by construction first shot at the new jobs, along with training; a commitment of $1 million for community parks and recreation; and 20 percent of the budget to be set aside for affordable housing within the complex.

The Figueroa Corridor Coalition was so successful and inspiring that another community coalition in the city scored a victory with Los Angeles International Airport's expansion plan and its own impressive Community Benefits Agreement.

Service Employees International Union Security Officers Campaign

The Service Employees International Union (SEIU) has challenged the private security industry—which enjoys billions of dollars in profits every year—to share more of its profits with workers from our community in the form of wages and benefits.

Private security is one of the 10 fastest-growing occupations in America. More than 1 million private security officers—more than twice the number of police officers—are employed in the United States; the workforce is disproportionately drawn from the African American community (for example, in Los Angeles, African American officers account for 65 percent of the workforce).

Despite the increased concerns about security following the events of Sept. 11, 2001, most security officers in major cities are paid poverty wages, have few benefits, and receive minimal training; the average annual pay for security officers is less than $19,000; health insurance—if it is offered—is unaffordable; and officers do not receive paid sick days or holidays.

If security companies provided officers with raises and benefits, hundreds of millions of dollars would flow into our nation's African American communities and poor neighborhoods. Simply achieving parity in pay and benefits for security officers in Los Angeles with janitorial workers would add more than $100 million a year into the communities of South Los Angeles. Furthermore, if security jobs provided greater opportunities for training and a career ladder, officers would have greater future prospects and provide more security for their families

The SEIU is deeply involved in the struggle for benefits and a living wage for all private security officers.[24]

What Every Leader and Elected Official Can Do

- Invest in the African American community.
- Monitor and prevent predatory lending.
- Establish tax-free homeownership savings accounts.
- Consistently provide Community Benefits Agreements.
- Commit to a national job training and career counseling effort for youth.
- Guarantee unionization and benefits for all workers.
- Support Individual Development Accounts.
- Expand Earned Income Tax Credits.
- Increase the minimum wage to a living wage.

Invest in the African American Community

Homeownership

The homeownership gap can be closed by lowering down payment requirements and making mortgages more available and affordable to all. Government officials must strengthen the Community Reinvestment Act (CRA), a civil rights law prohibiting discrimination by banks against low- and moderate-income neighborhoods.[25]

The CRA imposes an affirmative and a continuing obligation on banks to satisfy the need for credit and banking services of all the communities in which they are chartered, specifically in African American neighborhoods. Federal auditors must consistently monitor banks to ensure that they are making loans, investments, and other financial services available to low- and moderate-income communities of color.[26]

Entrepreneurship

Our elected officials at the federal level can increase business development and entrepreneurship in the African American community by doubling the amount of financing of the New Markets Tax Credit Program that provides money to entrepreneurs in urban areas identified by the U.S. Department of the Treasury.

The program is a federal tax initiative designed to increase the amount of investment capital in low-income communities. It is the most significant federal tax initiative to support community development in nearly 20 years.[27] While this is impressive, officials must extend the program to reach even more Black small businesses.

Local officials should also streamline the city permitting and zoning process to make it easier for new businesses to start up and small businesses to grow. Oftentimes there are so many rules and regulations that even those entrepreneurs with the resources to open a small business are unable to get their ventures off the ground.

Monitor and Prevent Predatory Lending

Because of their greater flexibility and speed, state governments must enact and enforce regulatory laws as necessary to protect citizens from predatory lending; deceitful lenders will inevitably find loopholes in federal laws. To protect all consumers, the ideal solution is a partnership between the federal government and state officials, wherein the federal government sets reasonable minimum standards and the states maintain their authority to address local issues.[28]

Predatory lenders target elderly, poor, and uneducated borrowers to strip the equity from their homes. Some predatory lenders trap borrowers in bad loans through the imposition of prepayment penalties that require the payment of a significant penalty to refinance into a more favorable loan. While the borrower may be able to qualify for a lower-cost loan, the prepayment penalty charge often prevents the refinancing. Prepayment penalties often provide kickbacks by lenders to brokers (yield-spread premiums) for placing borrowers in loans at a higher interest than the borrower could otherwise qualify for.[29]

Federal officials must make "yield-spread premiums" illegal. There should be no incentives for lenders to provide predatory loans to borrowers.

Establish Tax-Free Homeownership Savings Accounts

Congress should strive to close the homeownership gap by creating a new tool, such as "Individual Homeownership Development Accounts," that will allow working Americans to save money for a down payment on a home tax free. This concept is similar to the legislation Congress passed to establish 401(k) accounts years ago to encourage employee savings.

The federal government must make it truly feasible for working and middle-class African Americans to save for a home, with no penalties.

Consistently Provide Community Benefits Agreements

City officials must ensure that public investments be accountable to communities and provide community benefits. An accountable development (or community benefits) movement is growing, based on the premise that public investments must yield defined public benefits, such as good jobs, affordable housing, and childcare. The movement is being driven by diverse coalitions that include labor unions, community builders, housing developers, neighborhood advocates, and environmentalists.

Community Benefits Agreements should include hiring programs for neighborhood residents, livable-wage employment opportunities, training and/or educational opportunities, increased transit access and services, health-care and childcare services, increased access to technology, increased affordable housing opportunities, opportunities for ownership/profit sharing for community residents and institutions, and neighborhood amenities (e.g., parks and cultural centers).

For economic development projects that require physical development, city officials should require contracting with locally owned, minority-owned, and women-owned businesses for project design, construction, and ongoing operations.

Commit to a National Job Training and Career Counseling Effort For Youth

Today and in the future, jobs are and will become more technological, skilled, and learning-oriented. There must be massive public and private investment in science and technological education, as they are more important than ever. The federal, state, and local branches of government must fund many more science-oriented schools as well as programs tailored to stimulate interest in science and technology in elementary and middle schools.

Supporting mentorship programs and employment clubs and identifying entrepreneurial role models and work-based incentives are important. Community leaders and city officials must collaborate to provide paid internships, training, scholarships, and jobs for youth. Junior college and trade school tuition should be freely given to all who need it. There should be programs in these schools and in correctional facilities that combine high school equivalency with technical and vocational training.

There must also be nationwide efforts to break the class and race segregation in job markets, particularly in the fastest-growing industries. African Americans are vastly underrepresented in the high-tech industry—one of the key industries for America's future economic success. All large corporations, including the leading high-tech ones, must fund and put in place programs specifically geared to recruiting and training minority applicants for these industries and jobs.

Guarantee Unionization and Benefits for All Workers

The federal government should guarantee health insurance for all workers and their dependents. By so doing, businesses that spend a substantial amount of money on employee health care would realize huge savings and be better able to pay their employees a living wage. Along with the incentive to take good care of workers, a portion of the savings should underwrite skills training programs for the community.

Moreover, all workers must retain the right to belong to a union. State representatives should work to pass the Employee Free Choice Act, which will help correct the broken process through which workers form unions. This important legislation would ensure that workers have a fair chance to exercise their democratic right to choose a union. If Congress passes this Act, stronger enforcements would be in place to deter violations of labor law and help workers reach contracts quickly and fairly through a mediation process, instead of getting dragged through multiyear negotiations.[30]

Support Individual Development Accounts

Individual Development Accounts (IDAs) are matched savings accounts for people with low incomes that enable them to save money and build assets.[31] Every dollar that is saved in an IDA will be matched with donations from government agencies, nonprofit organizations, and private companies.[32]

Often these savings are used to buy a house, pay for education, or start a small business. It is crucial that our elected officials take responsibility for encouraging and helping low-income African American working families save enough money to buy an asset. Assets provide financial security for the future.

Federal funds must be allotted for IDAs. Not only should the government provide resources to match all accounts, but they should also require financial institutions to offer these accounts. In partnership with federal officials, all states should also consider supplementing federal donations with local funds.

Expand Earned Income Tax Credits

Earned Income Tax Credits (EITCs) reduce tax burdens and supplement wages for low-income working families.[33] Because the credit is refundable, workers receive any remaining amount of credit over their tax liability. It is important to reward low-wage workers and for those who are not full-time employees, provide them with an incentive to spend more time working.[34]

The federal government should enlarge the small Earned Income Tax Credit, as a means of reducing poverty and hardship for hardworking low-income African American individuals and families. In addition, for those who are eligible it can be difficult to understand the EITC filing process. In order for workers to take advantage of this great benefit, officials must simplify and make readily available information on the tax credit, and how one may receive it.

Increase the Minimum Wage to a Living Wage

Congress should raise the minimum wage to a living wage and link future increases to an objective standard.

Full-time adult workers need to earn enough to lift themselves out of poverty. For this to become a reality, the federal minimum wage must increase. At the city level, employers who are receiving any kind of government contracts or tax benefits should be required to pay their workers more, which will actually benefit cities, in the long run, because the more pervasive ordinances are across the country, the less room there will be for firms to move from city to city looking for the cheapest locality.[35]

Most low-wage workers, primarily employed in the service sector, are the people who perform some of the most essential services in this country. They are the ones whom we must fight for so that they, too, may achieve a dignified lifestyle.[36]

A Final Word

By investing in the Black community; by tracking and eliminating predatory lending; by boosting savings through various instruments and initiatives; and by training present and future generations of workers, we can ensure that all Americans will have a fair opportunity to access living-wage jobs, wealth, and economic prosperity.

CWBA
TEN YEARS LATER

ACCESSING GOOD JOBS, WEALTH, AND ECONOMIC PROSPERITY

Since this chapter was originally published in 2006, the United States—along with the majority of the developed world—experienced the most severe economic crisis since the Second World War. The Great Recession—triggered by the collapse of Lehman Brothers and the financial markets—led to the loss of homes, jobs, and investments; shrank the middle class; and swelled the ranks of the poor. The distress that accompanied such a historic economic downturn was widespread, but this *Covenant* update reveals that white America has begun to recover financially while Black America is even worse off than it was during the depths of the recession.

As the gap between rich and poor has widened, so has the wealth gap between Black and white Americans. Importantly, the increased disparity comes not from the income gap—which has remained relatively steady—but from progressively disproportionate accumulated wealth. Thus, while the income gap remains a critical and unresolved issue, for African American families to have access to key resources such as emergency savings, home ownership, and higher education (let alone retirement accounts), the path forward must also prioritize providing poverty relief, health insurance, and access to the tools of financial planning and security.

With respect to income, progress has stalled. In 1995 the median household income, measured in terms of real inflation-adjusted dollars, was $31,000 for African Americans and $55,000 for white workers. In 2013 it was $34,598 for Black Americans and $58,270 for white Americans. The contrast is even starker when comparing African American earnings to those of the highest-earning group—Asian Americans, whose median household income reached $67,065 in 2013.

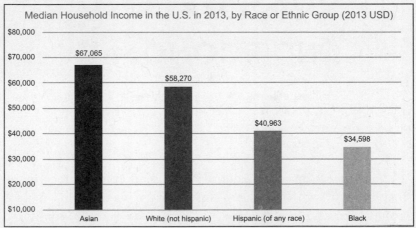

Source: DeNavas-Walt, Carmen, and Bernadette D. Proctor. "Income and Poverty in the United States: 2013." Current Population Reports (2014): 1-61.US Census Bureau. Web. 12 Oct. 2015.

Figure 1 – Median household income, 2013

Real Median Household Income by Race and Origin (1995–2012) (2012 USD)

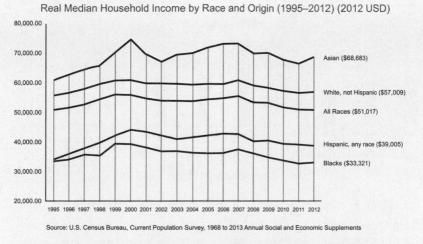

Source: U.S. Census Bureau, Current Population Survey, 1968 to 2013 Annual Social and Economic Supplements

Figure 2 – Inflation-adjusted median income, 1995–2012

As Figure 2 demonstrates, the median household income disparities among families of different racial and ethnic groups have remained both significant and relatively steady since 1995. Black Americans remain the lowest-earning group, reflecting both lack of access to higher-compensated professions and a minimum wage that is lower today in inflation-adjusted dollars than it was in 1997.

With respect to accumulated wealth, however, the disparity has become more severe. The rapid deterioration of the U.S. economy during the Great Recession led to a decrease of 39.4 percent in the average net worth of all American households, dropping from $135,700 in 2007 to $82,300 in 2013. Although losses since 2007 can be seen across all ethnic groups, since 2010 white household wealth has increased, while Black household wealth has continued to plummet. The modest increase of 2.4 percent in white household net worth contrasts with a 33.8 percent decrease in net worth among Black families, as illustrated in Figure 3.

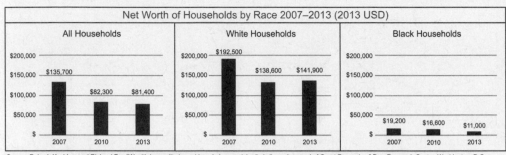

Source: Rakesh Kochhar and Richard Fry. "Wealth inequality has widened along racial, ethnic lines since end of Great Recession." Pew Research Center, Washington, D.C. (December 12, 2014). http://www.pewresearch.org/fact-tank/2014/12/12/racial-wealth-gaps-great-recession/, accessed on September 25, 2015.

Figure 3 – Household net worth, 2007–2013

Black household wealth is presented in proportion to white household wealth in Figure 4. The median net worth of white families in 2007 was ten times that of Black families. Although the gap narrowed during the course of the Great Recession to a proportion of approximately 8:1, the nation's collective economic recovery benefitted white Americans substantially more than African Americans in terms of net worth, with white households 12.9 times wealthier than Black households in 2013.

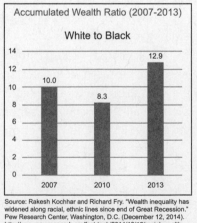

Source: Rakesh Kochhar and Richard Fry. "Wealth inequality has widened along racial, ethnic lines since end of Great Recession." Pew Research Center, Washington, D.C. (December 12, 2014). http://www.pewresearch.org/fact-tank/2014/12/12/racial-wealth-gaps-great-recession/, accessed on September 25, 2015.

Figure 4 – Accumulated wealth ratio, 2007–2013

In 2013, median household wealth among white Americans was $141,900, while the median among African Americans was

$11,000—less than 8 percent of that of white families. This tremendous disparity is far vaster than the wage gap, in which African American median income is approximately 59 percent that of white workers. To understand the difficulties Black Americans face in building financial security, we therefore need to look not only at median income but also at factors such as poverty rates, health insurance coverage, and educational attainment.

What is not immediately apparent in median income is the stark contrast in poverty rates between Black and white Americans. In 2012, 15 percent of Americans fell below the federal poverty level. Among white Americans, the incidence of poverty was 9.7 percent. For African Americans, the poverty rate was 27.2 percent. For these one in four African American families, whose household income was below $23,050 for a four-person family, the challenge of meeting basic needs makes wealth accumulation all but impossible.

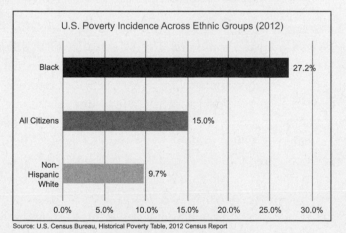

Source: U.S. Census Bureau, Historical Poverty Table, 2012 Census Report

Figure 5 – Poverty Incidence, 2012

Another key factor in financial stability is health insurance, as those without insurance are more likely to delay needed care and to face expensive medical bills when health problems become severe. In 2012, the rate of uninsurance among white Americans was 11 percent. Among Black Americans, 19 percent had no insurance coverage, leaving nearly one in five African Americans at risk of insurmountable medical debt. Disparity in health coverage is also evident among children, as 6.6 percent of white children have no insurance, compared to 9.3 percent of Black children.

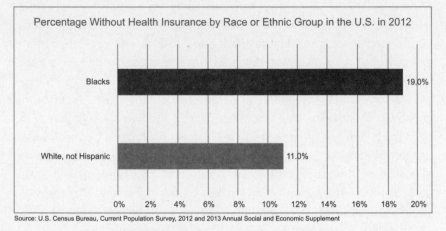

Percentage Without Health Insurance by Race or Ethnic Group in the U.S. in 2012

Blacks — 19.0%

White, not Hispanic — 11.0%

Source: U.S. Census Bureau, Current Population Survey, 2012 and 2013 Annual Social and Economic Supplement

Figure 6 – Rates of uninsurance, 2012

Finally, ongoing disparities in educational attainment continue to affect the wage gap and compound the difficulty of wealth accumulation. Figure 7 demonstrates that in 2013, more than one in five white students (21 percent) completed four-year bachelor's degrees, compared to 13 percent of Black students. White Americans were twice as likely as African Americans to go on to more advanced degrees, with 12 percent of white students completing master's degrees or doctorates compared to 6 percent of Black students. Viewed cumulatively, one in three white Americans (33 percent) attained a bachelor's degree or higher, compared to just one in five (19 percent) African Americans. The educational attainment gap forms a vicious cycle with the income and wealth accumulation gaps, as African American families are less able to afford college and graduate degrees, resulting in younger generations earning less than their white counterparts, and likewise lacking the means to send their own children to college.

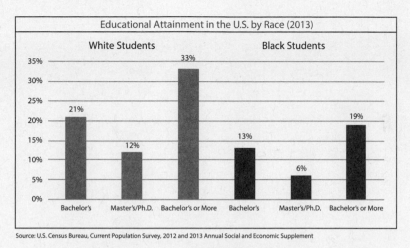

Source: U.S. Census Bureau, Current Population Survey, 2012 and 2013 Annual Social and Economic Supplement

Figure 7 – Educational attainment, 2013

In conclusion, in the ten years since this book was first published, the financial status of African Americans has deteriorated not only during the Great Recession but also in the ensuing years, when white Americans enjoyed a modest economic recovery. This disparity in household wealth can be only partially explained by the continuing wage gap. While it is critical to address earning power, the magnitude of the wealth gap is far greater than income alone can explain. Access to health care, higher education, and poverty relief, along with the provision of the financial tools and services described in this chapter, must be pursued as part of a comprehensive approach to long-term stability and prosperity.

—*Prepared by David Audretsch, Ph.D., Distinguished Professor, Indiana University; Ameritech Chair of Economic Development; Director, Institute for Development Strategies; Director, SPEA Overseas Education Program; Bloomington, Indiana*

✦ ✦

IX.

ASSURING ENVIRONMENTAL JUSTICE FOR ALL

Introductory Essay
by Robert D. Bullard

All communities are not created equal. If a community happens to be poor, Black, or of color, it receives less protection than does an affluent white community. The environmental justice framework defines "environment" as where we live, work, play, worship, and go to school, as well as the physical and natural world. Environmental justice is built on the principle that all Americans have a right to equal protection of our nation's environmental, health, housing, transportation, employment, and civil rights laws and regulations. Environmental protection is a basic human right.[1]

The environmental justice movement has come a long way since its humble beginning in Warren County, North Carolina, where a PCB landfill ignited protests and over 500 arrests. Those protests also led the United Church of Christ's Commission for Racial Justice in 1987 to produce *Toxic Wastes and Race,*[2] the first national study to correlate waste facility sites and demographic characteristics. Race was found to be the most potent variable in predicting where these facilities were located—more powerful than poverty, land values, and home-ownership. In 1990, *Dumping in Dixie: Race, Class, and Environmental Quality*—the first book on environmental racism—documented discriminatory policies and practices that allowed polluting facilities to be concentrated in Black communities.

In 1992, after much prodding from environmental justice advocates, the U.S. Environmental Protection Agency (EPA) finally acknowledged its mandate to protect all Americans.[4] And on Feb. 11, 1994, environmental justice reached the White House, when President Bill Clinton signed Executive Order 12898, "Federal Actions to Address Environmental Justice in Minority Populations and Low-Income Populations."[5] The order mandated federal government agencies to incorporate environmental justice into all of their works and programs.

Today, millions of Americans are concerned about the threat of exposure to chemical and biological agents. The tragic events of September 11, 2001 (terrorist attacks on the World Trade Center in New York, the Pentagon in Washington, and the plane crash in rural Pennsylvania), and the anthrax scare heightened concern and worry about disaster preparedness.

Toxic chemical assaults, however, are not new for too many African Americans and other people of color who are forced to live next to and often on the fence line with chemical industries that spew their poisons into the air, water, and ground. These residents experience a form of "toxic terror" 24 hours a day and seven days a week. When chemical accidents occur, government and industry officials tell residents to "shelter in place."[6]

Hurricane Katrina exposed the world to the naked reality of environmental racism. Environmental racism refers to any policy, practice, or directive that differentially affects or disadvantages (whether intended or unintended) individuals, groups, or communities based on race or color.[7] Environmental racism combines with public policies and industry practices to provide benefits for whites while shifting costs to people of color.[8] Katrina presented in living color clear links among race, poverty, land use, environmental risk, and unequal protection.[9] Poverty impacts health because it determines how many resources poor people have and defines the amount of environmental risks they will be exposed to in their immediate environment.[10]

Race maps closely with the geography of environmental risks and devastation: Katrina laid bare the "dirty little secret" of poverty in America.[11] The U.S. poverty rate is 12.5 percent.[12] Blacks, who are disproportionately poor, comprise a significantly large share of the three Gulf Coast states hardest hit by Katrina—Louisiana, Mississippi, and Alabama. Blacks comprise 32.5 percent of the population in Louisiana, 36.3 percent in Mississippi, and 26 percent in Alabama. New Orleans is nearly 68 percent Black;[13] about 28 percent of its residents live below the poverty level, more than 80 percent of whom are Black. The African American population in the coastal Mississippi counties where Katrina struck ranged from 25 percent to 87 percent Black.

Before Katrina, New Orleans was struggling with a wide range of environmental justice and health concerns, including an older housing stock with lots of lead paint. More than 50 percent (some studies place this figure at around 70 percent) of children living in the inner-city neighborhoods of New Orleans had blood lead levels above the current guideline of 10 micrograms per deciliter (μg/dL), which is defined as the "level of concern" by the Centers for Disease Control and Prevention.[14] Childhood lead poisoning in some New Orleans Black neighborhoods was as high as 67 percent.

Environmental health problems related to environmental exposure were hot-button issues in New Orleans long before Katrina's floodwaters emptied out the city. New Orleans' location on the Mississippi River Industrial Corridor increased its vulnerability to environmental threats. Dozens of toxic "time bombs" along this chemical corridor—the 85-mile stretch from Baton Rouge to New Orleans—made "Cancer Alley" a major environmental justice battleground.[15]

There are questions about what a "new" New Orleans should look like. There is even talk about some "low-lying" neighborhoods, inhabited largely by African Americans, not being rebuilt, such as the sealed-off Lower Ninth Ward. It is no accident that Blacks tend to live in the lowest-lying areas of the city.[16] Residents fear environmental reasons—location in flood plain and environmental contamination and new zoning codes—may be used to kill off their neighborhoods.

Black residents have deep-seated fears and resentment that they will once again be left out of rebuilding, with decisions driven more by race than by topography. Some of New Orleans' white power elites—heads of law firms, tourist businesses, and conservation groups—have a vision and plan for the recovery, restoration, and rebuilding of New Orleans: "smaller and more upscale."[17]

Before rebuilding and reconstruction in New Orleans and the Gulf Coast can begin in earnest, mountains of debris and toxic wastes must be cleaned up and disposed of in an environmentally sound way. Katrina left behind "a complex array of environmental health problems."[18] Katrina dumped over 63 million cubic yards of debris in Louisiana and 62.5 million cubic yards of debris in Mississippi. In contrast, Hurricane Andrew generated 20 million cubic yards of debris in 1992. Louisiana officials are faced with the challenge of disposing of mountains of debris from Katrina. Some of the disposal methods have come under fire from environmentalists, environmental justice leaders, and the EPA.

The Army Corps of Engineers is charged with cleaning up miles of sediments laced with cancer-causing chemicals, toxic metals, industrial compounds, petroleum products, and banned insecticides—all at levels that pose potential cancer risks or other long-term hazards.[19] This is likely to be the "mother of all toxic cleanups."[20] Much of the contaminated topsoil where 110,000 New Orleans flooded homes sit can be scooped up and replaced with clean soil. However, cleaning up the muck that seeped into houses is a major challenge.

Health officials are now seeing a large number of evacuees afflicted with "Katrina cough," an illness believed to be linked to mold and dust.[21] Individuals who otherwise do not have allergies have been coming down with the illness. It is especially worrisome for people with health problems—AIDS, asthma, and other serious respiratory illnesses—who may reenter their homes. Molds are not just an irritant; they can trigger episodes and set up life-threatening infections when normal immune systems are weakened. Mold spores are known triggers of asthma attacks—an illness that disproportionately affects African Americans.

Generally, government air quality tests focus on toxins, such as benzene, in areas where Katrina caused oil spills. The government does not have regulatory standards for either indoor or outdoor levels of mold spores. Independent tests conducted by the Natural Resources Defense Council (NRDC) in mid-November found dangerously high mold counts in New Orleans air.[22] The spore counts outdoors in most flooded neighborhoods tested by NRDC—New Orleans East, the Lower 9th Ward, Chalmette, Uptown, Mid-City, and the Garden District—showed levels as high as 77,000 spores per cubic meter at one site in Chalmette and 81,000 spores per cubic meter at another site in the Uptown area. The National Allergy Bureau of the American Academy of Allergy and Immunology considers any outdoor mold spore level of greater than 50,000 spores per cubic meter to be a serious health threat.

Hurricane Katrina and its aftermath are just the tip of the environmental racism iceberg; the bright side is that they are instructive and inform what we must do. To assure environmental justice for all, we must address all of the inequities that result from human settlement, industrial facility siting, and industrial development. We must educate and assist groups in organizing and mobilizing, empowering ourselves to take charge of our lives, our communities, and our surroundings. We must address power imbalances and the lack of political enfranchisement; we must redirect our resources so that we can create healthy, livable, and sustainable communities for *all* of us.

Power rests in all of us; when we operate as a collective, that's when we are most powerful and move forward as a unit. Katrina can be the issue that mobilizes us, organizes us, and creates the catalyst that unites us to work for justice in environmental protection, justice in terms of enforcement of regulations, and justice in terms of our children's being able to live, play, and go to school in environments that are not hazardous to their health.

As we said in the beginning: the environment is everything—where we live, work, play, and go to school, as well as the physical and natural world. We cannot separate the physical environment from the cultural environment. We have to talk about making sure that justice is integrated throughout all of the stuff that we do.

✢

ROBERT D. BULLARD, Ph.D., is Ware Professor of Sociology and Director of the Environmental Justice Resource Center (EJRC) at Clark Atlanta University in Atlanta, Georgia. Formed in 1994, the EJRC serves as a research, policy, and information clearinghouse on issues related to environmental justice, race and the environment, civil rights, facility siting, land use planning, brownfields, transportation equity, suburban sprawl, and Smart Growth. A prolific author, Bullard is one of the pioneering scholars and activists in the environmental justice movement. For more information: http://www.ejrc.cau/edu.

THE FACTS ON ENVIRONMENTAL JUSTICE

CHILDHOOD LEAD POISONING

- Lead poisoning continues to be the number-one environmental health threat to children of color in the United States, especially poor children and children living in inner cities.[23]

- Black children are five times more likely than white children to have lead poisoning.[24]

- One in seven Black children living in older housing has elevated blood lead levels.[25]

- About 22 percent of African American children living in pre-1946 housing are lead poisoned, compared with 6 percent of white children living in comparable types of housing.[26]

- Recent studies suggest that a young person's lead burden is linked to lower IQ, lower high school graduation rates, and increased delinquency.[27]

- Lead poisoning causes about two to three points of IQ lost for each 10 µg/dL lead level (µg/dL = 10 micrograms of lead in a deciliter—one-tenth of a liter—of blood).[28]

TOXIC NEIGHBORHOODS

- Nationally, three out of five African and Latino Americans live in communities with abandoned toxic waste sites.[29]

- The U.S. General Accounting Office (now known as the Government Accountability Office) estimates that there are between 130,000 and 450,000 brownfields (abandoned waste sites) scattered across the urban landscape from New York to California—most of which are located in or near low-income, working-class, and people-of-color communities.[30]

- Over 870,000 of the 1.9 million (46 percent) housing units for the poor—mostly minorities—sit within a mile of factories that reported toxic emissions to the Environmental Protection Agency.[31]

- More than 600,000 students—mostly African American—in Massachusetts, New York, New Jersey, Michigan, and California attended nearly 1,200 public schools located within one-half mile of federal Superfund or state-identified contaminated sites.[32]

- More than 68 percent of Black Americans live within 30 miles of a coal-fired power plant—the distance within which the maximum effects of the smokestack plume are expected to occur—compared with 56 percent of white Americans.[33]

KATRINA TOXIC CONTAMINATION AND HEALTH THREATS

- Katrina caused six major oil spills, releasing 7.4 million gallons of oil, or 61 percent as much as the 11 million gallons that leaked into Alaska's Prince William Sound from the Exxon *Valdez* in 1989.[34]

- The storm hit 60 underground storage tanks, five Superfund sites, and 466 industrial facilities that stored highly dangerous chemicals before the storm; it disabled more than 1,000 drinking-water systems, creating a "toxic soup" with *e. coli* in the floodwaters far exceeding EPA's safe levels.[35]

- Katrina left behind an estimated 22 million tons of debris, with more than half—12 million tons—left in Orleans Parish.[36]

- Flooded homes containing over one million pieces of "white goods," such as refrigerators, stoves, and freezers, require disposal.[37]

- An additional 350,000 automobiles must be drained of oil and gasoline and then recycled; 60,000 boats may need to be destroyed; and 300,000 underground fuel tanks and 42,000 tons of hazardous waste must be collected and properly disposed of at licensed facilities.[38]

- Government officials peg the numbers of cars lost in New Orleans alone at 145,000.[39]

FLOODED HOMES

- An estimated 140,000 to 160,000 homes in Louisiana may need to be demolished and disposed of.[40]

- More than 110,000 of New Orleans' 180,000 houses were flooded, and half sat for days or weeks in more than six feet of water.[41]

- As many as 30,000 to 50,000 homes in New Orleans may have to be demolished, while many others could be saved with extensive repairs.[42]

FLOODED SCHOOLS

- Katrina displaced more than an estimated 350,000 school children in the Gulf Coast—187,000 in Louisiana, 160,000 in Mississippi, and 3,118 in Alabama.[43]

- The powerful storm closed the New Orleans school system and left a trail of toxic muck in classrooms and on playgrounds. Over 93 percent of New Orleans' 125,000 public school children are African American.[44]

What the Community Can Do

Hurricane Katrina exposed the systematic weakness of the nation's emergency preparedness and response to disasters. The powerful storm also exposed the racial divide in the way the U.S. government responds to natural and manmade disasters in this country. It is time for *all* Americans to receive equal environmental protection. African Americans must demand that government agencies charged with protecting them use uniform cleanup standards to ensure equal protection of public health and environmental justice: (1) what gets cleaned up, (2) where the waste is disposed, (3) what gets rebuilt, and (4) where it gets rebuilt are key environmental and social equity issues.

Because of the enormous human suffering and environmental devastation, the rebuilding of New Orleans and the Louisiana, Mississippi, and Alabama Gulf Coast region will test the nation's ability and commitment to address lingering social inequality and institutional barriers that created and maintained the racial divide of "two Americas," one Black and poor and the other white and affluent.

What Every Individual Can Do Now:

- Do not forget the victims of Katrina. The rebuilding effort will go on for several years. Write to your congressional representatives and demand follow-up action and support.

- Educate yourself, your family, and your friends about issues of environmental justice.

- Find out about air quality, water quality, and toxic waste sites in your community.

- When you hear about environmental concerns in your communities, help to organize meetings, attend all gatherings, and encourage others to do the same.

- Make sure your home is free from the hazards of lead poisoning.

MOST OF ALL:

- Hold all leaders and elected officials responsible and demand that they change current policy.

What Works Now:

Several communities across America have been in the vanguard of seeking and securing environmental justice. A few of their stories follows.

West Harlem Environmental Action (WE ACT)

West Harlem Environmental Action (WE ACT) was founded to address ongoing West Harlem community struggles around the poor management of the North River Sewage Treatment Plant and the construction of the sixth bus depot across from an intermediate school and a large housing development—a densely populated and heavily trafficked area.[45] WE ACT evolved into an environmental justice organization committed to empowering the community to become a vocal, an informed, and a proactive force that determines and implements its vision of what its environment can and should be.

WE ACT had three key objectives: to force the City of New York to fix the North River Plant, to participate in determining future siting and planning decisions in West Harlem, and to affect the public policy agenda by positioning environmental justice as a major political issue. The organization has succeeded in meeting these objectives.

Through its perseverance and dedication to the community, WE ACT has achieved a number of environmental justice victories, including starting the New York City Environmental Justice Alliance (NYCEJA), through which WE ACT and its partnering community organizations reached a settlement of their lawsuit against the city. It established a $1.1 million fund related to environmental health and quality of life. It also gave WE ACT the leverage to ensure that the city completed its five-year, $55 million fixup of the North River Sewage

Treatment Plant. WE ACT also convinced the EPA to conduct the first assessment of Northern Manhattan's air quality. The assessment revealed that harmful particulates were more than 200 percent higher than the air quality standards for diesel soot.[46]

While there are far too many accomplishments to describe here, WE ACT has created significant change in Harlem.

Detroiters Working for Environmental Justice

Residents of Detroit are coming together to "Take a Stand for the Land in the Neighborhoods" as Detroiters Working for Environmental Justice (DWEJ).[47] Its mission is to stop the rise of asthma and other upper respiratory problems in the community. This is particularly important because Wayne County ranks fifth in the country demonstrating the greatest increase in asthma-related deaths among the African American population; it has some of the worst air quality in America.

The organization also works to reduce and eliminate the number of lead-poisoned children. Detroit has two-thirds of the known lead poisoning cases among children for the entire state of Michigan. This may be because of the disproportionate number of polluting facilities—incinerators, factories, small manufacturing companies, and gas stations—near homes, playgrounds, and schools.

DWEJ has also pledged to clean up contaminated land; stop "illegal dumping" in neighborhoods throughout the city that have been targeted as prime sites to dump construction debris, tires, trash, and barrels that contain contamination; and to improve water quality.

This organization of concerned citizens believes that community participation must be increased in land use decisions. Residents must have the opportunity to participate in decisions about what happens in their neighborhoods. Too many African Americans live near facilities that may be polluting the air and land without their knowledge.

DWEJ is committed to increasing the voice of the people when it comes to making decisions that impact the quality of their lives.

Louisiana Environmental Action Network (LEAN)

LEAN was founded to help Louisiana citizens change the balance of power and challenge the continued economic and ecological suicide of the community. By empowering more than one hundred grassroots community organizations and countless individuals, LEAN has already helped in gaining a tremendous foothold in the war to make Louisiana's communities safer, healthier places to live. LEAN's expanded efforts will allow the progress already made to continue.[48]

LEAN's purpose is to foster cooperation and communication between individual citizens and corporate and government organizations in an effort to assess and correct the environmental problems in Louisiana. LEAN's goal is the creation and maintenance of a cleaner and healthier environment for all of the state's inhabitants.

One of its key programs is "Healthy Schools, Healthy Students," designed to educate young students about the required safety when handling pesticides and about the programs and laws that Louisiana has concerning pesticides within and around schools.

Its specific goals are to: raise public awareness regarding pesticide safety; empower youth through environmental education, artistic creativity, and civic participation; and ensure safe and healthy educational learning facilities for all school children. While LEAN has been working to protect the health of Louisiana communities for many years, it is now focused on the future: school children. Throughout the United States, pesticides are being used in and around schools to control pests and to curb sanitary and health problems. Through the years citizens and public officials have come to realize that the exposure of youth to these chemicals may have harmful effects.[49]

In addition to its work in Louisiana's schools, LEAN has been instrumental in helping those who lost everything during Hurricane Katrina. It is determined to rebuild the devastated cities and fight for environmental justice for all of Louisiana's residents.

What Every Leader and Elected Official Can Do

- Enforce existing environmental and health standards in ensuring environmental justice for all.

- Implement Environmental Justice Executive Order 12898.

- Create and maintain healthy, clean, and safe schools for children.

- Clean up and rebuild historically Black colleges and universities (HBCUs) and develop partnerships with them.

- Manage debris.

- Involve impacted communities in environmental decision-making.

Enforce Existing Environmental and Health Standards

The U.S. Environmental Protection Agency (EPA) should uniformly enforce the environmental laws that are on the books. Toxic waste and cleanup standards should not be weakened or compromised in low-income and minority neighborhoods.

In Dickson, Tennessee, located 35 miles west of Nashville, an African American family is engaged in a heated battle against environmental racism practiced by the city, county, and state governments, as well as the federal EPA. The Dickson County Landfill first opened as a city dump in the heart of the mostly Black Eno Road community in 1968. The Harry Holt family home is within 500 feet from the landfill where the Scovill-Shrader Automotive manufacturing plant buried drums of industrial waste.[50]

Government records indicate that trichloroethylene (TCE), a suspected carcinogen, was found in the Harry Holt and Lavinia Holt wells as early as 1988, the same year the Tennessee Department of Environment and Conservation (TDEC) issued a permit to Dickson County for operation of the facility as a sanitary landfill. The TDEC approved the Dickson County landfill permit on Dec. 2, 1988—even though test results completed the month before on the Harry Holt and Lavinia Holt wells showed TCE contamination.[51]

Six days after the landfill permit was approved, TDEC sent the Holts letters dishonestly stating that their water was of good quality and that excessive levels of toxic substances were because of a sampling or lab error. In fact, government tests found five times above the established Maximum Contaminant Level (MCL) of TCE in the Holt wells. Three years later, EPA officials sent another letter to the Holt family, informing them "use of your well water should not result in any adverse health effect."[52]

The TDEC sampled the Holt family wells again about 10 years later and noted the presence of TCE at 29 times the MCL.[53] It was only after the extraordinarily high TCE levels in 2000 that a Dickson County landfill official visited the Holt family, informing them that their wells were unsafe. No written test results were sent to the family on the 2000 tests. The Holt family was placed on the county tap water system in December 2000, 12 years after government tests first detected TCE in their wells.

Governmental agencies treated white families in Dickson very differently from the Black Holt family. Nine white families whose wells were found to have TCE contamination were notified within 48 hours of that determination and informed not to drink the well water.[54] On the other hand, various levels of government knowingly allowed the Holt family to drink TCE-contaminated well water from 1988 to 2000. The case is still pending in the Dickson County courts.

Officials at all levels of government must equally protect all citizens. It is unjust to allow African Americans to live in hazardous conditions while warning and saving their white neighbors. Allowing waivers of environmental standards could compound the harm already caused by previous disasters and current ones such as Katrina; they undermine health protection of the most vulnerable members of our society.

Enforce the Environmental
Justice Executive Order 12898

On Feb. 11, 1994, President Clinton signed Executive Order 12898 requiring that all federal agencies address environmental justice in minority populations and low-income populations.[55]

To ensure equal funding, equal cleanup standards, and equal protection of public health in minority and low-income communities, the EPA, FEMA, and the Army Corps of Engineers need to enforce the Environmental Justice Executive Order 12898 in cleaning up and rebuilding the hurricane-affected Gulf Coast region. These agencies should report to Congress on their compliance with this provision monthly for the next 24 months to ensure that minority and low-income communities do not receive disparate treatment.

Create and Maintain Healthy,
Clean, And Safe Schools

It is imperative that schools and the land on which they sit are safe, clean, and free from health-threatening contamination. Existing schools and school grounds should be tested and remediated to the most protective, existing cleanup guidelines set by the EPA.

Repairs, rehabilitation, and construction of new schools should use the best green construction and "green-building" technology to ensure healthy indoor air, nontoxic materials for construction, maximum design for energy efficiency, and natural light for improved learning. Children learn faster and do better on standardized tests in classrooms with more daylight.

Clean Up, Rebuild, and Partner With Historically
Black Colleges and Universities (HBCUs)

Government and community-driven cleanup and rebuilding efforts must include restoring Black cultural and educational institutions, especially the historically Black colleges and universities in New

Orleans—Dillard University, Xavier University, and Southern University—that were damaged by Katrina.

A defined role for HBCUs in close proximity to brownfields redevelopment and related pilot programs should be included in the remediation process from local to federal levels. Many of the nation's 105 HBCUs are located in or near communities suffering from environmental problems. Urban universities, with their multiple social and physical sciences specialists, are natural partners in land use decision-making in environmental remediation.

Manage Debris

Hurricane Betsy struck the State of Louisiana and the City of New Orleans in 1965, hitting the mostly Black and poor New Orleans' Lower Ninth Ward especially hard. Debris was buried in the Agricultural Street Landfill—located in a predominately Black New Orleans neighborhood.[56] Over 390 homes were built on the northern portion of the 95-acre landfill site from 1976 to 1986. The Agricultural Street Landfill neighborhood was added to the National Priorities List as a Superfund site in 1994 because of toxic contaminants such as metals, polycyclic aromatic hydrocarbons (PAHs), volatile organic compounds, and pesticides.

The actual cleanup began in 1998 and was completed in 2001. The Concerned Citizens of Agriculture Street Landfill filed a class-action suit against the city for damages and cost of relocation. It took nine years to bring this case to court.[57] The case was still pending when Katrina struck.

Weeks after Katrina hit, the Louisiana Department of Environmental Quality (LDEQ) allowed New Orleans to open the 200-acre Old Gentilly Landfill to dump construction and demolition waste from the storm.[58] Federal regulators had ordered the unlined landfill closed in the 1980s. LDEQ officials insist that the old landfill meets all standards, while residents and environmentalists disagree, questioning the safety and suitability of dumping at the old landfill. Even some high-ranking elected officials have expressed fear that reopening the

Old Gentilly Landfill could create an ecological nightmare.[59] The land-fill caught fire four days after environmentalists filed a lawsuit to block the dumping.[60]

Wastes and debris from Katrina should be recycled and disposed of using methods that meet existing environmental and health standards. It is equally imperative that cleanup standards, building codes, and land use designations not be used as tools to discriminate against and ultimately kill off "low-lying" Black neighborhoods.

Involve Impacted Communities in Environmental Decision-Making

Promote Environmental Justice-Driven Community Development

Impacted residents must be involved in all environmental health decisions made regarding the cleanup, recovery, and rebuilding of damaged communities and brownfields. The EPA and other federal agencies must work closely with the local communities most affected by environmental problems in decisions on cleanup, recovery, and rebuilding to ensure a democratic and safe process.

Local officials must also strengthen policy requirements and enforcement mechanisms to safeguard environmental health for all brownfields projects. (A brownfield is a property that the expansion, redevelopment, or reuse of may be complicated by the presence or potential presence of a hazardous substance, pollutant, or contam-inant.)[61] Hurricane Katrina has created brownfields across the Gulf Coast region. Removing health risks must be the main priority of all brownfields action plans.

Government agencies, community members, and environmental justice organizations should all become involved in and support one another in redeveloping local neighborhoods to integrate brownfields priorities into long-range neighborhood redevelopment plans. This will allow for the use of Tax Increment Finance (TIF) funds accrued by the redevelopment process to fund the cleanup and redevelopment of brownfields sites for community-determined uses.

Institute Anti-Displacement
Provisions in Brownfields Redevelopment

City officials should not only prevent displacement, but must also support community-driven planning and programming activities that minimize or eliminate displacement of incumbent residents. Government funding should support efforts to expand opportunities for community-based organizations to purchase and redevelop properties in their neighborhoods, in partnership with African American business entrepreneurs through existing brownfields redevelopment programs. Government agencies at all levels—particularly at the local and regional levels—should provide tax benefits and subsidies typically given to private institutions.

A Final Word

The environmental justice movement demands an end to environmental racism and development policies and practices that endanger the health of the environment and displace people from their homes and neighborhoods. African Americans and other people of color have a right to a clean, safe, just, healthy, and sustainable environment. Unless the issue of environmental justice is addressed squarely in the aftermath of Hurricane Katrina, there will not be any Black New Orleans neighborhoods to recover or redevelop.

ASSURING ENVIRONMENTAL JUSTICE FOR ALL

In 1994 President Clinton issued Executive Order 12898, Federal Actions to Address Environmental Justice in Minority Populations and Low-Income Populations,[1] directing federal agencies to identify and address disproportionate adverse environmental effects on minority and low-income populations. The Environmental Protection Agency (EPA) has defined environmental justice as:

> The fair treatment and meaningful involvement of all people regardless of race, color, national origin, or income with respect to the development, implementation, and enforcement of environmental laws, regulations, and policies. Fair treatment means that no group of people, including racial, ethnic, or socioeconomic group should bear a disproportionate share of the negative environmental consequences resulting from industrial, municipal, and commercial operations or the execution of federal, state, local, and tribal programs and policies.[2]

In the 2006 first print edition of this text, Robert D. Bullard focused on several issues in the field of environmental justice, noting that race maps closely with the geography of environmental risks. He explained that lead poisoning was the number-one environmental health threat to children of color in the United States, especially poor children and children living in inner cities. Race was found to be the most important variable—more so than poverty, land values, and homeownership—in predicting where toxic waste facilities were located, with three out of five African and Latino Americans living in communities with abandoned toxic waste sites.

How has the situation changed in the last decade? Certainly, the issue has gained prominence. In 2010, the U.S. EPA administrator, Lisa Jackson, announced that "expanding the conversation on environmentalism and working for environmental justice" would be one of seven top priorities for the agency.[3] And while at one time, environmental justice in the not-for-profit world was a subset of either environmental or civil rights initiatives, today there appear to be more organizations dedicated specifically to the topic. But have environmental outcomes and institutional performance followed developments in the rhetoric and activities?

To interpret the detailed description originally provided by this chapter in 2006, and to understand the developments that have happened since, it is important to start outside the realm of environmental justice; one must start with economic justice. Disparities in environmental quality occur not only across races, but also across incomes. However, this is a distinction without much difference.

In 2014, the median annual income of white households was approximately $60,000. For Black and Hispanic households, the figures were $35,000 and $42,000 respectively.[4] Approximately 25 percent of the Black and Hispanic population lived in poverty, compared to only 10 percent of the white population. Thus, whether environmental justice occurs across racial boundaries or economic strata, the burden lies disproportionately on minorities.

One of the implications of a world where households are mobile and low-income households (for reasons of economizing on housing) are inclined to settle in areas with environmental disamenities is that over time minority households could disproportionately migrate to areas that expose them to high levels of environmental risk.[5] The combination of household mobility and economic disparities means that it is not enough to prevent new environmental risks from entering predominantly minority neighborhoods. Rather, to end environmental disparities, either environmental risk must be substantially ameliorated in all neighborhoods or economic disparities across races must be eliminated.

Turning specifically to environmental justice, overall there seem to be improvements in the general quality of the environment, but the disparities across racial and income groups have by no means disappeared. It is challenging to get a precise read on developments over the past decade because many of the recent studies are using data that predate 2006.[6] That alone indicates one of the sources of the problem: there are challenges just in documenting trends over time.

Environmental justice is not only about substantive and procedural issues, it is about process.[7] Substantive justice and distributional justice involve unequal exposure to risk, unequal enforcement of regulations, and unequal responsiveness to remedial needs. Process justice involves disparate access to information on exposure, unequal access to the rule making process, and under-representation during the development of research priorities. Issues in process make it more difficult to assess issues in substantive outcome and procedure.

In 2006, lead poisoning was reported to be the top environmental threat to children of color in the United States. The CDC considers levels of blood lead concentrations above 5 µg/dL to warrant public health concerns. In samples taken between 2003 and 2006 from Black and white children (aged 1 to 5 years), 12.1 and 2.3 percent, respectively, had blood lead levels at or above that threshold. The mean blood levels found in that testing were 2.4 and 1.5 µg/dL, respectively.[8]

Through strategies to eliminate lead in vehicle fuels, in paint, and in products for children, there have been substantial improvements in a relatively short time. The regulatory changes, coupled with "identification and increased screening of populations at high risk," have led to significant reductions in blood lead levels, especially among

Black fellow citizens and low-income groups.[9] Testing between 2007 and 2010 showed that while the percentage of children with elevated blood lead levels had remained essentially constant among white children, it had fallen to 5.6 percent among Black children, a more than 50 percent drop. During that same period, the average blood lead level among Black children had dropped by 25 percent. This is welcome news, indeed.

Recent studies also indicate, however, that racial disparities in the location of hazardous waste facilities continue. A 2012 national-scale study found that both poor and predominantly minority communities are more likely to contain brownfield sites than other communities. (As defined by the EPA, brownfields are locations that are "complicated by the presence or potential presence of a hazardous substance, pollutant, or contaminant.") Perhaps more significant, sites located in poor communities tend to be cleaned up relatively quickly, but those sites in communities with predominantly minority populations tend to be cleaned up relatively slowly.[10]

The burden of pollution emissions also continues to fall disproportionately on minorities and low-income households. For example, a 2011 study found that where monitoring data exists, both low-income and minority communities have higher exposures to particulate matter (known as PM 2.5) and ozone.[11] There is also recent evidence that ethnic and racial disparities in exposure to air toxics are greatest among low-income neighborhoods (those with households whose median annual income is lower than $25,000).[12]

The data and analysis with respect to both the siting of hazardous facilities and exposure to pollution emissions does not provide a complete picture of recent developments; it is difficult to identify clear trends over the past decade in these two areas. However, two conclusions are clear. First, minority communities tend to live nearer to hazardous waste facilities, though not all studies agree on the causal mechanism behind this. Second, minority communities are exposed to higher levels of air pollutants than non-minority communities, and these exposures result in adverse health outcomes for those communities. Thus, on distributional and procedural grounds, there is much work to be done.

Turning to the process elements of environmental justice, the record is mixed. For example, the EPA has recently released a new tool, the Environmental Justice Screening and Mapping Tool, or EJSCREEN, that provides geographic information on the distribution of 12 indicators related to air, waste, lead paint, and water quality.[13] EJSCREEN also provides data on six demographic indicators related to income, race, education, and age. This tool promises to provide a means for researchers and activists to examine and document patterns that are important to assessing environmental justice outcomes.

Following Administrator Jackson's 2011 announcement that the agency would increase its environmental justice focus, the Agency released Plan EJ 2014, a road map to guide EPA integration of environmental justice into its programs.[14] The plan identifies ambitious goals and outlines a path forward. Each year the agency develops a report to track progress on the plan. This is a step toward transparency and inclusion.

In another positive move, the Agency's Environmental Justice Small Grants Program, established in 1994, had awarded over 1,000 grants by 2007. However, it is not apparent from the EPA website how funding for the program has evolved since 2007, only that it continues to operate. Moreover, with relatively minimal funding (peaking at $3,000,000 in 1995 and bottoming at $423,545 in 2004), the program appears to have more symbolic than substantive impact.[15] In fact, one of the products of that program, the "Emerging Tools for Local Problem-Solving," has not been updated in more than seven years.[16]

Similarly, there are other disturbing signs of EPA's lack of diligence in addressing environmental justice, evidenced by even a casual perusal of the agency's Environmental Justice webpages. All of the documents on the Project Reports page are more than a dozen years old.[17] The Action Plans and Accomplishment/Progress Reports page doesn't appear to have been updated for over five years.[18] The EJ Fact Sheets have not been updated in the past three years.[19] In short, if the EPA Environmental Justice webpages are intended to share information and signal the EPA's energetic treatment of the issue, they need substantial work.

In sum, this brief review of environmental justice developments over the past decade seems to support the conclusions of the excellent treat of the issue in the recent book, *Failed Promises: Evaluating the Federal Government's Response to Environmental Justice*:[20] "While the conclusion [of this book] is that the federal government has thus far failed to live up to the promise of the executive order [EO 12898], the contributors also find a new concern for environmental justice at the EPA, with significant steps being taken to translate the initial concerns into specific changes in rulemaking, permitting, enforcement, and community engagement."

—Prepared by Kenneth R. Richards, Ph.D., J.D., Professor of Environmental and Energy Policy, School of Public and Environmental Affairs; Affiliated Professor of Environmental and Energy Law, Maurer School of Law; Affiliated Faculty, Vincent and Elinor Ostrom Workshop in Political Theory and Policy Analysis, Indiana University, Bloomington, Indiana

✢ ✢

X.

CLOSING THE RACIAL DIGITAL DIVIDE

INTRODUCTORY ESSAY
BY TYRONE D. TABORN

Within a span of six decades, there have been four revolutionary advancements in computer-based technology. Since World War II, computer technology has advanced from automation, to information technology, to the personal computer, and now to digital technologies. In each succeeding wave, companies were created, lifestyles changed, and fortunes made and lost. Ironically, when these windows of opportunity opened, African Americans could not exploit them. Blacks were shut out at the birth of digital technologies, when the most wealth was created. When they came in, they participated mainly as consumers.

In recent years, there has been much discussion surrounding Black participation in digital technology. Studies and reports have exposed the gap between Blacks and whites in computer ownership and Internet access. Both are important subjects, but narrow in their scope. More recently, the discussion has advanced to digital inclusion, as well as African American participation in areas such as business development and content creation.[1]

Global forces in technology, research, science, and telecommunications make it clear that the future will not hold much promise for generations of Blacks if the trends that limit African American participation in the global digital technology economy are not reversed. Young Blacks entering an information-based, technology-driven marketplace without the necessary technological skill sets will not only be unemployable, they will be irrelevant.

Trends and America's Changing Status

In his book *The World is Flat: A Brief History of the Twenty-first Century,* Thomas Friedman describes how rapidly the world is changing and talks about major trends driving that change—digital and technological world globalization, the growth of outsourcing, and the commodity of jobs.[2]

Interesting as these factors are in explaining the digital globalization of the world, what is more profound is how Friedman and others were unprepared for these social and economic shifts. Americans went to sleep, only to wake up and find themselves in a fight for survival. It all happened that quickly.

What happened was that many nations once happy with second-hand shoes wanted to make their own. With accessibility to technology and information created by the personal computer revolution, these nations amassed the knowledge, workers, and technology infrastructure to do just that.

Advancements in digital technologies and telecommunications allowed other nations to challenge the United States' global standing. Players were no longer just Japan or Europe; India and China were also in the technology game, and the rules had changed. Now they were calling some of the shots.

So how, in the span of 30 years, did the United States go from being an unchallenged technology leader to a nation falling behind in innovation? And what does that mean for African Americans?

One explanation seems obvious. Many business leaders underestimated the impact that personal computers would have in the hands of millions and the speed of change to follow. But there were other, historical reasons why no one believed the United States would ever really be challenged as the world's technology leader.

World War II had resulted in breakthroughs in computer technology that would soon be of commercial value. Most War Department investments in the U.S. technology base contributed to industry's technological innovation in automation and mass production techniques. From the start of the computer age in the 1940s and through the 1980s, the U.S. economy had been good at exporting blue-collar and manufacturing jobs overseas to a cheaper labor market. Workers moved from performing the tasks to operating the machines that replaced them. Therefore, skilled craftsmen and tradesmen were no longer needed to operate machinery, and fewer workers were needed in general. The American workers' jobs became commodities that were easily exported to a cheaper labor force.

Those jobs were then replaced with new ones requiring greater skill sets that could not be easily exported. U.S. colleges and universities turned out tens of thousands of highly skilled science, engineering, and technology workers. Immigrants coming to the United States, though creating a brain drain in their homelands, filled vacancies in research and industry. Because of the huge amount of capital required to develop a national technology infrastructure, few challenged American companies.

But all that changed as the personal computer ushered in the digital revolution. Because of IBM's Mark Dean, Ph.D., an African American engineer who co-invented key components of the IBM computer, the personal computer would move from labs to millions of desktops and homes in less than 30 years. The power of the personal computer fundamentally changed the world, as programmers, designers, and manufacturers brought ideas and new business models to life. Just as important, the affordability of computing power allowed new players in the technology field.

Numerous entrepreneurs seized opportunities in the beginning of the personal computer revolution to make fortunes. Notable examples are Bill Gates at Microsoft and Michael Dell of Dell Computers. But while billions of dollars were being made both in the United States and abroad in the growing technology market, the attention of Blacks would be elsewhere. Lagging in employment, income levels, and health-care access, few African Americans were able to benefit from these opportunities. During this period, when the role of technology and computers was being explored in businesses and government agencies, Blacks were focused on securing public accommodation in education, employment, housing, and government.

Meanwhile, in Taiwan, Korea, and other Asian countries, new technology and technology suppliers were being born as well. All of these economic entrants proved that technology could provide opportunities and huge financial returns in a realistic time frame.

If investing billions of dollars in oil refineries may have been out of reach for many developing nations, investing in data processing was not. Governments seized opportunities that digital technologies would create, and the Internet and high-speed telecommunications removed geographical barriers.

Politicians also realized that the low-skilled workers who filled America's outsourced manufacturing jobs were not prepared to meet the demands of technical positions. Creating skilled workers became a priority for nations such as India and China; they embarked on ambitious educational agendas that would yield a technologically capable workforce and were soon willing to compete for jobs. Before long, it was not the steel or textile worker whose job was going overseas; engineering, law, accounting, and medical technician jobs were also going begging in the United States.

With a growing supply of talent, investors, and technically educated citizens, India and China could take on America at innovation and research. Plus, because of tighter immigration rules put in place after the September 11, 2001, terrorist attacks, foreign workers started looking for opportunities closer to home. For the first time in history, America faces a reverse brain drain.

It is important to grasp where we are now, because this is where we African Americans can establish ourselves as an invaluable part of society. If not, we risk becoming a permanent lower class with decreasing influence.

How Do We Compete?

The world's need for technology will only grow, creating endless opportunities. Of course, it is imperative for Blacks to close the gap of computer ownership, access to broadband Internet, and computer and technology literacy to participate and compete in the digital economy. But computers are no more than tools that enable greater productivity if used correctly. There are other hurdles that remain.

First, to play a meaningful role in the digital economy, Blacks must deal with the quality of education in schools. Today, almost every job requires technology skills or computer knowledge, so every Black child must understand that the world is becoming a technology-driven place, and the number of Black students prepared to participate in the higher levels of technology must be increased.

According to John Slaughter, Ph.D., President of the National Action Council for Minorities in Engineering (NACME), more than one-half million minority students will graduate from high school this year. Only 32,000 of them will complete the necessary science and math courses to be considered for entry into engineering school; of that number, about 15,000 will enroll. At the end of the undergraduate process, fewer than 4,000 Black engineers will join the ranks of 72,000 other U.S. engineering graduates.[3] This does not come close to the 219,563 India will produce or the 400,000 China will add to its workforce.[4]

Our historically Black colleges and universities (HBCUs) are a great source of talent. Yet, they receive a mere fraction of our federal research dollars.[5] I believe that our HBCUs with accredited schools of engineering need about $1 billion for the investments and infrastructure to produce real and meaningful results for our nation. The small program grants that they now receive do little more then keep a few faculty members on staff. We are at a critical point, and with real funding, these schools can increase their output in key areas.

We need something significant: perhaps a unified federal research lab on homeland security, rather than the current system, wherein every single university tries to build its capacity but will never match those of Cornell, MIT, or Johns Hopkins. There could be one institution to which all of the HBCUs send their best and brightest, a place with sufficient resources invested to make a true impact with immediate and notable results.

In addition to improving education, Black participation in the business side of technology is critical. There were 1.2 million Black-owned businesses in 2002, but only 94,862 Black-owned businesses had paid employees, and their receipts totaled $69.8 billion, or an average of $735,586 per firm.[6]

Black-owned businesses with no paid employees numbered 1.1 million, up 51 percent from 1997. They had receipts of $22.9 billion, up 54 percent from 1997. The average receipts of these businesses were $20,761 per firm. One-quarter of the businesses in Washington, DC, were Black-owned. Black-owned businesses accounted for 12–15 percent of firms in Maryland, Georgia, Mississippi, and Louisiana.[7]

Blacks also need to increase their representation in corporate America. They still make up only a small percentage of the technology workforce and top management.[8] Increasing these numbers will have many benefits. Black corporate leaders can influence their employers to purchase from Black-owned companies; invest in Black colleges, banks, and institutions; and build branches and plants in Black communities, thus helping to drive investments.

The Black community must take ownership of the development of its youth. Many parents in the Black community have abdicated responsibility, while others simply lack the skills to advocate and maneuver the system. In the past two decades, the percentage of Black families headed by both husband and wife has dropped from 70 percent to 48 percent.[9]

Several factors in the community can help young people choose math and science. A role model is a major factor that sparks a child's interest in science and technology, but given that there are so few in our communities, many Black children will not meet a mentor. Science-based after-school programs and field trips also influence children to choose science and technology. Churches and community groups can play a powerful role in increasing science and technology by providing programs and support resources that many Black households cannot provide.

So: (1) improving the education of Black students, (2) increasing federal grants to and perhaps initiating federal programs for HBCUs, (3) heightening Black participation in business, (4) boosting Black representation in corporate America, and (5) fostering and utilizing our resources in the Black community are realistic and necessary goals for reversing current trends. They are important issues to focus on when it comes to Black involvement in the digital technology revolution, and they are just as important as focusing on computer ownership and Internet access.

Now is the time to push for change within our schools and businesses and communities, because far-reaching, unpredictable global changes are occurring rapidly. This is a critical time in history, and the stakes could not be higher. And the truth is that we will not succeed—as a culture or as a nation—without the inclusion and full participation of Black people.

÷

TYRONE D. TABORN, Ph.D. (honoris causa), is Editor-in-Chief, Publisher, and Chief Executive Officer of Career Communications Group, which has created an integrated and inspiring group of magazines, dynamic websites, and outstanding annual national conferences that provide a powerful forum for organizations to find and retain the best and brightest minority technologists. He is the founder of the Black Family Tech Week program, which is sponsored by the IBM Corporation, as well as the founder of La Familia Technology Awareness Week and the Native American Technology Awareness Project. For more information: www.ccgmedia.com.

THE FACTS ON THE DIGITAL DIVIDE

DIMENSIONS OF THE RACIAL DIGITAL DIVIDE

- Nearly 51 percent of African Americans have access to a home computer compared to 74.6 percent of whites. In terms of Internet access, only 40.5 percent of African Americans have access to the Internet at home compared to 67.3 percent of whites.[10]

- While 52.8 percent of African American children have access to a computer at home, fully 85.5 percent of white children do. Forty-one percent of African American children have access to the Internet at home, but 77.4 percent of white children have such access.[11]

- Nearly 14 percent of African Americans have access to broadband Internet at home—the strongest predictor of intensity and sophistication of Internet use, even more so than years of Internet experience—while 26.1 percent of whites do.[12]

EDUCATIONAL IMPLICATIONS

- Black children are roughly 35 percent less likely to have a computer at home and have Internet access than white children.[13] Given that fact and considering the following, African Americans are at an educational disadvantage:

  - Teenagers with access to a home computer are 6 to 8 percent more likely to graduate from high school than teenagers who do not have computers at home.[14]

  - Sixty-eight percent of Internet users who searched for colleges stated the Internet played a role in their choice.[15]

EMPLOYMENT IMPLICATIONS

- African Americans are at a disadvantage in terms of employment because, on the job, 60 percent of all workers use a computer and 46 percent use the Internet. For jobs that require a college degree, 85 percent of workers use a

computer and 74 percent use the Internet. Even less educated workers must increasingly have computer skills. For
those with only a high school diploma, 43 percent use a
computer at work and 27 percent use the Internet.[16]

USAGE

- Of African American adults who use the Internet: 47
  percent look for religious and spiritual information, 34
  percent search for political information, and 63 percent
  conduct research for school or training.[17]

- Seventy-eight percent of African American teen Internet
  users spend time communicating by e-mail; 50 percent of
  them regularly use Instant Messenger.[18]

What the Community Can Do

Information technology permeates every aspect of life. Not only
must we be concerned about making sure our children, families, and
communities have access—which has been the goal of efforts to
close the digital divide—but we must also make sure we are using
technology to close the *historical* divide. Through effective use, we
can bridge the health divide, the educational divide, and the wealth
divide that have prevented Black people from being able to fully participate and prosper.

What Every Individual Can Do Now:

- If you do not have a computer at home, identify your
  closest community learning center; inquire about
  computer training courses it has available.

- Invest in a home computer, especially if you have
  children.

- Make sure your home computer is connected to the
  Internet.

- Encourage your child's school to offer computer literacy courses, including word processing, web design, and Internet research techniques.

MOST OF ALL:

- Hold all leaders and elected officials responsible and demand that they change current policy.

What Works Now:

Following are some instructive as well as inventive examples of what communities are doing to close the racial digital divide.

Rosa L. Parks Learning Centers

The Rosa L. Parks Learning Centers, in Michigan and California, have developed a program where youths mentor seniors in basic computer literacy. Mrs. Parks was a graduate of the first class in 1997.[19] By the end of the session, senior citizens demonstrate increased motor activity and motivation to learn, while they impart wisdom based on their life experiences as a part of the interactive learning experience.[20]

The program exposes young people to the common sense of the community's elders while also enhancing their own academic skills. Youth are rarely given the opportunity to teach others, but in this case they empower themselves and achieve an even greater sense of self-worth by passing on their knowledge.

In addition, society often assumes that senior citizens do not need to be intellectually stimulated or taught new skills. The Rosa L. Parks Learning Centers recognize that no member of the Black community can be forgotten.

Eastmont Computing Center

This Community Learning Center in East Oakland operated by the Oakland Citizens Committee for Urban Renewal is dedicated to providing universal access and employment-focused progressive training to underserved communities in Oakland. Eastmont Computing Center's emphasis is on youth; however, it is a resource for all members of the city's underserved communities.[21] The organization's services include free computer and Internet access; job training and placement for youth; and technology resources for local schools, libraries, and nonprofits that do not have their own access. Eastmont Computing Center is unique in its efforts, considering the fact that it serves over 30,000 people living within one mile of the center.[22]

There are a number of exciting programs housed at Eastmont, among them: the Intel Computer Clubhouse and the Computer Community Service Project. The Clubhouse "provides a creative and safe after-school learning environment where young people . . . work with adult mentors to explore their own ideas, develop skills, and build confidence in themselves through the use of technology."[23]

During each three-month Community Service class, youth complete two to three community service projects using the skills they have learned. Sixty students per year have the opportunity to learn up to three of six possible areas in depth: Desktop Support, Community Information Web Publishing, Community Information Paper Publishing, Community Information Video Publishing, Networking and Technical Services, and Office Database Administration.[24]

National Black Family Technology Awareness Week

National Black Family Technology Awareness Week—a program founded and developed by Career Communications Group, Inc. (CCG)—educates and empowers African American families through technology.[25] CCG's overall mission is "to promote significant minority achievement in engineering, science, and technology,"[26] and it believes that the family unit is a perfect place to start.

CCG outlines the following agenda for National Black Family Tech Awareness Week. On Black Family Technology Sunday, stimulate interest in the Black Family Technology Awareness program by explaining why this event is of great importance, present the action that each family should very seriously consider when the week is over, and ensure all participants that a community organization will work with and help them to bridge the digital divide if they are willing to make the needed commitments of time, energy, and money. The remaining breakout: Business Opportunity Monday, Technology Health Tuesday, Technology Education Wednesday, Discover Your Future Thursday, Technology Pioneers Friday, and Technology Everybody Can Play Saturday.[27]

Over the course of the week, participants empower themselves and their families, learn how to access health and nutrition information on the Internet, become informed of educational resources for adults and children, discover the wealth of online employment opportunities, and learn how the "web weaves itself around [all aspects] of our lives today."[28] Black families will be able to change their lives by the end of the program.

What Every Leader and Elected Official Can Do

- Increase computer ownership among youths and families.

- Increase training opportunities and resources to develop digital literacy and advanced skills.

- Create state funding sources to extend the Internet to organizations that serve low-income communities.

- Protect and support the ability of local governments to ensure affordable broadband access.

- Make universal broadband access a credible goal of state and local policy.

Increase Computer Ownership Among Youths and Low-Income Families

The alarming trend of a widening digital divide between African American and white children demands policy responses that seek to extend to *all* children the educational and economic opportunities that computers can offer. The prohibitive cost of computers for many low-income African American families means that state and local governments, as well as the philanthropy community, have a critical role to play in ensuring universal computer ownership in families with children.

Several states have taken the lead in pioneering initiatives to help remedy this problem. In 2002, Maine inaugurated an ambitious plan to equip every seventh and eighth grade student and teacher with a laptop computer.[29] Known as the Maine Learning Technology Initiative, this bold statewide strategy seeks to eliminate the digital divide and to create some of the most technology savvy students in the world. Seeing schools as a critical, but not the only, venue by which computers can have an impact on the lives of children, the state opted for a policy approach that would extend the benefits of computer use to the homes of children as well. Maine sets a compelling example for its sister states to follow in bridging the digital divide.

The state of Washington has begun to help remedy the digital divide affecting its low-income families. In 2005, the legislature enacted revisions to its law pertaining to Individual Development Accounts (IDAs) to allow purchases of home computers.[30] IDAs are a state-supported, asset-building approach for low- to moderate-income families. Families are provided with a savings account with a special incentive: the state matches every dollar the participating family contributes. States across the country should extend their IDA programs to incorporate computer purchases for low-income families to help reduce one of the biggest barriers to participating in the digital economy.

Increase Training Opportunities and Resources to Develop Digital Literacy and Advanced Skills

In addition to providing public access to the Internet in places such as libraries, schools, and community technology centers, public policy should invest in training and education services to equip inexperienced Internet and computer users with the means to take full advantage of what these technologies have to offer. State elected officials can help encourage the advancement of digital literacy by providing subsidies, loans, and tax breaks to encourage individuals and families to acquire needed skills.

Moreover, state programs are needed to expand training opportunities made available at public venues such as the ones mentioned earlier. Access to computers and the Internet, while critical, are only part of the solution to the digital divide. Training and skill development are the new frontier in the ability of public policy to help ensure digital opportunity.

Create State Funding Sources to Extend the Internet to All Organizations That Serve Low-Income Communities

Just as it is important to ensure that African Americans have access to computers and the Internet at home, it is also important to equip community-based organizations that serve African American communities with the technology resources they need to best serve those communities. One way is through creating state digital-divide funding sources. One such source in California—the California Teleconnect Fund—was created by the legislature to ensure that the state's schools, libraries, and health-care facilities were equipped with the broadband Internet access that is increasingly necessary to provide adequate services to communities in need.

Seeing its success in serving these public institutions, the state expanded the funding source to apply to community-based organizations as well. Financed using a small surcharge placed on the phone bill of the state's telephone consumers, a funding pool such as the

California Teleconnect Fund should be replicated in other states to help ensure that the community organizations providing critical social services have the needed technology tools at their disposal.

Furthermore, telecommunications mergers provide windows of opportunity for elected officials to secure financial backing for closing the digital divide. In California and Ohio, the state public utility commissions have opened the process for reviewing mergers among telecom companies to include consideration of community need and to demand resource contributions for helping to close the digital divide. Other states, too, should pursue similar, effective strategies.

Protect and Support the Ability of Local Governments to Ensure Affordable Broadband Access

The federal government has called for universal and affordable broadband access for every American by the year 2007. However, many of the urban areas in which African Americans live lack the availability of high-speed Internet connections at affordable prices. Consequently, many cities are seeking to build broadband networks of their own to make universal affordable broadband access a reality. Philadelphia and San Francisco are among the cities that have launched ambitious plans to blanket their entire communities with wireless broadband Internet access, offered at rates that are anticipated to be less than half of those offered by cable and telephone companies.

Telecommunications companies, reacting to the possibility of competition from local governments that may undercut pricing and erode profits, have convinced 13 state legislatures across the country to outlaw this very type of local policy approach to reducing the broadband digital divide.[31] In response, the Community Broadband Act of 2005 has been introduced to prevent state governments from excluding local governments desiring to provide broadband Internet access at affordable rates to their citizens. This proposed legislation requires the support of local, state, and federal elected officials to ensure that when private-sector providers fail to meet the broadband technology needs of local communities, those communities reserve the right to build broadband networks for themselves.

In addition to supporting, and if necessary enforcing, the Community Broadband Act, state and local elected officials should explore the feasibility of municipal broadband networks and launch statewide initiatives to actively encourage publicly owned broadband networks where possible. Local elected officials must also explore approaches to regional cost-sharing to expand the possibility of public broadband networks for small towns and communities.

Make Universal Broadband Access a Credible Goal of State and Local Policy

Broadband Internet access is increasingly becoming the infrastructure of opportunity and participation in American society. Once regarded as a luxury, telephone service is now universally considered to be a basic necessity for participating in all spheres of society. It was because of a set of federal and state policies known as "universal service" that telephone service reached the levels of penetration among the U.S. population that we see today. For a world in which communication technologies have undergone revolutionary changes, federal and state policies related to telecommunications should be extended to make universal broadband access a central goal.

At the local level, governments that do not pursue initiatives to build affordable broadband networks themselves should pursue policies to increase the deployment of broadband service in low-income communities. These may include: (1) simplifying the process for issuing permits to ensure that bureaucratic inefficiencies are not a barrier to broadband deployment; (2) coordinating municipal public works planning in partnership with private telecommunications providers to identify and maximize public benefits; (3) using cable franchise renewal negotiations to leverage public benefits such as cable system upgrades or price breaks; and (4) pooling their demand for telecommunications services with other local governments and major institutions to obtain deployment or pricing benefits for local communities.

A Final Word

If we make sure that our children always have computer and Internet access; if we empower our families, businesses, and community organizations by learning about the World Wide Web and all it has to offer; and if we hold our elected officials responsible for increasing computer ownership and training opportunities to develop digital literacy skills among youth and families as well as for making universal broadband access available to all, then and only then can we close the racial digital divide.

CLOSING THE RACIAL DIGITAL DIVIDE

The "digital divide" is the inability of persons and geographical regions to access technology due to socio-economic factors.[1] While this divide is closing for some citizens, a decade after this text was first published, core structural problems remain. The Pew Research Center reported that 2014 saw 15 percent of American adults without access to the Internet, and 30 percent lack broadband access in the home, this latter statistic most heavily impacting the poor, the elderly, and racial minorities. Michael Brick, in an article for *Newsweek,* writes: "At a time of vast income inequality, experts say the so-called digital divide perpetuates cycles of poverty. Internet access holds the key to education, employment, government services, and much more. As the role of the Internet in everyday life expands at dizzying speed, those left behind face a dangerous level of isolation."[2]

The news is encouraging with respect to Black America's linkages to the digital world. One recent study shows that white and Black access to the Internet is virtually the same. Eighty-seven percent of whites use the Internet regularly, and 84 percent of Black consumers report using the Internet; there is no statistically significant difference between usage across the two races.[3] The same study shows that the percentage of cell-phone owners across the races is virtually identical.[4] Thus, technology usage by individuals does not appear to be stratified by race or ethnicity.

These statistics, however, do not reveal the whole story. Smartphone-only access is a big part of the total percentage of minorities reaching the Internet. The digital divide becomes clearer when looking at the percentage of households who have broadband, computer-based Internet access in the home. Whereas more than 77 percent of households headed by whites have Internet access at home, just 61 percent of Black households have home Internet access.[5] Additionally, smartphones can't do everything. As Robert Schoon of the *Latin Post* notes: "Try doing something other than checking social media, reading news, and quick Wikipedia reference—like applying for jobs, applying for college, accessing government services, or doing homework—on a daily basis for a couple weeks, and you'll quickly realize that the digital divide isn't realistically closed by smartphones."[6]

The real divide is based in a "racial wealth gap" that holds millions back from adopting broadband because a computer can rarely be purchased from their yearly income. Computers have to be bought out of savings or one's wealth. Citizens who cannot afford a computer or who access the Internet using their smartphones out of necessity are the same citizens who are on the other side of the racial wealth gap.[7] The cost of Internet connectivity and computers is thus the biggest problem. A recent report showed 26 percent of respondents did not have Internet at home because they could not afford it, and 13 percent did not have a computer. On average, those in both categories earned less than $25,000 annually.[8]

Brent Wilkes, National Executive Director for the League of United Latin American Citizens, cites a Pew Research Center study in saying, "Broadband use at home is game changing and has an impact on employment opportunities. For those who do not have home access, it creates barriers . . . You need a computer."[9] If one is upper income, well educated, or young, race does not appear to drive usage.[10] Wealth is a direct factor in determining the level of digital access.

One critical problem that needs to be addressed is the lack of equipment and/or broadband access in America's schools. Just as individual and household access is demarcated by class, so too is it in primary and secondary schools. A typical school has about the same connection speed as the average American home, but it serves about 200 times as many users. Some schools even have to ration out Internet time to students.[11] According to one nonprofit watchdog organization, less than one-half of all schools meet the connectivity necessary to improve the educational achievement of students. The group estimates that 40 million students lack broadband and that the goal of high-speed connectivity in all schools will not be reached until at least 2021.[12] Just 14 percent of low-income students have high-speed connectivity, which affects urban schools with predominantly Black enrollments.[13]

The goal of connecting all citizens to broadband is a worthy one, but reaching that goal for poor and/or Black citizens requires action by both the public and private sectors. In June 2013, the Obama administration introduced the ConnectED initiative, which was created to equip practically every school in the country with a high-speed broadband connection by 2018. However, this program appears to be too small to dramatically advance Black households and students. Additionally, a new initiative was launched in 2015 called ConnectHome, which is a partnership dedicated to expanding high-speed broadband to more families across the country. The pilot program is launching in 27 cities and one tribal nation and will initially reach over 275,000 low-income households and nearly 200,000 children with the support needed to access the Internet at home. Internet service providers, nonprofit organizations, and the private sector will offer broadband access, technical training, digital literacy programs, and devices for residents in assisted housing units.

The U.S. has made great strides in closing the longtime problem of a digital divide. Black America has greater access to digital technology compared to a decade ago, and government programs are trying to close the remaining gaps. However, until families can afford the basic technological necessities—a computer being one—and gain broadband access from home, a digital divide along class and racial lines will remain.

—*Prepared by Michael McGuire, Ph.D., Executive Associate Dean, School of Public and Environmental Affairs, Indiana University, Bloomington, Indiana*

✢ ✢

A CALL TO ACTION

CORNEL WEST

This book is an historic document that extends the rich tradition of deep democracy in America, a tradition of struggle—from Harriet Tubman, Frederick Douglass, Ida B. Wells-Barnett, and A. Philip Randolph to Martin Luther King, Jr. This tradition has always tried to energize and organize those whom Sly Stone called "everyday people" in order to take back power in the face of the elite abuse of power. And the history of America is, at its best, the history of abused Black people boldly confronting an entrenched status quo in order to expand justice and freedom for all. We have been and remain the moral conscience of this country. Like the blues, jazz, and hip-hop, Black democratic visions and actions are invaluable gifts to this nation.

This book is the brainchild of the visionary and courageous Tavis Smiley. His renowned annual gatherings on C-SPAN, alongside his nightly TV shows, weekly radio shows, lectures, and books, generate an unprecedented forum for public dialogue about the state of Black people in America. He boldly decided to use his celebrity status and high visibility in service to Black freedom and deep democracy. That is why this book is not only a call to action; it is also itself a form of action. He boldly decided—again—that Black people would organize best if we had a common agenda and a democratic vision that bring us together. So in spite of all the distrust of and even the disrespect we sometimes have for each other, he forged ahead with a project few could deny. To love a people taught to hate themselves for 400 years may be difficult, but it is as delicious as it is desirable for Black democratic action—as we best see in Black music.

Tavis Smiley coordinated Black leaders to support this call to action. He solicited Black educators to lay bare the facts of our situation. He spoke in Black churches and mosques to preserve a strong spiritual dimension to the call. And he worked with the younger generation to keep the call rooted in their experiences. That is why this book itself is an act of full-fledged Black self-determination as well as a call for each one of us to act and do something in order to be an organized force for good in our struggle for justice and freedom.

Our *Covenant* is neither a contract nor a compact. A contract is too selfish and a compact is too seasonal. Now is the time for us to keep faith with our spiritual, moral, and political covenant bequeathed to us by great foremothers and forefathers that simply says: "Stand with grace and dignity and take action with courage and compassion, with malice toward none yet a righteous indignation against injustice, so that everyday people—and especially their precious children—can flower and flourish as the sun shines and the stars shout with joy."

✣ ✣

ENDNOTES

Covenant I: Securing the Right to Health Care and Well-Being

1. http://www.cdc.gov/nchs/data/nhis/earlyrelease/insur200412.pdf.

2. *Ibid.*

3. http://www.ama-assn.org/ama/pub/category/12930.html.

4. Healthy People 2010 provides a framework for prevention for the nation. It is a statement of national health objectives designed to identify the most significant preventable threats to health and to establish national goals to reduce these threats. For more information, see http://www.healthypeople.gov/About/.

5. http://www.aboutlead.com/lead_poisoning/children.html.

6. http://www.cdc.gov/omh/AMH/factsheets/mental.htm.

7. *Ibid.*

8. For more information, *see* http://ncmhd.nih.gov or visit http://www.nih.gov.

9. W. Parker, "Black-White Infant Mortality Disparity in the United States: A Societal Litmus Test," *Public Health Reports,* Volume 118, July–August 2003, 336.

10. "Diet-Related Chronic Diseases That Disproportionately Affect African American Men," http://5aday.gov/aahealth/aamen/diet/pdfs/NY state.pdf.

11. "How Diet Affects African American Men's Health: High Blood Pressure," http://5aday.gov/aahealth/aamen/diet/pressure.html.

12. *Ibid.*

13. "Fact Sheet: African American Women and Cardiovascular Disease," http://www.blackwomenshealth.org/siteNews2?news_iv_ctr1=-18cpage=NewsArticle&id=5157, Black Women's Health Imperative.

14. *Ibid.*

15. *Diabetes in African Americans Fact Sheet,* National Diabetes Information Clear-inghouse, National Institute of Diabetes and Digestive and Kidney Diseases, NIH Publication No. 98-3266, June 1998.

16. *Ibid.*

17. K. Wright, "The Time Is Now! The State of AIDS in Black America," Black AIDS Institute, Los Angeles, CA, February 2005, pp. 5, 8.

18. *Ibid.,* p. 6.

19. "Centers for Disease Control and Prevention, HIV/AIDS Fact Sheet," http://www .cdc.gov/omh/AMH/factsheets/hiv.htm#1.

20. *HIV/AIDS Surveillance Report 2003,* U.S. Department of Health and Human Ser-vices, CDC, Atlanta, GA, Volume 15.

21. K. Wright, *op. cit.,* p. 7.

22. "Asthma: A Concern for Minority Populations," October 2001, http://www.niaid .nih.gov/factsheets/asthma.htm2001, National Institute of Allergy and Infectious Diseases.

23. *Ibid.*

24. "Minority Health Disparities at a Glance," www.omhrc.gov/healthdisparities/ glance.htm, Healthy Human Services.

25. "2001 Health Care Quality Survey," The Commonwealth Fund, New York, NY, November 2001, chart 37.

26. "Child Health: General Health Facts," http://www.childrensdefense.org/child health/generalhealthfactsd.aspx, Children's Defense Fund.

27. K. Wright, *op. cit.,* p. 7.

28. A.M. Butz, P.A. Eggleston, K. Huss, C.S. Rand, K.A. Riekert, M. Winkelstein, "Care-giver-Physician Medication Concordance and Under Treatment of Asthma among Inner-City Children," *Pediatrics,* Vol. 111, No. 3, March 2003, p. 217.

29. "Environmental and Economic Injustice: Fact Sheet," http://www.ejrc.cau.edu/ NBEJNEJFS.html, National Black Environmental Justice Network.

30. R. Flournoy and S. Treuhaft, "Healthy Food, Healthy Communities," The Califor-nia Endowment and PolicyLink, Oakland, CA, September 2005, p. 10.

31. "Five a Day: Fresh Facts," http://www.dhs.ca.gov/ps/cdic/cpns/press/fresh _facts/2004-02.html, California Department of Health Services.

32. R. Flournoy, "Regional Development and Physical Activity: Issues and Strategies for Promoting Health Equity," PolicyLink, Oakland, CA, November 2002, p. 10.

33. *Ibid.,* p. 11.

34. "Air Quality and African Americans," http://www.lungusa.org/ site/pp.asp?c=d vLUK900E&b=308865, American Lung Association.

35. P. Sherer, "The Benefits of Parks: Why America Needs More City Parks and Open Space," The Trust for Public Land, San Francisco, CA, 2003, p. 4.

36. "Research Agenda," http://www.who.int/peh-emf/research/agenda/en/, World Health Organization.

37. "Mental Health: Culture, Race, and Ethnicity," http://www.surgeongeneral.gov/ library/mentalhealth/cre/execsummary-6.html, U.S. Department of Health and Human Services.

38. R. Flournoy and S. Treuhaft, *op. cit.,* September 2005, p. 9.

39. S. Castro Uribes, "Southwest Fresno Group Lobbies for Major Grocery Store," *Fresno Bee,* June 17, 1995, Metro section, p. Bl.

40. L. Mikkelsen and S. Chehimi, "The Links Between the Neighborhood Environment and Childhood Nutrition," Prevention Institute, Oakland, CA, Fall 2004.

41. "A Place for Healthier Living: Improving Access to Physical Activity and Healthy Foods," Joint Center for Political and Economic Studies and PolicyLink, 2004, p. 5.

42. "Fayette County Public School District, Field Network Demographics," http:// www.uky.edu/Education/OFE/table.doc, University of Kentucky.

43. "School Foods Tool Kit," Center for Science in the Public Interest, Washington, DC, September 2003, cited by "A Place for Healthier Living: Improving Access to Physical Activity and Healthy Foods," Joint Center for Political and Economic Studies and PolicyLink, 2004, p. 6.

44. "History of the Bucket Brigade Movement," http://www.labucketbrigade.org/ about/history.shtml, Louisiana Bucket Brigade.

45. "Chemical Body Burden: Tools for Communities," http://www. chemicalbody burden.org/tools, Coming Clean.

46. *Ibid.*

47. *Ibid.*

48. "History of the Bucket Brigade Movement," *op. cit.*

49. *Ibid.*

50. *Ibid.*

51. *Ibid.*

CWBA TEN YEARS LATER: Covenant I

1. Figure 1 of Federal Reserve Bank of St. Louis, "This Recession's Effect on Employment," available at https://www.stlouisfed.org/publications/bridges/winter-20092010/this-recessions-effect-on-employment-how-it-stacks-up-for-blacks-whites-men-and-women

2. Source: Table 21 http://www.cdc.gov/nchs/data/nvsr/nvsr63/nvsr63_07.pdf

3. This conclusion is also emphasized in Aron, L. Urban Institute. "Despite Fifty Years of Improvement in Infant Mortality, Large Black-White Gap Remains Unchanged." August 26, 2013. http://www.urban.org/urban-wire/despite-fifty-years-improvements-infant-mortality-large-black-white-gap-remains-unchanged. Accessed on 8/25/15.

4. Figure 5 in http://www.cdc.gov/nchs/data/hus/hus14.pdf#029

5. Magaly Olivero. March 2, 2014. "Hypertension: Disparities Widen for Black Women." Connecticut Health I-Team. http://c-hit.org/2014/03/02/hypertension-disparities-widen-for-black-women/ Accessed on 8/26/15.

6. The State of Obesity. September 2014. "Special Report: Racial and Ethnic Disparities in Obesity." http://stateofobesity.org/disparities/blacks/#footnote-2 Accessed 8/26/15.

7. Source: CDC. "Fast Facts: HIV Among Youth." http://www.cdc.gov/hiv/group/age/youth/index.html. Accessed on 10/8/15.

8. Gohl et al. 2015. "Exposure To Harmful Workplace Practices Could Account For Inequality In Life Spans Across Different Demographic Groups" Health Affairs. http://content.healthaffairs.org/content/34/10/1761.full

9. Figure 2 of http://www.prb.org/Publications/Articles/2011/us-smoking-trends.aspx

10. Whitt-Glover, M., et al. "Disparities in Physical Activity and Sedentary Behaviors Among US Children and Adolescents: Prevalence, Correlates, and Intervention Implication." *Journal of Public Health Policy*. 2009; Vol. 30, pgs. S309–S334.

11. "The House and Senate Fail to Fund Critical Healthy Food Financing Initiative." May 23, 2014. The Reinvestment Fund. http://www.trfund.com/house-and-senate-fail-to-fund-critical-healthy-food-financing-initiative/. Accessed on 8/31/15.

12. Pope et al (2013) show that subsequent to media coverage of a 2007 study highlighting widespread racial discrimination in professional basketball refereeing statistics, this phenomenon has completely disappeared. http://www.nber.org/papers/w19765.

Endnotes

Covenant II: Establishing a System of Public Education in Which All Children Achieve at High Levels and Reach Their Full Potential

1. J.S. Coleman, E.Q. Campbell, C.J. Hobson et al., *Equality of Educational Opportunity.* (Washington, DC: U.S. Government Printing Office, 1966).

2. The College Board, *Reaching the Top: A Report of the National Task Force on Minority High Achievement* (New York: The College Board, 1999).

3. J. Ogbu, *Minority Education and Caste: The American System in Cross-cultural Perspective* (New York: Academic Press, 1978).

4. *See* R.J. Herrnstein and C. Murray, *The Bell Curve: Intelligence and Class Structure in American Life* (New York: The Free Press, 1994); A.R. Jensen, "How much can we boost IQ and scholastic achievement?," *Harvard Educational Review* 39,1969, pp. 1–23; O. Lewis, *A Puerto Rican Family in the Culture of Poverty* (New York: Random House, 1966); and W. Shockley, "Dysgenics, Geneticity, Raceology: A Challenge to the Intellectual Responsibility of Educators," *Phi Delta Kappa* 53(5), 1972, pp. 297–307.

5. F. Riessman, *The Culturally Deprived Child* (New York: Harper and Row, 1962).

6. S. Fordham and J. Ogbu, "Black Students' School Success: Coping with the burden of 'acting white,'" *Urban Review* 18, 1986, pp. 17–206.

7. C.M. Steele, "A Threat in the Air: How Stereotypes Shape Intellectual Identity and Performance," *American Psychologist* 52(6), 1997, pp. 613–629.

8. *See* K. Clark, *Dark Ghetto* (New York: Harper & Row, 1965); Coleman et al., *op. cit.*; G.D. Jaynes and R.M. William, eds., *A Common Destiny* (Washington, DC: National Academy Press, 1989); J. Kozol, *Savage Inequalities: Children in America's Schools* (New York: Crown Publishers, 1991); L.S. Miller, *An American Imperative: Accelerating Minority Educational Advancement* (New Haven: Yale University Press, 1995); F.F. Piven and R.A. Cloward, *Regulating the Poor: The Functions of Public Welfare* (New York: Pantheon Books, 1971); and V. Sexton, *Education and Income Inequalities of Opportunity in Our Public Schools* (New York: Viking Press, 1961).

9. W.E.B. Du Bois, *The Souls of Black Folks* (New York: New American Library, 1969 [1903]).

10. H. Price, *Achievement Matters: Getting Your Child the Best Education Possible* (New York: Kensington Publishing Corporation, 2002); and the College Board, *op. cit.*

11. E.W. Gordon, ed., *Education and Justice: A View from the Back of the Bus* (New York: Teachers College Press, 1999); Gordon, "Affirmative Development of Academic Abilities," *Pedagogical Inquiry and Praxis 2* (New York: Teachers College, Columbia University, Institute for Urban and Minority Education, September 2001); and Gordon, "Affirmative Development: Looking Beyond Racial Inequality," *College Board Review* 195, 2002, pp. 28–33.

12. Miller, *op. cit.*

13. The College Board, *op. cit.*

14. P. Bourdieu, "The Forms of Capital," in J. Richardson, ed., *Handbook of Theory and Research for the Sociology of Education* (Westport, CT: Greenwood, 1986), pp. 241–258.

15. http://www.idra.org/Research/edstats.htm#earlychildhood.

16. "African American Achievement in America," http://www2.edtrust.org/NR/rdon lyres/9AB4AC88-7301-43FF81A3-EB94807B917F/0/AfAmer_Achivement.pdf, The Education Trust.

17. Llagas, *op. cit., p. 48.*

18. Ibid., pp. 122, 123.

19. "African American Achievement in America," *op. cit.*

20. Llagas, *op. cit., p. 38.*

21. *Ibid.*

22. *Ibid., p. 40.*

23. *Ibid., pp. 92, 94.*

24. http://wwwjbhe.com/features/45_student_grad_rates.html.

25. For more information, *see* http://www.hcz.org/project/mis sion.html.

26. http://www.hcz.org/project/sites.html.

27. *Ibid.*

28. http://www.freedomschools.org.

29. http://www.freedomschools.org/mission/default.aspx.

30. http://www.freedomschools.org/history/ freedomschools1964.aspx.

31. http://www.freedomschools.org/history/default.aspx.

CWBA TEN YEARS LATER: Covenant II

1. http://www.nationsreportcard.gov/reading_math_2013/#/student-groups

2. http://nces.ed.gov/nationsreportcard/naepdata/report.aspx

3. http://blogs.edweek.org/edweek/curriculum/2013/06/naep_report_a_closer_look_at_the_achievement_gap.html

Endnotes

4. http://www.nationsreportcard.gov/reading_math_2013/#/student-groups

5. http://nces.ed.gov/nationsreportcard/naepdata/report.aspx

6. http://www.brookings.edu/research/papers/2012/08/16-student-retention-west

7. https://nces.ed.gov/programs/digest/d14/tables/dt14_104.40.asp?current=yes

8. http://nces.ed.gov/programs/digest/d13/tables/dt13_302.60.asp

9. http://nces.ed.gov/programs/digest/d14/tables/dt14_306.10.asp?current=yes

10. *Whither Opportunity? Rising Inequality, Schools, and Children's Life Chances,* by Greg J. Duncan and Richard J. Murnane, Eds., New York, NY: Russell Sage Foundation, 2011, 551 pp., $48.70 hardcover.

11. http://kff.org/other/state-indicator/poverty-rate-by-raceethnicity/

12. U.S.Department of Education Office of Civil Rights. 2014. Civil rights data collection data snapshot: school discipline. Available online at: http://ocrdata.ed.gov/Downloads/CRDC-School-Discipline-Snapshot.pdf

13. Arcia, E. 2006. Achievement and enrollment status of suspended students: outcomes in a large, multicultural school district. *Education and Urban Society*, 38(3): 359–69.

14. *Ibid.*

15. Fabelo, T., Thompson, M., Plotkin, M., Carmichael, C., Marchbanks, M., & Booth, E. 2011. Breaking schools' rules: a statewide study of how school discipline relates to students' success and juvenile justice involvement. Available online at: http://csgjusticecenter.org/youth/breaking-schools-rules-report/

16. For example, the expulsion rate in the Noble Network of Charter Schools—a high-performing, "no excuses" charter school network in Chicago that predominantly serves low-income and minority students—was 1.53 percent in the 2013–14 academic year, as compared to just 0.08 percent in Chicago Public Schools.

17. https://credo.stanford.edu/documents/UNEMBARGOED%20National%20Charter%20Study%20Press%20Release.pdf

18. http://www.researchconnections.org/files/childcare/pdf/OPRERestoPolicyBrief1_FINAL.pdf

19. http://www.bostonpublicschools.org/site/Default.aspx?PageType=3&DomainID=4&PageID=1&ViewID=047e6be3-6d87-4130-8424-d8e4e9ed6c2a&FlexDataID=3439

Covenant III: Correcting the System of Unequal Justice

1.   In the book *Body Count: Moral Poverty . . . And How to Win America's War Against Crime and Drugs* (New York: Simon & Schuster, 1996) that Dilulio co-wrote with William Bennett and John Walters, Dilulio suggests that "a late 1990s juvenile-crime explosion will be driven by a rising tide of . . . deeply troubled young men." He had earlier "attracted uncritical attention from the left and the right for his talk of the growth of a 'super-predator' caste of feral young males born of the absence of civil society, families, and churches in many parts of America." Excerpted from "The Real John Dilulio" by Eli Lehrer of The Heritage Foundation, February 7, 2001, archived at http://www.heritage.org.

2.   Marc Mauer and Ryan Scott King, "Schools and Prisons: 50 Years After *Brown v. Board of Education,*" http:www.sentencingproject.org/pdfs/ brownvboard.pdf, The Sentencing Project.

3.   http://www.ojp.usdoj.gov/bjs/pub/pdf/wo.pdf.

4.   *In re Gault,* 387 U.S. 1(1967).

5.   Mauer and King, *op. cit.*

6.   Eleanor Roosevelt, remarks at presentation of a booklet on human rights, *In Your Hands,* to the United Nations Commission on Human Rights, United Nations, New York, March 27, 1958. (United Nations typescript of statement at presentation.)

7.   James Baldwin, *A Rap on Race,* 1971.

8.   "Incarcerated America," Figure 1, http://www.hrw.org/backgrounder/usa/incarceration/us042903.pdf, April 2003, Human Rights Watch.

9.   Mauer and King, *op. cit.*

10. "Felony Disenfranchisement Laws in the United States," http://www.sentencing project.org/pdfs/1046.pdf, September 2005, The Sentencing Project.

11. *Ibid.*

12. "Incarcerated America," Figures 4 and 5, http://www.hrw.org/backgrounder/usa/incarceration/us042903.pdf, April 2003, Human Rights Watch.

13. "Young Black Americans and the Criminal Justice System: Five Years Later" Report Summary, http://www.sentencingproject.org/pdfs/9070smy.pdf, April 2001, The Sentencing Project.

14. Mauer and King, *op. cit.*

15. *Ibid.*

16. *Ibid.*

Endnotes

17. *Ibid.*

18. Fatema Gunja, "Race and the War on Drugs Position Paper," http://www.aclu .org/Files/OpenFile.cfm?id=14089, May 2003, ACLU.

19. "African American Youth and the Juvenile Court System," http://www.juvjustice .org/resources/fs005.html, Coalition for Juvenile Justice.

20. http://wwwjuvjustice.org/resources/fs005.html.

21. "Volvo for Life Awards: Charmaney Bayton," http:// www.volvoforlifeawards .com/cgi-bin/iowa/english/heros/hero2004/5119.html.

22. *Rule of Law: Citizens' Rights in a Georgia Court of Law*, http://www.sentencing project.org/pdfs/ruleoflaw.pdf, The Sentencing Project.

23. Reentry National Media Outreach Campaign, http:// www.reentryme diaoutreach.org.

24. http://www.drugsense.org/wodclock.htm, http://www.aclu.org/Files/OpenFile .cfm?Id=14089.

25. http://cnnstudentnews.cnn.corn/TRANSCRIPTS/0308/04/ldt.00.html.

26. Michael Coyle, "Race and Class Penalties in Crack Cocaine Sentencing," http:// www.sentencingproject.org/pdfs/5077.pdf, The Sentencing Project.

27. *Ibid.*

28. *Ibid.*

29. *Ibid.*

30. Eric Lotke, Jason Colburn, and Vincent Schiraldi, "Three Strikes and You're Out," http://wwwjusticepolicy.org/article.php?id=450, Justice Policy Institute.

31. Jeremy Travis, "But They All Come Back: Rethinking Prisoner Reentry," Sentenc- ing & Corrections: Issues for the 21st Century, No. 7, http://www.ncjrs.org/ pdffilesl/nij/181413.pdf.

32. "Bill Summary & Status for the 109th Congress: Second Chance Act of 2005," http://thomas.loc.gov/cgi-bin/bdquery/z?d109:HR01704:@@@L&summ2=m8c.

33. Lenora Lapidus et al., "Caught in the Net: The Impact of Drug Policies on Wom- en and Families," ACLU, *Break the Chains: Communities of Color and the War on Drugs,* The Brennan Center at NYU School of Law, March 22, 2005, p. 61.

34. *Ibid.*

35. http://thomas loc.gov/cgi-bin/query/z?c109:S.1352.IS.

36. *Ibid.*

37. "Education on Lockdown: The Schoolhouse to Jailhouse Track," The Advancement Project, March 2005, p. 7.

38. *Ibid.*, p. 15.

39. *Ibid.*, p. 11.

40. *Ibid.*, p. 46.

41. Malcolm Young and Patricia Allard, "Prosecuting Juveniles in Adult Court: Perspectives for Policymakers and Practitioners," http://www.sentencingproject.org/pdfs/2079.pdf, The Sentencing Project.

42. *Ibid.*

43. *Ibid.*

CWBA TEN YEARS LATER: Covenant III

1. *The Covenant*, Chapter III, p. 49.

2. "U.S. at a unique time in history for justice reform, says Attorney General Lynch," PBS Interview (Oct. 8, 2015), accessed at http://www.pbs.org/newshour/bb/u-s-unique-time-history-justice-reform-says-attorney-general-lynch/.

3. E. Ann. Carson, *Prisoners in 2014*, NCJ 248955, Bureau of Justice Statistics (Sept. 2015), at 16 and Table 11.

4. Monica Anderson, "Vast majority of blacks view the criminal justice system as unfair," Pew Research Center (Aug. 12, 2014).

5. E. Ann. Carson, *Prisoners in 2014*, supra n. 2, at 15. See also generally Michelle Alexander, *The New Jim Crow: Mass Incarceration in the Age of Color Blindness* (The New Press 2010).

6. Executive Office of the President, ECONOMIC COSTS OF YOUTH DISADVANTAGE AND HIGH-RETURN OPPORTUNITIES FOR CHANGE (July 2015), at 14 and n. 75.

7. Id. at 13 and n. 73.

8. Id. at 14 and n. 79.

9. U.S. Sentencing Comm'n, Report to the Congress: Cocaine and Federal Sentencing Policy 98–104 (2007); see Mo. Rev. Stat. § 195.222(2) (2013) (18.5-1); Ariz. Rev. Stat. §§ 13-3408(A)(2), (B)(2) (12-1); 13-3401(36)(b), (c); N.H. Rev. Stat. § 318- B:26(I)(a)(1), (3) (28-1).

10. Drew DeSilver, "Feds may be rethinking the drug war, but states have been leading the way," Pew Research Center (Apr. 2, 2014), accessed at http://www

.pewresearch.org/fact-tank/2014/04/02/feds-may-be-rethinking-the-drug-war
-but-states-have-been-leading-the-way/. Examples include "lowering penalties for
possession and use of illegal drugs, shortening mandatory minimums or curbing
their applicability, [and] removing automatic sentence enhancements." Id.

11. See http://www.governing.com/gov-data/state-marijuana-laws-map-medical-rec
reational.html; http://norml.org/aboutmarijuana/item/states-that-have-decrimi
nalized.

12. James M. Cole, Deputy Attorney General, Memorandum for All United States
Attorneys (Aug. 29, 2013), accessed at http://www.justice.gov/iso/opa/resourc
es/3052013829132756857467.pdf.

13. Pub. L. No. 111–220, 124 Stat. 2372.

14. Kara Gotsch, *Breakthrough in U.S. Drug Sentencing Reform: The Fair Sentencing
Act and the Unfinished Reform Agenda*, Washington Office on Latin America (Nov.
2011), at 4.

15. Michael Coyle, "Race and Class Penalties in Crack Cocaine Sentencing," The
Sentencing Project, accessed at http://www.prisonpolicy.org/scans/sp/Raceand
Class.Sentencing.pdf.

16. *United States v. Blewett*, F.3d (6th Cir. en banc 2013), at 7–8.

17. *Dorsey v. United States*, 567 U.S. ___ (2012).

18. U.S. Sentencing Commission, *Final Crack Retroactivity Data Report Fair Sentencing
Act* (Dec. 2014) at 8 and and Tables 5 and 8, accessed at http://www.ussc.gov/
sites/default/files/pdf/research-and-publications/retroactivity-analyses/fair-sen
tencing-act/Final_USSC_Crack_Retro_Data_Report_FSA.pdf

19. https://www.washingtonpost.com/world/national-security/justice-department
-about-to-free-6000-prisoners-largest-one-time-release/2015/10/06/961f4c9a
-6ba2-11e5-aa5b-f78a98956699_story.html; https://www.themarshallproject.
org/2015/10/09/meet-the-federal-prisoners-about-to-be-released (summarizing
U.S. Sentencing Commission 2014 Drug Guidelines Amendment Retroactivity
Data Report (Aug. 2015)).

20. See https://www.washingtonpost.com/world/national-security/obama-com
mutes-sentences-of-46-non-violent-drug-offenders/2015/07/13/b533f61e-2974
-11e5-a250-42bd812efc09_story.html.

21. See http://famm.org/wp-content/uploads/2015/10/10-01-15-Sentencing-Re
form-and-Corrections-Act-Summary1.pdf and http://famm.org/famm-house-sen
tencing-reform-compromise-another-step-in-right-direction/.

22. Id.

23. U.S. Sentencing Commission, *Recidivism Among Offenders Receiving Retroactive
Sentence Reductions: The 2007 Crack Cocaine Amendment* (May 2014) (finding
30.4% recidivism rate among crack offenders receiving sentence reductions

under a 2007 sentencing guidelines revision, and 32.6% rate for those serving full sentences).

24. See https://www.washingtonpost.com/posteverything/wp/2015/08/03/with-one-decision-obama-could-totally-reform-the-criminal-justice-system/.

25. http://www.economist.com/news/united-states/21621799-how-prosecu
tors-came-dominate-criminal-justice-system-kings-courtroom; http://www.econo
mist.com/news/leaders/21621784-american-prosecutors-have-too-much-power-hand-some-it-judges-plea-change; see also Rakoff, "Why Innocent People Plead Guilty," New York Review of Books (Nov. 20, 2014), accessed at http://www.nybooks.com/articles/archives/2014/nov/20/why-innocent-people-plead-guilty/.

26. Jeremy Travis, Invisible Punishment: An Instrument of Social Exclusion, in INVIS-IBLE PUNISHMENT: THE COLLATERAL CONSEQUENCES OF MASS IMPRISON-MENT 15, 16 (Marc Mauer & Meda Chesney-Lind eds., 2002).

27. http://sentencingproject.org/doc/publications/fd_Felony%20Disenfranchise
ment%20Primer.pdf

28. Alexander, supra n. 5.

29. 559 U.S. 356 (2010).

30. Padilla, 559 U.S. ___ and n. 9 (collecting cases).

31. National Inventory of Collateral Consequences of Conviction (NICCC) Project Description, at http://www.abacollateralconsequences.org/description/ (last visited October 9, 2015).

32. "After Fifty Years, a State of Crisis for the Right to Counsel," NPR (March 19, 2013), transcript accessed at http://www.npr.org/2013/03/19/174753333/after-50-years-a-state-of-crisis-for-the-right-to-counsel.

33. Available at http://www.abacollateralconsequences.org/.

34. See http://www.sentencingproject.org/doc/publications/fd_Felony%20Disen
franchisement%20Primer.pdf.

35. The State of Sentencing 2014: Developments in Sentencing Law and Practice, The Sentencing Project (2015), accessed at http://sentencingproject.org/doc/publi
cations/sen_State_of_Sentencing_2014.pdf.

36. See, e.g., http://www.wsj.com/articles/criminal-records-haunt-hiring-initia
tive-1436736255.

37. See "Research Supports Fair Chance Policies," National Employment Law Project Fact Sheet (April 2015) and sources cited therein.

38. Equal Employment Opportunity Commission Office of Legal Counsel, Enforce-ment Guidance No. 915.002 (April 25, 2012), accessed at http://www.eeoc.gov/laws/guidance/arrest_conviction.cfm.

39. Michelle Natividad Rodriguez and Nayatara Mehta, *Ban the Box: U.S. Cities, Counties, and States Adopt Fair Hiring Policies to Reduce Barriers to Employment of People with Conviction Records*, National Employment Law Project (Sept. 2015). Some high-profile private employers have already banned the box, see Fredreka Schouten, "Koch Industries drops criminal-history question from job applications," USA Today (Apr. 27, 2015), accessed at http://www.usatoday.com/story/news/2015/04/27/koch-industries-criminal-justice-job-applications/26325929/.

40. Id.

41. See http://www.nelp.org/campaign/ensuring-fair-chance-to-work/.

42. "U.S. Department of Education Launches Second Chance Pell Pilot Program for Incarcerated Individuals," 7/31/2015.http://www.ed.gov/news/press-releases/us-department-education-launches-second-chance-pell-pilot-program-incarcerated-individuals.

43. Davis, Lois M., Jennifer L. Steele, Robert Bozick, Malcolm Williams, Susan Turner, Jeremy N. V. Miles, Jessica Saunders and Paul S. Steinberg. How Effective Is Correctional Education, and Where Do We Go from Here? The Results of a Comprehensive Evaluation. RAND Corporation (2014), accessed at http://www.rand.org/pubs/research_reports/RR564.

44. Id.

45. 29 USC 3101 et seq.

46. Connecticut, for example, used this money to provide community college academic and vocational post-secondary courses and transition services to 377 students at 9 sites during the 2007–2008 school year; 270 students completed the program. Connecticut Department of Correction Unified School District #1 Annual Report 2007-2008, accessed at http://www.ct.gov/doc/lib/doc/PDF/PDF Report/EducationStatistics0708.pdf.

47. Some argue that zero-tolerance policies, in addition to anti-Muslim sentiments, led to the highly publicized case of ninth-grader Ahmed Mohamed, who brought a home-made clock, not a weapon, to school in Texas and was placed in handcuffs by police. See Eva-Marie Ayalaz, "Zero-tolerance policies may have been another factor in Irving case," Dallas Morning News (Sept. 16, 2015), accessed at http://www.dallasnews.com/news/community-news/irving/headlines/20150916-zero-tolerance-policies-may-have-been-another-factor-in-irving-case-experts-say.ece. The spokeswoman for the Texas school district where Mohamed attended school said, "We were doing everything with an abundance of caution to protect all of our students," and a spokeswoman for the Association of Texas Professional Educators said that in light of school shootings and other deadly events in public venues, an educator is more likely to be overly cautious in reporting something questionable. Id.

48. Tony Fabelo, Michael D. Thompson, et. al, "Breaking Schools' Rules: A Statewide Study of How School Discipline Relates to Students' Success and Juvenile Justice Involvement," (July 2011), accessed at https://csgjusticecenter.org/youth/break

ing-schools-rules-report/ (study of nearly 1 million Texas students shows suspension and expulsion overused and discriminatory based on race and educational disabilities).

49. U.S. Department of Education and U.S. Department of Justice, *Supportive School Discipline Initiative* (2014), accessed at https://www2.ed.gov/policy/gen/guid/school-discipline/appendix-3-overview.pdf.

50. Id.; see also U.S. Department of Education, *School Climate and Discipline* website at http://www2.ed.gov/policy/gen/guid/school-discipline/index.html, and U.S. Department of Education, *Guiding Principles: A Resource Guide for Improving School Climate and Discipline* (Jan. 2014), at 7, accessed at http://www2.ed.gov/policy/gen/guid/school-discipline/guiding-principles.pdf.

51. Melinda D. Anderson, "Will School-Discipline Reform Actually Change Anything?," *The Atlantic* (Sept. 14, 2015), accessed at http://www.theatlantic.com/education/archive/2015/09/will-school-discipline-reform-actually-change-any thing/405157/

52. Id.; Cal. Educ. Code Sec. 48900.

53. STUDENT CODE OF CONDUCT FOR CHICAGO PUBLIC SCHOOLS (EFFECTIVE SEPTEMBER 8, 2015) Section: 705.5 Board Report: 15-0722-PO1 Date Adopted: July 22, 2015; Chicago Public Schools, *Suspensions and Expulsions Reduction Plan and Data Highlights* (Feb. 26, 2014), accessed at *http://www.cpsboe.org/content/documents/student_suspension_and_expulsion_reduction_plan.pdf*; CPS Announces Mid-Year Data (March 19, 2015), accessed at http://cps.edu/News/Press_releas es/Pages/PR1_3_19_2015.aspx.

54. CPS Announces Mid-Year Data (March 19, 2015), supra n. 49.

55. See *Roper v Simmons*, 543 US 551 (2005), *Graham v. Florida,* 560 US 48 (2010), and *Miller v. Alabama,* 132 S.Ct. 2455 (2012).

56. *The State of Sentencing 2014: Developments in Sentencing Law and Practice,* supra n. 32, at 13.

57. Campaign for Justice State Snapshot http://www.campaignforyouthjustice.org/state-work/state-snapshot

58. See Colorado Juvenile Defender Center, "New Direct File Law: 2012 Legislative Session," accessed at http://cjdc.org/wp/wp-content/uploads/2012/06/direct -file-bill-summary-2012.pdf.

59. David Gottesman and Susan Wilde Schwartz, "Juvenile Justice in the U.S.: Facts for Policymakers," National Center for Children in Poverty (July 2011), at 3.

60. Gottesman and Schwartz, supra n. 59.

Covenant IV: Fostering Accountable Community-Centered Policing

1.   "Incarcerated America," Figure 1. http://www.hrw.org/backgrounder/usa/incar-ceration/us042903.pdf, April 2003, Human Rights Watch; U.S. Census Bureau, "The Black Population in the United States: March 2002," available at http://www.census.gov/prod/2003pubs/p20-541.pdf.

2.   *See,* e.g., U.S. Sentencing Commission, "Special Report to Congress: Cocaine and Federal Sentencing Policy" (February 1995), available at http://www.ussc.gov/crack/execsum.pdf ("the 1991 Household Survey shows that 52 percent of those reporting crack use in the past year, as opposed to distribution, were white"); The Sentencing Project, "Crack Cocaine Sentencing Policy: Unjustified and Unreasonable," available at http://www.sentencingproject.org/pdfs/1003.pdf ("approximately 2/3 of crack users are white or Hispanic").

3.   For example, *see* Ed Chen, "Naming Names—Racism's Double Standard" (June 1999), available at http://www.aclunc.org/opinion/990618-littleton.html ("In places like San Jose and Orange County, 97 percent of listed gang members are minorities"). As for the arrest rates, *see* Center on Juvenile and Criminal Justice, "The Impact of Juvenile Curfew Laws in California" (Abstract, June 1998), available at http://www.cjcj.org/pubs/curfew/curfew.html ("In Ventura County, curfew arrests of Hispanic and Black youths are 8.4 times and 7.4 times higher, respectively, than those of white youths. In Fresno and Santa Clara counties, Hispanic youths are five times, and Black youths three times, more likely to be arrested for curfew violations than are white youths. Los Angeles authorities arrest Hispanic and Black youths for curfew violations at rates two to three times that of whites").

4.   "Contacts between Police and the Public: Findings from the 2002 National Survey," Bureau of Justice Statistics, Washington, DC, April 2005, p. 10.

5.   David A. Harris, "The Stories, the Statistics, and the Law: Why 'Driving While Black' Matters," *Minnesota Law Review,* 84, 1999, p. 265.

6.   *Ibid.*

7.   "Roster of U.S. Civilian Oversight Agencies," September 2005, http://www.nacole.org/RosterCivilianOversightAgencies0905.pdf, NACOLE.

8.   *Ibid.*

9.   Kathleen Maguire and Ann L. Pastore, *Sourcebook of Criminal Justice Statistics,* http://www.albany.edu/sourcebook/, pp. 48, 53.

10.   *Ibid.,* p. 53.

11.   Rosann Greenspand and David Weisburd, "Police Attitudes Toward Abuse of Authority: Findings From a National Study," National Institute of Justice, May 2000, p. 9.

12.   "Police Use of Force in America," International Association of Chiefs of Police, 2001, p. 44.

13. *Ibid.*, p. 45.

14. "Oversight and Police Accountability: A Statement of Principles," http://www
.policeaccountability.org/statementopa.htm, UNO Police Accountability Initiative.

15. *Ibid.*

16. "Bullets in the Hood: A Bed-Stuy Story," http://www.dctvny.org/ bullets/, DCTV.

17. "The Ella Baker Center's Mission Statement," http://www.ellabakercenter.org/
page.php?pageid=191, The Ella Baker Center.

18. "About Bay Area PoliceWatch," http://www.ellabakercenter.org/page.php?page
id=115, The Ella Baker Center.

19. "Bay Area PoliceWatch: Social and Legal Services," http://www.ellabakercenter
.org/page.php?pageid=125, The Ella Baker Center.

20. "Bay Area PoliceWatch: Campaigns and Media Work," http://www.ellabakercen
ter.org/page.php?pageid=126, The Ella Baker Center.

21. *Ibid.*

22. *Ibid.*

23. "Police Accountability Issues," http://policeaccountability.org/issue facts.htm,
UNO Police Accountability Initiative.

24. City of Berkeley, Ordinance No. 4644-N.S., Section 10.

25. *Ibid.*

26. *Ibid.*, Section 2.

27. M Harris West, "Community-Centered Policing: A Force for Change," PolicyLink
and The Advancement Project, 2001, p. 86.

28. *Ibid.*, p. 96.

29. City of Berkeley, *op. cit.*, Section 10.

30. William White (Chair of the Berkeley Police Review Commission), interviewed by
Maya Harris West, October 3, 2000.

31. West, *op. cit.*, p. 28.

32. *Ibid.*, p. 29.

33. Herman Goldstein, *Policing a Free Society* (Cambridge, MA: Ballinger Publishing
Co., 1977), p. 270, cited by M. Harris West, "Community-Centered Policing: A
Force for Change," PolicyLink and The Advancement Project, 2001, p. 30.

34. West, *op. cit.*, p. 29.

35. *Ibid.,* p. 31.

36. *Ibid.*

37. *Ibid.,* p. 35.

38. *Ibid.,* p. 37.

39. Goldstein, *op. cit.,* p. 28.

40. *Ibid.*

41. West, *op. cit.,* p. 44.

42. *Ibid.,* p. 63.

43. *Ibid.,* p. 64.

44. *Ibid.*

45. "Police Accountability: Definitions of Terms," http://www.policeaccountability .org/defterms.htm, UNO Police Accountability Initiative.

46. "Oversight and Police Accountability: A Statement of Principles," *op. cit.*

47. "Shielded from Justice: Summary and Recommendations: Investigation and Discipline," http://www.hrw.org/reports98/police/ uspol2.htm, Human Rights Watch.

48. S. Quinn, "Varieties of Civilian Oversight: Similarities, Differences, and Expectations," NACOLE, December 2004, p. 1.

49. "Shielded from Justice," *op. cit.*

50. "Shielded from Justice: Summary and Recommendations: Obstacles to Justice," http://www.hrw.org/reports98/police/uspoll.htm, Human Rights Watch.

51. *Ibid.*

52. "Shielded from Justice: Summary and Recommendations: Public Accountability and Transparency," http://www.hrw.org/reports98/ police/uspol3.htm, Human Rights Watch.

53. "Revisiting *Who Is Guarding the Guardians?* A Report on Police Practices and Civil Rights in America," U.S. Commission on Civil Rights, Washington, DC, November 2000, Executive Summary.

CWBA TEN YEARS LATER: Covenant IV

1. Braga, A. A. & Brunson, R. K. (2015). The Police and Public Discourse on "Black-on-Black" Violence. New Perspectives in Policing Bulletin. Washington, D.C.: U.S. Department of Justice, National Institute of Justice, 2015. NCJ 248588.

2. Bayley, D. H., Davis, M. D. and Davis, R. L. (2015). Race and Policing: An Agenda for Action. New Perspectives in Policing Bulletin. Washington, DC: U.S. Department of Justice, National Institute of Justice. NCJ 248624.

3. Robinson, C. D. (1975, p.278). The Mayor and the Police - the Political Role of the Police in Society. In G. L. Mosse (Ed.). *Police Forces in History*. Vol. 2. Beverly Hills, California: Sage.

4. Brunson, R. K. (2007). Police don't like black people: African American young men's accumulated police experiences. Criminology and Public Policy, 6(1), 71–102.

5. Rahr, S. and Rice, S. K. (2015). From Warriors to Guardians: Recommitting American Police Culture to Democratic Ideals. New Perspectives in Policing Bulletin. Washington, D.C.: U.S. Department of Justice, National Institute of Justice. NCJ 248654.

6. Bureau of Justice Statistics. Law Enforcement Management and Administrative Survey. Years 2007 and 2013. U.S. Washington, DC: Department of Justice.

7. Reaves, B. A. (2015). Local Police Departments, 2013: Personnel, Policies, and Practices. Washington, DC: Bureau of Justice Statistics. U.S. Department of Justice. NCJ 248677.

8. Terry v. Ohio, 392 U.S. 1, 1968

9. Skogan, W. G., and Frydl, K. (Eds). (2004). *Fairness and Effectiveness in Policing: The Evidence*. Washington, DC: National Academies Press.

10. We the Protestors. Campaign Zero. Retrieved from http://www.joincampaignzero.org/#vision

11. Police Executive Research Forum. (2015). Re-Engineering Training on Police Use of Force. Washington, DC. Critical Issues in Policing Series. Retrieved from http://www.policeforum.org/assets/reengineeringtraining.pdf

12. Milgram, A. and Straub, F. (2015). How to restore trust in the police. *The Crime Report.* September.

13. Tillyer, R. (2014). Opening the black box of officer decision-making: An examination of race, criminal history, and discretionary searches. *Justice Quarterly*, 31(6), 961–985.

14. Langton, L., and Durose, M. (2013). Police Behavior during Traffic and Street Stops, 2011. Washington, DC. Bureau of Justice Statistics. NCJ 242937.

15. Cochran, J. S. and Warren, P. Y. (2012). Racial, ethnic, and gender differences in perceptions of the police. The salience of officer race within the context of racial profiling. *Journal of Contemporary Criminal Justice*, 28(2), 206-227.

16. Ridgeway, G. (2007). Analysis of Racial Disparities in the New York Police Department's Stop, Question, and Frisk Practices. RAND. Santa Monica, CA.

17. Carter, J. G. (2015). How close do police mirror the communities they serve? Working paper. School of Public and Environmental Affairs. Indiana University-Purdue University Indianapolis.

Covenant V: Ensuring Broad Access to Affordable Neighborhoods That Connect to Opportunity

1. "Transportation and Poverty Alleviation," Transact, citing the Federal Transit Administration, at http://www.transact.org/library/facsheets/Transportation%20 and%20Poverty%20Alleviation.DOC. *See also* Robert Garcia, "Transportation Equity in Los Angeles: The MTA and Beyond," *Environmental Defense,* available at http://www.enviromentaldefense.org/article.cfm?contentid=1238.

2. Lance Freeman, *Siting Affordable Housing: Location and Neighborhood Trends of Low-Income Housing Tax Credit Development in the 1990s* (Washington, DC: Brookings Institution Center on Urban & Metropolitan Policy, 2004).

3. Scott Allard and Sheldon Danziger, "Proximity and Opportunity: How Residence and Race Affect the Employment of Welfare Recipients," Housing Policy Debate, Vol. 13, No. 4 (2003): 682, Fannie Mae Foundation.

4. Margery Austin Turner et al., *Discrimination in Metropolitan Housing Markets: National Results from Phase I HDS 2000* (Washington, DC: The Urban Institute, 2002); *see also* subsequent phases of the same study.

5. *Ibid.*

6. U.S. Bureau of the Census, 2004; available at http://www.census.gov.

7. "Out of Reach 2004," a report by the National Low Income Housing Coalition, Washington, DC.

8. *The State of Working America 2002–2003* (Washington, DC: Economic Policy Institute, 2003).

9. U.S. Bureau of the Census, "Census 2000," available at http://www.census.gov/ PressRelease/www/releases/archives/income_wealth/000417.html.

10. National Organization for Women - California, available at http://www.canow .org.

11. *See* http://www.knowledgeplex.org/kp/text_document_summary/scholarly_arti cle/relfiles/hpd_0302_downs_pt01.pdf.

12. Thomas Sanchez, Rich Stolz et al., "Moving to Equity: Addressing Inequitable Effects of Transportation Policies on Minorities," Joint Report of the Civil Rights Project at Harvard University and the Center for Community Change, June 2003.

13. Excerpted from http://www.volvoforlifeawards.com/cgibin/iowa/english/heros/ hero2004/8543.html.

14. http://www.bethelnew1ife.org/hous.html.

15. http://www.bethelnewlife.org/about.html.

16. http://sf.indymedia.org/news/2005/08/1718887.php and Public Advocates, http://www.publicadvocates.org/Bay%20Area%20Bus%20 Riders%20File%20 Federal%20Civil%20Rights%20Lawsuit%20 (for%2 Oweb%2Oposting) %20 04.19.05.htm.

17. *Ibid.*

18. Ghungmei Lee, *Racial Segregation and Educational Outcomes in Metropolitan Boston,* Harvard Civil Rights Project, 2004.

19. Freeman, *op. cit.*

20. Rolf Pendall, "Local Land-Use Regulation and the Chain of Exclusion," *Journal of the American Planning Association,* Vol. 66, No. 2 (2002): 125–142.

21. *See* PolicyLink, *Equitable Development Toolkit on Inclusionary Zoning,* http://www .policylink.org/Projects/IZ/.

22. Source: U.S. Bureau of the Census, *op. cit.*

23. Kalima Rose and Judith Bell, *Expanding Opportunity: New Resources to Meet California's Housing Needs,* PolicyLink, Winter 2005.

24. Austin Turner et al., *op. cit.*

25. Press release, "New Study: African Americans and Hispanics Feel Unwelcome in Metro Boston; Racial Discrimination Seen as Common Occurrence," http://www .civilrightsproject.harvard/edu/news/pressreleases/discrimination_boston.php.

26. Frank Hobbs and Nicole Stoops, "Demographic Trends in the 20th Century: Census 2000 Special Reports," November 2002.

27. William Apgar and Allegra Calder, "The Dual Mortgage Market," *The Geography of Opportunity,* edited by Xavier Briggs, Brookings Institution, 2005.

28. Millennial Housing Commission, *Meeting Our Nation's Housing Challenge,* 2002.

29. Allard and Danziger, *op. cit.*

30. Paul G. Lewis et al., *Federal Transportation Policy and the Role of Metropolitan Planning Organizations in California* (San Francisco, CA: Public Policy Institute of California, 1997); *see also* Seth B. Benjamin et al., "MPOs and Weighted Voting," *Intergovernmental Perspective,* 20 (1994): 31–36.

CWBA TEN YEARS LATER: Covenant V

1. Sharp, Gregory, and Matthew Hall 2014. Emerging Forms of Racial Inequality in Homeownership Exit, 1968–2009. *Social Problems*, 61(3): 427–447.

2. http://www.slate.com/articles/news_and_politics/politics/2014/07/black_home ownership_how_the_recession_turned_owners_into_renters_and_obliterated. html

3. Census.gov

4. ibid

5. http://www.pewresearch.org/fact-tank/2014/10/09/for-most-workers-real-wag es-have-barely-budged-for-decades/

6. Blackdemographics.com

7. http://www.bloomberg.com/news/articles/2013-09-03/black-homeowner ship-dying-where-obama-revitalized

8. http://time.com/3700741/black-hispanic-mortgage-disparity/

9. http://www.civilrights.org/fairhousing/laws/

10. http://nationalmortgageprofessional.com/news/55927/hud-awards-38-million -fight-housing-discrimination

11. http://www.huffingtonpost.com/ralph-da-costa-nunez/black-homelessness _b_1341912.html

12. http://www.icphusa.org/filelibrary/ICPH_Homeless%20Black%20Families.pdf

Covenant VI: Claiming Our Democracy

1. Voting rights attorney Armand Derfner of Derfner, Altman & Wilborn appeared before the House Judiciary Committee's Subcommittee on the Constitution at an oversight hearing, "Voting Rights Act: An Examination of the Scope and Criteria for Coverage Under the Special Provisions of the Act," on October 20, 2005.

2. Letter from J. Michael Wiggins, Acting Assistant Attorney General, Civil Rights Division, U.S. Department of Justice, to Wallace Shaw, Esq., August 18, 2002, available at http://www.usdoj.gov/crt/voting/sec_5/pdfs/1_081202.pdf.

3. Taken from an op-ed article, "Needed: A 'Citizenship' Right to Vote," by Rep. Jesse L. Jackson, Jr. (D-IL), April 26, 2004, in which the Congressman quotes Harvard University's Dr. Alex Keyssar: "108 democratic nations constitutionally guarantee the right to vote to their citizens, and eleven do not." Available at http://wwwjessejacksonjr.org/ query/creadpr.cgi?id=%22006813%22.

4. Minority Staff, Special Investigations Division, Committee on Government Reform, "Income and Racial Disparities in the Undercount in the 2000 Presidential Election," July 9, 2001.

5. *Ibid.,* at 10.

6. *United States v. Charleston County,* 365 F.3d 341, 350 (4th Cir. 2004).

7. *See* http://www.cavalierdaily.com/Cvarticle.asp?ID=24181&pid=1329.

8. "Felony Disenfranchisement Laws in the United States," http://www.sentencing project.org/pdfs/1046.pdf, September 2005, The Sentencing Project.

9. http://www.pfaw.org/pfaw/dfiles/file_462.pdf.

10. http://www.fairvote.org/pr/amy_intro.htm.

11. http://www.congressionalblackcaucus.net.

12. Chris Jenkins, "Felon Voting Rights Pushed in Va.," *Washington Post,* April 29, 2005, p. A5, available at http://www.washingtonpost.com/wp-dyn/content/arti cle/2005/04/28/AR2005042801631.html.

13. *Ibid.*

14. http://www.aamia.org/aboutus.htm.

15. *Ibid.*

16. http://sites.pfaw.org/mt/aamia/2005/10/breaking_victor.html.

17. Excerpted from the HSAN mission statement and program strategy, available at http://www.hsan.org/content/main.aspx?pageid=7.

18. *Ibid.,* p. 8.

19. *Ibid.*

CWBA TEN YEARS LATER: Covenant VI

1. United States Census Bureau, File, T., The Diversifying Electorate – Voting Rates by Race and Hispanic Origin in 2012 (and Other Recent Elections) (2013), https://www.census.gov/prod/2013pubs/p20-568.pdf.

2. http://www.nytimes.com/interactive/2015/10/11/us/politics/2016-presidential -election-super-pac-donors.html?_r=0 .

3. National Commission on Voting Rights, Protecting Minority Voters: Our Work is Not Done, p. 34 (2014), http://votingrightstoday.org/ncvr/resources/discrimina tionreport.

4. Lopez, T., Brennan Center for Justice, Shelby County: One Year Later (2014), http://www.brennancenter.org/sites/default/files/analysis/Shelby_County_One_Year_Later.pdf.

5. American Civil Liberties Union, "Veasey v. Abbott" (Aug. 5, 2015), https://www.aclu.org/cases/veasey-v-abbott.

6. Lopez, T., Brennan Center for Justice, Shelby County: One Year Later (2014), http://www.brennancenter.org/sites/default/files/analysis/Shelby_County_One_Year_Later.pdf.

7. American Civil Liberties Union, "League of Women Voters versus North Carolina" (July 30, 2015), https://www.aclu.org/cases/league-women-voters-north-carolina-et-al-v-north-carolina.

8. http://www.cnn.com/2015/10/02/politics/alabama-dmv-drivers-license-hillary-clinton/

9. Leadership Conference on Civil and Human Rights, The Persistent Challenge of Voting Discrimination: A Study of Recent Voting Rights Violations by State (2014), http://www.civilrights.org/press/2014/Racial-Discrimination-in-Voting-Whitepaper.pdf.

10. https://leginfo.legislature.ca.gov/faces/billNavClient.xhtml?bill_id=201520160AB1461

11. Pew Research Center, "114th Congress is Most Diverse Ever" (2015), http://www.pewresearch.org/fact-tank/2015/01/12/114th-congress-is-most-diverse-ever/

12. Demos, Shanton, K., The Problem of African American Underrepresentation on Local Councils (2014), http://www.demos.org/sites/default/files/publications/Underrepresentation_0.pdf.

13. National Commission on Voting Rights, Protecting Minority Voters: Our Work is Not Done, p. 34 (2014), http://votingrightstoday.org/ncvr/resources/discriminationreport.

14. United States Department of Justice Civil Rights Division, Investigation of the Ferguson Police Department (March 4, 2015), http://www.justice.gov/sites/default/files/opa/press-releases/attachments/2015/03/04/ferguson_police_department_report.pdf.

15. http://www2.ed.gov/about/offices/list/ocr/letters/colleague-201401-title-vi.pdf; http://www.usccr.gov/pubs/School_Disciplineand_Disparate_Impact.pdf.

16. Uggen, C., Shannon, S., and Manza, J., State-Level Estimates of Felon Disenfranchisement in the United States (2012), http://sentencingproject.org/doc/publications/fd_State_Level_Estimates_of_Felon_Disen_2010.pdf.

17. http://www.theatlantic.com/politics/archive/2015/03/do-the-koch-brothers-really-care-about-criminal-justice-reform/386615/

18. The Washington Post, "How Black Lives Matter moved from a hashtag to a real political force" (Aug. 19, 2015), https://www.washingtonpost.com/news/the-fix/wp/2015/08/19/how-black-lives-matter-moved-from-a-hashtag-to-a-real-politi cal-force/.

19. FairVote: The Center for Voting and Democracy, "Right to Vote Amendment Secures Unanimous Backing of DNC Executive Committee" (2015), http://www.fairvote.org/research-and-analysis/blog/right-to-vote-amendment-secures-unani mous-backing-of-dnc-executive-committee/.

20. HJ Resolution 25, Proposing an amendment to the Constitution of the United States regarding the right to vote, https://www.congress.gov/114/bills/hjres25/BILLS-114hjres25ih.pdf.

21. DC Vote, Chronology of the District of Columbia's Denial of Democracy (2015), http://www.dcvote.org/sites/default/files/documents/Chronology%20of%20 DC%20Denial%20of%20Democracy_2015.pdf.

Covenant VII: Strengthening Our Rural Roots

1. The essay authors are grateful for the inspiration behind these first two para- graphs from a website, "In Motion, The African American Migration Experience," presented by the Schomburg Center for Research in Black Culture, New York Public Library; the National Geographic has published a companion book; for more information on both: http://www.inmotionaame.org/home.cfmjsession id=8030917861133898935789?bhcp=1.

2. "Race and Ethnicity in Rural America: Labor Force Activity," Economic Research Service, U.S. Department of Agriculture, available at http://www.ers.usda.gov/briefing/raceandethnic/laborforce.htm.

3. "Race and Ethnicity in Rural America: Measures of Economic Well-Being—Health Insurance Coverage by race and ethnicity, 1990–2000," U.S. Department of Agriculture, available at http://www.ers.usda.gov/briefing/raceandethnic/well being.htm.

4. *Ibid.*

5. Robert Gibbs, ed., "Rural Education at a Glance," January 2004, available at http://www.ers.usda.gov/publications/RDRR98.

6. *Ibid.*

7. *Ibid.*

8. "The Black Population in the United States: 2002," U.S. Census Bureau, available at http://www.census.gov/prod/2003pubs/p20541.pdf.

9. Rita Price, "Leaving the land," *The Columbus Dispatch,* November 6, 2005, avail- able at http://www.blackfarmers.org.

10. Miessha Thomas et al., "What Is African American Land Ownership?," Federation of Southern Cooperatives Land Assistance Fund, available at http://www.federa tionsoutherncoop.com/aalandown04.htm.

11. "The Restorative Development Initiative Pioneering with the Federation of Southern Cooperatives," Bioneers, available at http://www.bioneers.org/programs/ food_farming/fedfarm.php.

12. "U.S. Department of Agriculture Stonewalls African American Farmers in Landmark Civil Rights Settlement," Environmental Working Group Report, available at http://www.ewg.org/reports/blackfarmers/execsumm.php.

13. *See* the Mandela Farmers' Market, available at http://www. mobetterfood.com/ mfm_front%20_overview.htm.

14. Southern Rural Black Women's Initiative, Children's Defense Fund—Southern Office, available at http://www.cdfsro.org/SRBWI%20Brochure%20-%20Missis sippi%207-1-04.pdf.

15. *Ibid.*

16. "Fighting to Save Black-Owned Land Since 1967," Federation of Southern Cooperatives Land Assistance Fund, available at http://www.federationsoutherncoop .com/.

17. http://www.federationsoutherncoop.com/mission.htm.

18. http://www.federationsoutherncoop.com/overview.htm.

19. "Status of Public Education in Rural Areas and Small Towns—A Comparative Analysis," National Education Association Research, September 1998, available at http://www.nea.org/rural/companalrural.html.

20. *Ibid.*

21. PolicyLink, "Healthy Food, Healthy Communities," Fall 2005, available at http:// www.policylink.org.

22. http://www.ewg.org/reports/blackfarmers/part4.php.

23. "U.S. Department of Agriculture Stonewalls . . . ," *op. cit.*

24. *Ibid.*

25. "Federation/LAF Land Retention Services," Federation of Southern Cooperatives Land Assistance Fund, available at http://www. federationsoutherncoop.com/ landret.htm.

CWBA TEN YEARS LATER: Covenant VII

1. http://www.ers.usda.gov/media/1697681/eb26.pdf

2. http://ced.berkeley.edu/bpj/2013/04/the-color-of-elsewhere-identity-and-wealth
    -in-rural-america/

3. www.census.gov

4. http://srbwi.org/images/uploads/SRBWI_Report_Layout_for_web_low_res
    _%281%29.pdf

5. https://www.raconline.org/topics/social-determinants-of-health

6. http://srbwi.org/images/uploads/SRBWI_Report_Layout_for_web_low_res
    _%281%29.pdf

7. *Ibid.*

8. http://nonprofitquarterly.org/2015/08/13/philanthropy-is-largely-mia-on-condi
    tions-of-black-women-and-children-in-rural-south/

9. https://www.raconline.org/topics/social-determinants-of-health

10. http://ahrf.hrsa.gov/

11. https://ruralhealth.und.edu/projects/health-reform-policy-research-center/pdf
    /2014-rural-urban-chartbook-update.pdf

12. http://nonprofitquarterly.org/2015/08/13/philanthropy-is-largely-mia-on-condi
    tions-of-black-women-and-children-in-rural-south/

Covenant VIII: Accessing Good Jobs, Wealth, and Economic Prosperity

1. "Equality Index," *The State of Black America 2004: the Complexity of Black Progress* (New York: National Urban League, 2004).

2. *Ibid.*

3. *Ibid.*

4. Andrew Stettner and Sylvia A. Allegretto, "The Rising Stakes of Job Loss: Stubborn Long-Term Joblessness Amid Falling Unemployment Rates," EPI and NELP, available at http://www.nelp.org/docUploads/RisingStakes%2Epdf.

5. Dr. Samuel Myers, "African American Economic Well-Being During the Boom and Bust," in *The State of Black America 2004: the Complexity of Black Progress* (New York: National Urban League, 2004).

6. Thomas M. Shapiro, "The Racial Wealth Gap," in *The State of Black America 2005: Prescriptions for Change* (New York: National Urban League, 2005).

Endnotes

7. W.E.B. Du Bois, *The Souls of Black Folks* (New York: New American Library, 1969 [1903]).

8. Louis Uchitelle, "For Blacks, a Dream in Decline," *The New York Times,* October 23, 2005.

9. Service Employees International Union (SEIU), "It Takes a Nation of Millions: What's at stake for black workers as labor debates change," 2005, available at http://www.seiu.org/docUploads/It_Takes_A _Nation_of_Millions.pdf.

10. Uchitelle, *op. cit.*

11. *Ibid.*

12. Julianne Malveaux, Ph.D., "The Real Deal on Black Unemployment," available at http://www.findarticles.com/p/articles/mi_mODXK/ is_13_21/ai-n6169071.

13. SEIU, *op. cit.*

14. Renée Cameto et al., "Youth Employment," NLTS2 Data Brief, December 2003, available at http://www.ncset.org/publications/ viewdesc.asp?id=1310.

15. Charles Dervarics, "Minorities Overrepresented Among America's 'Disconnected' Youth," Population Reference Bureau, 2005, available at http://www.prb.org/ Template.cfm?Section=PRB8ctemplate=/ContentManagement/ContentDisplay .cfm&ContentID=11335

16. Nikitra S. Bailey, "Predatory Lending: The New Face of Economic Injustice," *Human Rights Magazine,* American Bar Association, available at http://www.abanet .org/irr/hr/summer05/predator.html.

17. Harry C. Alford, Jr., "Blacks Should Help in Doing Away with the 'Death Tax,'" Newspaper Association of America, available at http://lobby.la.psu.edu/027 _Estate_Tax/Organizational_Statements/NAA/NAA_Policy_Blacks_Help.htm.

18. Nikitra S. Bailey, *op. cit.*

19. *Ibid.*

20. "Small Business Notes: Definition of Sub-prime Lending," available at http:// www.smallbusinessnotes.com/glossary/defsubprime.html.

21. Nikitra S. Bailey, "Predatory Lending: The New Face of Economic Injustice," *Human Rights Magazine,* American Bar Association, available at http://www.abanet. org/irr/hr/summer05/predator.html..

22. "Farrah Gray," Black Entrepreneur's Hall of Fame, February 8, 2005, available at http://blackentrepreneurshalloffame blogspot.com/2005/02/farrah-gray.html.

23. For an update on the coalition's successful agreement, *see* Strategic Actions for a Just Economy, "Figueroa Corridor Coalition for Economic Justice," available at http://www.saje.net/programs/fccej.php.

24. SEIU, *op. cit.*

25. National Community Reinvestment Coalition, "The Truth about CRA and Plans to Eviscerate an Effective Law," available at http://www.ncrc.org.

26. *Ibid.*

27. Local Initiatives Support Coalition, "Bridging the Gap: LISC and the New Markets Tax Credit," available at http://www.lisc.org/resources/2003/01/bridging_l350 .shtml?Social+&+Economic+Development.

28. Nikitra S. Bailey, *op. cit.*

29. Debbie Goldstein and Stacy Strohauer Son, "Why Prepayment Penalties are Abusive in Subprime Home Loans," Center for Responsible Lending, available at http://www.responsiblelending.org/pdfs/PPP_Policy_Paper2.pdf.

30. American Rights at Work, "Employee Free Choice Act," available at http://www .americanrightsatwork.org/takeaction/efca/index.cfm.

31. Center for Economic Development, "Individual Development Accounts Focus," available at http://www.cfed.org/focus.m?parentid=31&siteid=374&id=374.

32. Center for Economic Development, "Individual Development Accounts," available at http://www.cfed.org/imageManager/IDAnetwork/IDAs.doc.

33. Robert Greenstein, "The Earned Income Tax Credit: Boosting Employment, Aiding the Working Poor," Center on Budget and Policy Priorities, August 17, 2005.

34. *Ibid.*

35. Jared Bernstein, "The Living Wage Movement: Pointing the Way Toward the High Road," Economic Policy Institute, *Community Action Digest,* Spring 1999, Vol. 1, Issue 1.

36. *Ibid.*

Covenant IX: Assuring Environmental Justice for All

1. Robert D. Bullard, *The Quest for Environmental Justice: Human Rights and the Politics of Pollution* (San Francisco: Sierra Club Books, 2005).

2. *Commission for Racial Justice, Toxic Wastes and Race in the United States: A National Report on the Racial and Socio-economic Characteristics of Communities with Hazardous Waste Sites* (New York: United Church of Christ, 1987).

3. Bullard, *Dumping in Dixie: Race, Class, and Environmental Quality* (Boulder, CO: Westview Press, 1990), chapter 1.

4. U.S. EPA, *Environmental Equity: Reducing Risk for All Communities* (Washington, DC: EPA, 1992).

5.   William J. Clinton, "Federal Actions to Address Environmental Justice in Minority Populations and Low-Income Populations, Exec. Order No. 12898," *Federal Register, 59*, No. 32, February 11,1994, available at http://www.epa.gov/compliance/resources/policies/ej/exec_order_ 12898.pdf#search='executive%20order%20 12898' and at http://www.fs.fed.us/land/envjust.html.

6.   Bullard, "It's not just pollution," *Our Planet,* Vol. 12, No. 2, 2001: 22–24.

7.   Bullard, *Confronting Environmental Racism: Voices from the Grassroots* (Boston: South End Press, 1993).

8.   *See* Robert D. Bullard, ed., *Confronting Environmental Racism: Voices from the Grassroots* (Boston: South End, 1993); Bullard, "The Threat of Environmental Racism," *Natural Resources & Environment 7* (Winter, 1993): 23–26; Bunyan Bryant and Paul Mohai, eds., *Race and the Incidence of Environmental Hazards* (Boulder, CO: Westview Press, 1992); Regina Austin and Michael Schill, "Black, Brown, Poor and Poisoned: Minority Grassroots Environmentalism and the Quest for Eco-Justice," *The Kansas Journal of Law and Public Policy 1* (1991): 69–82; Kelly C. Colquette and Elizabeth A. Henry Robertson, "Environmental Racism: The Causes, Consequences, and Commendations," *Tulane Environmental Law Journal 5* (1991): 153–207; and Rachel D. Godsil, "Remedying Environmental Racism," *Michigan Law Review* 90 (1991): 394–427.

9.   *See* Bullard, *Unequal Protection: Environmental Justice and Communities of Color* (San Francisco: Sierra Club Books, 1994).

10. Kenneth Olden, "The Complex Interaction of Poverty, Pollution, Health Status," *The Scientist,* Vol. 12, No. 2, (February 1998): 7. *See* NIEHS: Division of Extramural Research and Training: Health Disparities Research, available at http://www.niehs.nih.gov/dert/ programs/translat/hd/ko-art.htm.

11. Mark Sauer, "Dirty Little Secret: Disaster Laid Bare the Prevalence of Poverty in America," *The San Diego Union-Tribune,* September 18, 2005.

12. U.S. Bureau of the Census, "People: Poverty," available at http://factfinder.census .gov/jsp/saff/SAFFInfojsp?_pageId=tp8_ poverty.

13. U.S. Bureau of the Census, "Orleans Parish, Louisiana," *State and County Quick Facts,* 2000, available at http://quickfacts.census.gov/qfd/states/22/22071.html.

14. Felicia A. Rabito, LuAnn E. White, and Charles Shorter, "From Research to Policy: Targeting the Primary Prevention of Childhood Lead Poisoning," *Public Health Reports,* 119 (May/June 2004).

15. *See* Beverly Wright, "Living and Dying in Louisiana's Cancer Alley," in Robert D. Bullard, *The Quest for Environmental Justice,* pp. 87–107.

16. Jason DeParle, "Broken Levees, Unbroken Barriers: What Happens to a Race Deferred," *The New York Times,* September 4, 2005.

17. Evan Thomas and Arian Campo-Flores, "The Battle to Rebuild," *Newsweek,* October 3, 2005, available at http://www.msnbc.msn.com/id/9469300/site/ newsweek.

18. Centers for Disease Control and Prevention and EPA, *Environmental Health Needs and Habitability Assessment,* Atlanta: Joint Task Force Hurricane Katrina Response, Initial Assessment (September 17, 2005), found at http://www.bt.cdc.gov/di sasters/hurricanes/katrina/ pdf/envassessment.pdf#search='centers%20for%20 disease%20 control%20katrina%20contamination'.

19. Randy Lee Loftis, "Extreme Cleanup on Tap in New Orleans," *The Dallas Morning News,* November 6, 2005, available at http://www. dallasnews.com/sharedcon tent/dws/dn/latestnews/stories/110605dntswtoxic.c3d4a5d.html.

20. "The Mother of All Toxic Cleanups," *Business Week,* September 26, 2005, available at http://www.businessweek.com/magazine/ content/05_39/b3952055 .htm.

21. Scott Gold and Ann M. Simmons, "Katrina Cough Floats Around," *The Los Angeles Times,* November 4, 2005, available at http://www.latimes.com/news/nation world/nation/la-nacough4nov04,0,7514027.story?coll=la-home-headlines.

22. Natural Resources Defense Council, "New Private Testing Shows Dangerously High Mold Counts in New Orleans Air," Press Release, November 16, 2005, available at http://www.nrdc.org/media/pressreleases/051116.asp.

23. National Institute of Environmental Health Sciences, *Environmental Diseases from A to Z,* NIH Publication No. 96-4145, available at http://www.niehs.nih.gov.

24. Alliance for Healthy Homes, "Children at Risk, Disparities in Risk: Childhood Lead Poisoning," http://www.afhh.org/chil_ar_disparities.htm.

25. Trust for America's Health, "Browse by Topic: Health Disparities—Lead," http:// healthyamericans.org.

26. *Ibid.*

27. *See* U.S. Centers for Disease Control and Prevention (2000), MMWR, 49 (RR-14): 1–13; *see also* National Institutes of Health (NIH), National Institute of Environmental Health Sciences (NIEHS), Health Disparities Research, http://www.niehs .nih.gov/oc/ factsheets/disparity/home.htm.

28. Peter Montague, "Pediatricians Urge a Precautionary Approach to Toxic Lead," September 29, 2005, *Rachel's Democracy and Health News,* #827 (September 2005), http://www.rachel.org/bulletin/bulletin.cfm?Issue_ID=2513.

29. Commission for Racial Justice, *op. cit.*

30. R. Twombly, "Urban Uprising," *Environmental Health Perspective,* Vol. 105, (July 1997): 696–701.

31. "Study: Public Housing is Too Often Located Near Toxic Sites," *The Dallas Morning News,* October 3, 2000, available at http://www.cnn.com/2000/NA TURE/10/03/toxicneighbors.ap/.

Endnotes

32. "Child-Proofing Our Communities Campaign," *Poisoned Schools: Invisible Threats, Visible Actions* (Falls Church, VA: Center for Health, Environment and Justice, March 2001); *see also* http://www.childproofing.org/mapindex.html.

33. *See* the Air of Injustice report on the Clear the Air website at http://cta.policy.net/proactive/newsroom/release.vtml?id=23901.

34. Marla Cone and Ashley Powers, "EPA Warns Muck Left by Floodwaters is Highly Contaminated," *The Los Angeles Times,* September 16, 2005; *Associated Press,* "Katrina and the Environment," September 16, 2005, available at http://www.cbsnews.com/stories/2005/09/16/Katrina/main855409.shtml.

35. Marla Cone, "Floodwaters a Soup of Pathogens, EPA Finds," *The Los Angeles Times,* September 8, 2005, p. A18.

36. Ted Griggs, "Rebuilding to Be Slow, Expensive," *The Advocate,* September 11, 2005, p. 12A.

37. *Ibid.*

38. James Varney and Jan Moller, "Huge Task of Cleaning Up Louisiana Will Take at Least a Year," Newhouse News Service, October 2, 2005, available at http://www.newhousenews.com/archive/varney100305.html.

39. *Ibid.*

40. U.S. EPA and Louisiana Department of Environmental Quality, "News Release: Top State and Federal Environmental Officials Discuss Progress and Tasks Ahead After Katrina," September 30, 2005, available at http://www.deq.state.la.us/news/pdf/administratorjohnson.pdffsearch='katrina%20debris%20350%2C000%20automobiles'.

41. *Ibid.*

42. *Ibid.*

43. Marnie Hunter, "Schools Take in Displaced Students," CNN.com, September 12, 2005, found at http://www.cnn.com/2005/EDUCATION/09/07/katrina.schools/.

44. Annie Schleicher, "School Bells Ring for Children Displaced by Hurricane Katrina," *The NewsHour with Jim Lehrer,* September 7, 2005, found at http://www.pbs.org/newshour/extra/features/julydec05/katrina_9-07.html.

45. http://www.weact.org/history.html.

46. *Ibid.*

47. http://www.dwej.org/facts.htm.

48. http://www.leanweb.org/leaninfo.html.

49. http://www.leanweb.org/pesticid.html.

50. Tetra Tech EM, Inc., *Dickson County Landfill Reassessment Report: A Report Prepared for the U.S. EPA, Region iv,* Atlanta, March 4, 2004.

51. Permit Registration Number SNL221020065EXT, issued on December 2, 1988, J.W. Luna, Commissioner, Tennessee Department of Health and Environment.

52. Letter from Wayne Aronson, Acting Chief, Drinking Water Section, Municipal Facilities Branch, U.S. EPA to Mr. Harry Holt, December 3, 1991.

53. Tetra Tech EM, Inc., *op. cit.,* p. 28.

54. *Op. cit.,* "Chronology of Events, Dickson County Landfill," p. B-9.

55. http://www.epa.gov/region7/ej/aboutej.htm.

56. Alicia Lyttle, "Agricultural Street Landfill Environmental Justice Case Study," University of Michigan School of Natural Resource and Environment, found at http://www.umich.edu/—snre492/Jones/agstreet.htm.

57. Bullard, *The Quest for Environmental Justice, op. cit.*

58. Cain Burdeau, "New Orleans Area Becoming a Dumping Ground," *The Associated Press,* October 31, 2005.

59. Gordon Russell, "Landfill Reopening is Raising New Stink," *The Times-Picayune,* November 21, 2005, available at http://www.nola.com/news/t-p/frontpage/index.ssf?/base/news-4/1132559045240640.xml.

60. WDSU, "Hurricane Debris Catches Fire at Old Gentilly Landfill," November 4, 2005, available at http://www.wdsu.com/news/4611257/detail.html?rss=no&psp=news.

61. http://www.epa.gov/brownfields/about.htm.

CWBA TEN YEARS LATER: Covenant IX

1. 59 FR 7629; February 16 1994.

2. U.S. EPA, Final Guidance For Incorporating Environmental Justice in EPA'S NEPA Compliance Analysis 7–8 (1998)

3. http://www3.epa.gov/environmentaljustice/resources/publications/factsheets/fact-sheet-ej.pdf (all websites cited were last accessed October 10, 2015).

4. U.S. Census Bureau, Current Population Survey, 1968 to 2015 Annual Social and Economic Supplements.

5. See, e.g., Wolverton, A. 2009 "Effects of Socio-Economic and Input-Related Factors on Polluting Plants' Location Decisions." *The B.E. Journal of Economic Analysis & Policy* 9(1): Article 14; Wolverton, A. 2012. "The Role of Demographic and

Cost-Related Factors in Determining Where Plants Locate: A Tale of Two Texas Cities." In, *The Political Economy of Environmental Justice*. ed. Spencer Banzhaf, Stanford University Press.

6.   See, e.g., Bell ML, Ebisu K. 2012. Environmental Inequality in Exposures to Airborne Particulate Matter Components in the United States. *Environ Health Perspectives* 120:1699–1704; Clark LP, Millet DB, Marshall JD (2014) National Patterns in Environmental Injustice and Inequality: Outdoor NO_2 Air Pollution in the United States. *PLoS ONE* 9(4): e94431; Abel and White (2011) "Skewed Riskscapes and Gentrified Inequities: Environmental Exposure Disparities in Seattle, Washington." *Am J Public Health*. 2011 Dec;101 Suppl 1:S246–54.

7.   See, "Environmental Justice," http://deohs.washington.edu/environmental -justice.

8.   Center for Disease Control and Prevention. "Blood Lead Levels in Children Aged 1–5 Years — United States, 1999–2010." *Morbidity and Mortality Weekly Report* April 5, 2013 / 62(13);245–248. http://www.cdc.gov/mmwr/preview/mmwrht ml/mm6213a3.htm

9.   Ibid.

10. Eckerd, Adam and Andrew Keeler. "Going green together? Brownfield remediation and environmental justice." Policy Sciences, 2012, vol. 45, issue 4, pages 293–314

11. Miranda, M.L.; Edwards, S.E.; Keating, M.H.; Paul, C.J. Making the Environmental Justice Grade: The Relative Burden of Air Pollution Exposure in the United States. *Int. J. Environ. Res. Public Health* 2011, 8, 1755-1771.

12. Zwickl, Klara , Michael Ash, & James K. Boyce. "Regional variation in environmental inequality: Industrial air toxics exposure in U.S. cities." *Ecological Economics* 107 (2014) 494–509.

13. http://www2.epa.gov/ejscreen

14. http://www3.epa.gov/environmentaljustice/plan-ej/index.html

15. http://nepis.epa.gov/Exe/ZyPDF.cgi/60000OCK.PDF?Dockey=60000OCK.PDF

16. http://www3.epa.gov/environmentaljustice/grants/ej-smgrants.html

17. http://www3.epa.gov/environmentaljustice/resources/reports/annual-project -reports.html

18. http://www3.epa.gov/environmentaljustice/resources/reports/actionplans.html

19. http://www3.epa.gov/environmentaljustice/resources/publications/ej-fact-sheets .html

20. Konisky, D. 2015. *Failed Promises: Evaluating the Federal Government's Response to Environmental Justice.* MIT Press, page xi

Covenant X: Closing the Racial Digital Divide

1. National Telecommunications and Information Administration, "Falling Through the Net II: New Data on the Digital Divide," November 9, 2005, http://www .ntia.do.gov/ntiahome/net2/falling.html.

2. Thomas L Friedman, *The World Is Flat: A Brief History of the Twenty-first Century* (New York: Farrar, Straus and Giroux, 2005).

3. John Brooks Slaughter, 2003 Woodruff Distinguished Lecture: "The Search for Excellence and Equity in Higher Education: A Perspective from an Engineer," Georgia Institute of Technology, Atlanta, GA, April 10, 2003, National Action Council for Minorities in Engineering (NACME).

4. National Science Foundation, *Science and Engineering Indicators 2004* (Arlington, VA: National Science Foundation, May 2004), NSB 04-01.

5. National Science Foundation, Division of Science Resources Statistics, *Academic Research and Development Expenditures: Fiscal Year 2003,* NSF 05320.

6. U.S. Census Bureau, Commerce Department, *Preliminary Estimates of Business Ownership by Gender, Hispanic or Latino Origin, and Race: 2002* (issued July 28, 2005).

7. *Ibid.*

8. Census 2000 EEO Data Tool, EEO Residence Data Results for Total U.S., Percentage of Chief Executives by Race/Ethnicity, http://www.census.gov/eeo2000.

9. Joy Bennett Kinnon, "The Shocking State of Black Marriage: Experts Say Many Will Never Get Married," *Ebony,* November 2003, available at http://www.find articles.com/p/articles/mi_m1077/is_1_59/ai_110361377.

10. R. Fairlie, "Are We Really a Nation Online? Ethnic and Racial Disparities in Access to Technology and Their Consequences," Report for the Leadership Conference on Civil Rights Education Fund, University of California, Santa Cruz and National Poverty Center, University of Michigan, September 20, 2005.

11. *Ibid.*

12. J. Horrigan, "Broadband Adoption at Home in the United States: Growing but Slowing," paper presented to the 33rd Annual Telecommunications Policy Research Conference, George Mason University School of Law, Arlington, VA, September 24, 2005.

13. Fairlie, *op. cit.*

14. *See* Daniel Beltran et al., "Do Home Computers Improve Educational Outcomes? Evidence from Matched Current Population Surveys and the National Longitudinal Survey of Youth 1997," University of California, Santa Cruz, October 2005.

15. Respondents were asked whether they searched for a college within the past two years. Statistics reflect this subgroup of Internet users. *See* Nathan Kommers and Lee Rainie, "Use of the Internet at Major Life Moments: Research Briefing," Pew Internet and American Life Project, 2002.

16. Fairlie, *op. cit.*

17. M. Madden and L. Rainie, "America's Online Pursuits," PEW Internet & American Life Project, December 22, 2003, pp. 27, 33, and 36.

18. A. Lenhart, M. Madden, and P. Hitlin, "Teens and Technology," PEW Internet & American Life Project, July 27, 2005, p. 15.

19. http://www.rosaparks.org.

20. http://www.rosaparks.org/pages/program_overview.html.

21. http://www.eastmont.net/about_ecc.htm.

22. *Ibid.*

23. http://www.eastmont.net/clubhouse/CLUBHOUSE_test.html.

24. http://www.eastmont.net/services.htm.

25. http://www.blackfamilynet.net/v2/national_events.php.

26. http://www.blackfamilynet.net/v2/aboutus.php.

27. http://www.blackfamilynet.net/v2/agenda.php.

28. *Ibid.*

29. *See* Maine Learning Technology Initiative, available at http://www.state.me.us/mlte.

30. *See* Chapter 402, Laws of 2005, state of Washington, 59th Legislature, 2005 Regular Session, available at http://www.leg.wa.gov/pub/billinfo/2005- 06/Pdf/Bills/Session%20Law%202005/1408-S.sl.pdf.

31. F. Lautenberg, "Open the doors to broadband access; don't slam them shut," *The Hill,* July 13, 2005, retrieved from http://www.hillnews.com/thehill/export/TheHill/News/Frontpage/071305/ss_lautenberg.html.

CWBA TEN YEARS LATER: Covenant X

1. http://ivn.us/2013/12/27/economic-racial-digital-divide-creates-larger-education-gap-nationwide/

2. http://www.newsweek.com/2014/02/21/google-making-digital-divide-worse-245546.html

3. http://www.latinpost.com/articles/5751/20140109/study-digital-divide-not-race-based-and-bridged-by-smartphones-not-so-fast.htm

4. *Ibid.*

5. http://www.pewinternet.org/2015/09/22/digital-divides-2015/

6. http://www.latinpost.com/articles/5751/20140109/study-digital-divide-not-race-based-and-bridged-by-smartphones-not-so-fast.htm

7. http://www.huffingtonpost.com/david-honig/the-digital-divide-and-th_b_1317953.html

8. http://ivn.us/2013/12/27/economic-racial-digital-divide-creates-larger-education-gap-nationwide/

9. http://newsone.com/3082952/black-internet-usage-2014-statistics/

10. http://www.latinpost.com/articles/5751/20140109/study-digital-divide-not-race-based-and-bridged-by-smartphones-not-so-fast.htm

11. http://www.theatlantic.com/education/archive/2015/03/the-schools-where-kids-cant-go-online/387589/

12. http://www.educationsuperhighway.org/

13. http://www.theatlantic.com/education/archive/2015/03/the-schools-where-kids-cant-go-online/387589/

✢ ✢

ACKNOWLEDGMENTS

The original *Covenant with Black America* text, published in 2006, was a labor of love. So it is ten years later. Without the team I was fortunate to bring together, this vitally important data about the past, present, and future of Black lives in America could not have been assembled.

Let me commence by thanking the brilliant and highly regarded academic team at the Indiana University School of Public and Environmental Affairs (SPEA). The school's Dean, John Graham, and his able right hand, Susan Johnson, asked Executive Associate Dean Michael McGuire to spearhead this project. I could not have been more pleased with the all-star academics he recruited to assist in the research and writing of the various *Covenant* updates found at the conclusion of each chapter. At the end of each update you will find the names of the *Covenant* contributors for that section, all of whom I owe a debt I can never repay. Information is power; knowledge is power. Thanks to each of you for empowering us with the information we need to help make Black America better.

To the staff at Hay House—my longtime publishing and distribution partner—thank you a thousand times. And then some! To our founder, Louise Hay; our leader, Reid Tracy; our creative director, Christy Salinas, and her designer Tricia Breidenthal; our editor Perry Crowe and the rest of the crew he assembled to make this manifesto real: Nicolette Young, Celeste Phillips, Jessica Kelley, and Molly Brown.

Additionally, deep gratitude to all the *Covenant* contributors and supporters from a decade ago who gave us reason to believe, and an assignment to follow up on ten years later. We didn't drop the ball.

Finally, to my staff at The Smiley Group, Inc., and SmileyBooks: none of this would be possible were it not for your professionalism and abiding support.

✢ ✢

ABOUT THE AUTHOR

Tavis Smiley is currently the host of the late-night television talk show *Tavis Smiley* on PBS, as well as *The Tavis Smiley Show* from Public Radio International (PRI). He is also the founder of the nonprofit Tavis Smiley Foundation, which has undertaken a $3-million, four-year campaign called "ENDING POVERTY: America's Silent Spaces" in order to alleviate endemic poverty in America. *TIME* magazine named Smiley to its list of "The World's 100 Most Influential People."

✢ ✢

We hope you enjoyed this SmileyBooks publication.
If you'd like to receive additional information, please contact:

SMILEYBOOKS

Distributed by:
Hay House, Inc.,
P.O. Box 5100
Carlsbad, CA 92018-5100

(760) 431-7695 or (800) 654-5126
(760) 431-6948 (fax) or (800) 650-5115 (fax)
www.hayhouse.com® • www.hayfoundation.org

✢

Published and distributed in Australia by: Hay House Australia Pty. Ltd.,
18/36 Ralph St., Alexandria NSW 2015 • *Phone:* 612-9669-4299
Fax: 612-9669-4144 • www.hayhouse.com.au

Published and distributed in the United Kingdom by: Hay House UK, Ltd.,
Astley House, 33 Notting Hill Gate, London W11 3JQ • *Phone:* 44-20-3675-2450
Fax: 44-20-3675-2451 • www.hayhouse.co.uk

Published and distributed in the Republic of South Africa by: Hay House SA (Pty),
Ltd., P.O. Box 990, Witkoppen 2068 • info@hayhouse.co.za • www.hayhouse.co.za

Published in India by: Hay House Publishers India, Muskaan Complex,
Plot No. 3, B-2, Vasant Kunj, New Delhi 110 070 • *Phone:* 91-11-4176-1620
Fax: 91-11-4176-1630 • www.hayhouse.co.in

Distributed in Canada by: Raincoast Books, 2440 Viking Way, Richmond, B.C.
V6V 1N2 • *Phone:* 1-800-663-5714 • *Fax:* 1-800-565-3770 • www.raincoast.com